Through Hell
and out the other side

Stories of a Therapeutic Foster Mom

ELLEN HARLIE

Through Hell and Out the Other Side

Hard Cover ISBN: 978-0-9889601-1-4
Soft Cover ISBN: 978-0-9889601-0-7

Library of Congress Control Number: 2014935561
Printed in Saint Louis, Missouri, The United States of America

All photographs used in this book are original and were taken by Ellen Harlie with the exception of one which was taken by her father when she was a child.

Bobby Mac Press
4732 Kingbird Lane
Saint Louis, MO 63123
boilerdoctorab@gmail.com

Table of Contents

Acknowledgements

Thanks to my husband whose patience was infinite. He knew I had a story to tell but it would be an uphill battle because I had never used a computer or written anything. He listened to my endless stories, encouraged and supported me for four years as I worked on the book. Without his help the story would never have been told.

Thanks to my son for his contribution to the book. He relayed the forgotten and untold stories that surfaced as I was going down memory lane. His life was forever altered at the age of 14 when he shared his home and family with foster kids.

Thanks to my son-in-law who helped me in so many ways through the years. His presence had a positive and calming influence on the boys. He helped me through many difficult situations and I am grateful.

Thanks to my daughter who welcomed the boys, with all their baggage, into her home and included them in family activities. She came to my rescue countless times and, when I needed a shoulder to cry on, she was there.

About the Author

The author, who goes by Ellen Harlie in this work, is not using her real identity or the real identity of the 55 children who spent time in her home as foster children. In fact, her location is not revealed because it is imperative that she protect the privacy of the children she fostered and others she encountered on her journey.

She grew up on a farm, with one brother, where wheat fields spread to the horizon and oil wells dotted the landscape. Social life in the rural area revolved around a large, but close extended family, and church activities. She spent hours playing with dolls, hoping she would one day have lots of children. Her wish came true.

A mile and a half from the farmhouse she attended a one-room school through eighth grade. There were no school busses, so she drove to the high school in the town. After graduating from high school she attended college, and eventually moved out of the state.

The road of life led her into fostering. It was an amazing journey, with many roadblocks, and a story that needs to be told. After 18 years of fostering many of the more difficult children, she shares with the readers her insight on the system as well as details of individual placements she dealt with over the years.

Preface

You are about to embark on a journey through my life as a foster parent, wife and mother. I have chosen to present each child's story as their own chapter. There was always a constant overlap of boys coming and going and they often appear in several chapters as minor characters. From time to time, characters will show up in a story before they are formally introduced. As the stories unfold, they are in chronological order as best could be maintained. Some children were there as long as 13 years, some only a short time. Collectively, this series of short stories will provide the reader with an overview of my life as a therapeutic foster parent, caring for more than 55 children over the years.

Foster children wind up in the "system" for widely-differing reasons. Some enter foster care as infants; others are in their late teens before finding themselves in foster care. The reasons they are being fostered are totally beyond their control. Living in a good foster home can help the child to transition into a useful and productive citizen. Unfortunately, many enter the system so damaged their future is bleak, but they still deserve the opportunity.

Living in a rural area where the manufacture of crystal meth was prevalent, many children from dysfunctional drug homes were placed in the foster system. Availing myself of every training session offered to foster parents, I became qualified to handle the difficult cases. Many of my placements had been physically and/or sexually abused, as well as neglected, for years. By the time they were placed in my home, they had a lot of emotional baggage and not much else. Ineffective parenting during the formative years permanently affects a child.

Good foster parents are the backbone of the foster care system but they are handicapped by the system that created them. As soon as the county or state monitor sees improvement, the child is downgraded to a lower classification. When downgrading takes place it creates an opening for a new behavioral or therapeutic placement in the home where the downgrade took place. The incentive for foster parents to get the training and licensing to keep behavioral or therapeutic placements is the higher pay. Downgrading generally results in the child being relocated to a foster home with minimal training that is licensed to keep the lower classified placements. Removing a child from the home where they have achieved a modicum of integration into the extended family and community and placing them in a new situation further exacerbates their problems. The child's problems have been dormant, but once the familiar day-to-day environment is removed, the problems often return as the child is placed in the new foster home. The unsuspecting foster parents receive the child, often with re-emerging problems, to satisfy the system's budgetary constraints. The traditional foster parent may realize they can't handle the child and ask to have him moved and the cycle starts over.

The boys did not choose to be born into a dysfunctional family. They learned from an early age to fend for themselves and to get even when they felt wronged. So they stole from others in order to survive and often vandalized property as a means of retaliating for some perceived wrong done to them. Many therapeutic placements have violent outbursts, steal, lie and act out sexually. Our lives as therapeutic foster parents were impacted in other ways. Neighbors resented living next door to boys who stole at every opportunity. We were rarely invited into anyone's home; we weren't welcome. Some of the frustration, fears and joys, I underwent as I dealt with a houseful of troubled boys will be revealed in the following pages, as well as some of the more humorous moments.

Foster children fall into four basic classifications:

- Traditional placements are children without special needs.
- Medical placements are children who need ongoing medical treatment.
- Behavioral placements are children with moderate to severe behavioral problems.
- Therapeutic placements have severe behavioral problems, some are about to enter a residential or juvenile facility, and some are being released from one of those facilities and are being placed in a therapeutic foster home to transition into a family living environment.

Foster parents caring for medical or behavioral placements receive twice as much pay as those caring for traditional placements. Those caring for therapeutic-placement children receive the highest pay, twice that of the medical and behavioral placements.

1

THE FRAMEWORK
Ellen's Life and Reasons for Fostering

Three days after Christmas, the last foster child had left my home and I found myself following a moving van out of my driveway toward my new life. There was not much in the van because I had sold or given away almost everything. As I drove away from everything that was familiar, I had mixed emotions, thinking about how I had started fostering.

When I married Auggie, I was divorced with two sons, ages five and ten. We lived paycheck to paycheck, from what he earned at his truck-driving job. I was pregnant with my third child, Caroline, when the owner of the trucking company was shot and killed. Auggie not only lost a job and a boss, but he lost his best drinking buddy. It was not unusual for them to start drinking after work, pass out in the office, wake up the next morning and get into their trucks and hit the road.

We struggled while Auggie looked for a job. He managed to find a few low-paying jobs and was able to keep food on the table but little more. Occasionally he would meet up with Elmer, a drinking buddy from work, and while drinking heavily, they decided to open their own local drayage company. Auggie borrowed $2,000 and Elmer contributed $2,000. They would get together and drink their way into oblivion, all the while arguing about how to run a business. The business was going nowhere. Their office consisted of two diesel trucks parked under a bridge. The old trucks were always breaking down, probably because the drivers did their own mechanical work, usually while they were drinking. One night, after drinking and fighting, Elmer said he wanted his money back. Auggie agreed.

What followed was an amazing journey. Because Auggie was charismatic, he managed to get good accounts immediately. By the time Bert was born four years later, the business was a success. Auggie was making $40,000 a month and pulling out $20,000 as salary for a brief period. He was creative, always figuring out how every purchase could be declared a tax deduction. After his death, I sorted boxes filled with years of ledgers and paperwork, discovering just how much money had slipped through his fingers.

Auggie had season tickets to every sporting event the city had to offer. He belonged to the hockey team's private club and was occasionally invited to fly to out-of-town games with the team. He also belonged to the baseball team's private club. I had heard that he paid for drinks for everyone who would belly up to the bar to drink with him.

At the hockey games, he sat directly behind the visitors' bench, furnishing beer for the entire section. The home team owner phoned Auggie. He said, "This is a hockey game, not the Auggie show." Auggie responded, "If you'd put a decent team on the ice, it wouldn't be the Auggie show."

We had a split-foyer home in a subdivision and it didn't take long to fill the house. Auggie added a room with a basement and continued to buy stuff. In the backyard he had an awesome oak fort built for the children. It was on stilts and had a large room with a porch. There was a play area underneath with swings and a slide.

Auggie's buying frenzy continued. We moved to an executive home, twice as large as the split-foyer. The new house had four bedrooms, walk-in closets, an office, four bathrooms, a finished multi-level basement, three-car garage, and a beautiful kitchen. We ate in the finest restaurants on a regular basis. He was one of the biggest supporters of the church, giving both time and money.

Auggie decided he wanted a new suit. Bert was a restless seven-year-old with no interest in shopping for a suit. Auggie told him he would buy him a video game afterward if he was good. Auggie ended up buying four suits, along with shirts and ties, and a new game system for Bert along with seven games.

Bert was not happy in his fourth grade class. He didn't get along with the teacher, Mrs. Beggs, and begged to get out of her class. In Auggie's world, you didn't mess with his kids. He told the principal to take his son out of that class or he was taking his kid out of the school. Of course if Bert left the school, Auggie's donations would stop as well. In true Catholic fashion, within three days, Bert was moved to the other fourth grade class.

Auggie's drinking continued out of control. Although huge amounts of money were rolling in, his spending increased to match the income. One evening, while dead drunk, he decided we should go to the mall. He was staggering and bumping into walls. A group of boys was following him and laughing. I was humiliated. He steered me into an upscale store where he bought me a full-length mink coat with as little thought as if he were ordering a soda.

Auggie liked to hang out in the bars near the big trucking company hubs, rubbing elbows with the hard-drinking truckers. Although he drove home drunk, the police never stopped him despite the fact that he ran into the median barriers and hit the side of the garage.

On the rare occasions when he decided to go into the office, Auggie would call home frequently. I could tell how drunk he was by his voice. He began having blackouts and the business began to decline. Although there was less money coming in, his spending habits did not change. As I was mowing the lawn one morning, I watched the repo man tow away Auggie's $35,000 Lincoln.®

Everything became intensely secretive. He made it clear that I was not to get the mail or answer the phone. One evening while I was preparing dinner, no water came out of the faucet. Auggie said he simply forgot to send in the payment. Then the electric company showed up, telling me we had to pay up or they would shut us off. I went to the grocery store and they refused to take my check.

Things went from bad to worse. Auggie finally had to tell me the house was in foreclosure because we were seven months behind on payments. Defeated, he sat in a chair crying. He told me the box in the dining room was full of unopened mail, mostly bills that were long overdue. We were broke. The accounts had fizzled out. It was time to have another beer.

Totally disgusted, I sat in a bar watching him as he downed one drink after another. His speech was slurred and he was in a foul mood. I had reached my breaking point and told him, "You're nothing but a drunk and I'm not living this way another second. I will be filing for a divorce. I'll find my own way home." I had never threatened to file for divorce. I walked away, heading to the phone to find a ride. I believe he was stunned because he followed me and said he would take me home. On the way home, he screamed obscenities, furious that I had stood up to him. I did not back down and he realized I was serious. This seemed to sober him up and he begged me not to leave him. I didn't budge. I was done. He spent the night in his office. Years later, Caroline told me she had been flooded with both sadness and relief as she watched him drive away.

Auggie started calling after he got to his office. I refused to talk to him, but Caroline finally did. Sixteen-year-old Caroline told him he was a mean drunk, making our lives miserable. She spent several hours on the phone, pouring out her soul and begging him to stop drinking.

He came home the next day and agreed to quit drinking beer. I was thrilled, thinking maybe this was fixable. I was stupid. True to his word, he did stop drinking beer; however, he started drinking wine and was still drunk all the time. We had another meltdown. I slapped him and he slapped me. I called the police. When the responding officers arrived, I was totally embarrassed when I realized they were two brothers from our former neighborhood. I told them I was fed up with his drinking. I suggested they check the car where they would find a cup half full of wine. He liked to have a little drink while he was driving. The officers returned with the cup, telling Auggie to leave and warning him to stay away until he sobered up. They watched while he drove away.

Auggie came home the next morning, swearing he would never drink again, claiming he loved his family more than alcohol. He kept his word. It was years before he admitted booze had almost destroyed his family. He was a changed man and spent the rest of his life trying to make up for the harm done.

It was clear that Auggie wouldn't be able to solve our financial problems. I knew we would have to file bankruptcy so I called an attorney, intending to file Chapter Thirteen so we wouldn't lose our home. The lawyers I contacted said we would need to file Chapter Seven. We owed so much money, there was no way to salvage anything.

Continuing my quest to find a lawyer, I finally found one willing to help us file Chapter Thirteen. We were nearly $1 million in debt, but most of the debt was written off, a portion was reduced and we agreed to pay back $750 a month for four years. A friend loaned us the money to catch up on the mortgage payments.

I went back to work which made Auggie cry. I was chipping away at the mountain of debt. Auggie's nieces and nephews had loaned him thousands of dollars that all had to be repaid. One thing was clear: I needed a better job.

An article in the newspaper about the need for therapeutic foster parents caught my attention. It said there was a shortage of qualified foster homes and that it paid well. I knew I could handle the job. We had kept a challenging neighbor boy, Ryder, for several years and had handled the situation well.

I called immediately and made an appointment to start my journey as a foster parent. We would have to pass all the classes for behavioral placements, get a background check and be licensed for fostering. I was surprised that Auggie was able to pass the background check. We were licensed for two boys, ages 12 through 18.

We put our house on the market and bought a less expensive property in a rural area. The home was over 100 years old and had very few closets so I piled some of our clothes on the living room floor. The dog came along and pooped on them. The house was in the middle of a pasture with no lawn or trees. I cried for a week, then dried my eyes and got busy. I sowed grass, planted trees and filled my home with foster kids.

The drayage business had little income and it was shrinking by the day. Eventually there was no business left.

Auggie loved living in the country. His health had been poor for years and began deteriorating rapidly. He looked for something to occupy his time and enable him to earn a little money despite his health limitations. As foster parents, we discovered there were agencies needing drivers to transport children who lived in residential facilities for family visits, court dates or other reasons.

The kids liked him. He had been given handcuffs and shackles to use in securing problem transports but he never used them. Every transport included a visit to a fast food restaurant. Auggie would pull into a service station and ask the kids if they wanted a soda. He would casually mention that he couldn't give them cigarettes but was leaving his cigarettes on the seat. He took his time paying for the gas and came back, paying no attention to how many cigarettes were in the pack. The kids hoped Auggie would be the one picking them up and they never gave him any trouble.

Auggie's legs had been severely injured when he was a teenager. His foot had gotten caught in the side of a freight elevator and, as the elevator crawled up three floors, it pulled his legs down, mangling them badly. They were a broken, bloody mass of bones and flesh. The doctors were in doubt as to whether they would be able to save either leg, prompting his father to sign to have both legs amputated. The orthopedic surgeon came in and refused to amputate unless it was to save his life. A year later, Auggie left the hospital on crutches. Because of pure determination, he recuperated enough to play on a soccer team.

Despite his miraculous recovery, Auggie had to endure complications for the rest of his life. He became deathly ill with osteomyelitis, which left him weak and exhausted. He had chronic poor circulation in one leg. In an attempt to save the leg, a vein was removed from his arm and put in his leg. The surgical incision, which had been stapled, would not heal and the wound spread. He had oxygen therapy four hours a day, five days a week, but it didn't work. The wound grew to a length of about 10 inches, with the bone exposed. He was in tremendous pain, to the point of exhibiting dementia.

One day after he went into the walk-in closet to get some batteries, our son and I heard him screaming and ran to see what was wrong. He was hanging onto a shelf, unable to walk and unaware of his surroundings. Bert and my daughter-in-law, Kathleen, managed to get him out of the closet and back to bed. When he was finally coming back to reality, he said, "I never did get my fuckin' batteries."

After that, he was unable to get out of bed without help. He would awaken me during the night to get his pain medication or to use the bathroom. Although he was unable to walk, he refused to get a wheelchair so I wheeled him around in his office chair. In addition to helping him bathe, I spent thirty minutes every morning and every evening cleaning and dressing his wound.

I was exhausted. I had all of this to deal with in addition to the foster and adoptive children with varying degrees of behavioral problems.

The wound developed gangrene. I've never smelled anything worse. With all options exhausted and no hope left, his leg had to be amputated several inches above the knee. The circulation was so poor that cutting off the leg did not produce bleeding. Auggie was weak and still required a lot of care after the surgery. He never used his prosthetic leg. Eventually, the kids made a lamp out of it. A local garage still has it on display.

Three months after the amputation, I got sick. I had run a fever for several weeks but had been getting by on aspirin and Tylenol.® One Sunday morning I got up early and made potato salad to take to a foster parent support group picnic. I had been having chest pains for several days and was feeling worse than usual. I laid down on the bed. Since he had never seen me lie down like that, Auggie knew I was really sick. Eventually I agreed to let him take me to the emergency room.

Within minutes of arriving at the rural hospital, I was diagnosed as having had a heart attack accompanied by pneumonia. Blood tests revealed I also had septicemia and I was gently told I had a 50 percent chance of survival. I was then taken by ambulance to a large hospital in the city where I spent three days in intensive care before being moved to a ward.

After a couple of days I told the doctor, "I can't stay here. I have a one-legged husband and a house full of boys with behavioral problems." He agreed, knowing I would leave with or without his permission. "Try to take better care of yourself," he admonished.

Auggie did not handle my illness well. In fact, he was hysterical. Caroline had taken four days off of work to help her dad and take care of the boys. When she went back to work, Auggie called her and said, "You need to come over and fix dinner." As soon as I got home, I was as busy as ever.

Gradually Auggie got his strength back and seemed healthier than he had been in years. He finally relented and got both a standard and an electric wheelchair. After several months of therapy, he was back to transporting kids. He was driving a pickup but decided to buy a new van with automatic sliding doors to accommodate his wheelchair so he could be independent. He asked whether I thought he should take out the insurance that would pay for the van if he died. I said, "No." Three months later he was dead.

Auggie's orthopedic surgeon was also his best friend. When the leg was amputated he had told me he didn't expect Auggie to live more than a year. He lived 13 months. Death had knocked on the door so often that I was unprepared when it entered. He had cheated death so many times before. Auggie said, "My bags are packed and I'm ready to go. I'm tired of hurting."

The night before he died, he did not feel well but that was not unusual. He never mentioned that he was having chest pains. Noticing his entire body felt ice cold, I asked if he would like a sweatshirt. He was dying and I didn't know it. When the paramedics arrived, they asked him how bad his chest pains were on a scale of one to ten. He replied, "10". His heart stopped beating on the way to the hospital.

Mike stayed with the kids so Bert and I could follow the ambulance. Several foster kids showed up at the emergency room plus our kids and Kathleen. Paxton came in and threw himself over Auggie's lifeless body saying, "I've lost two dads in this same room." Someone asked Todd how he was doing. He said, "How the fuck do you think I'm doing? Everyone is crying because our dad just died." The man least likely to be a foster parent died surrounded by foster boys who loved him.

I was hysterical as I called from the hospital to tell Melanie, the social worker, that Auggie was dead. By the time I got home, the house was full of people. Some were from children's welfare and the mental health facility. Some were other foster parents. Neighbors dropped in as well. There was enough food to feed an army for a week.

We had planned to have a barbecue that Saturday and had invited family and friends. Instead of having a barbecue, we went to the funeral home to make the arrangements. Caroline, Bert and Kathleen went with me. Before we went, we decided we weren't going to let the funeral home run up our bill just because we were grieving. We picked out the cheapest casket - lime green. When asked if we wanted the obituary placed in the city paper, which charges by the word, Bert said, "Yeah. Auggie's dead. Van for Sale."

It was a 500-mile trip to the family cemetery. I was told by the funeral home that I would have to pay mileage plus pay for a motel for two drivers. I told Bert to take the seats out of the back of the van. He did and we put the casket in the van after getting a license through the funeral home to haul a body. Bert drove Auggie past all of his favorite places. The six-car procession made the 500-mile journey to deliver Auggie to his final resting place. Most of the passengers were former foster kids.

Numb and bewildered, I felt like someone had poured molasses in my brain. After a couple of weeks, I began cleaning out Auggie's belongings, starting with his night stand. I looked at his array of powerful pain killers and realized every container was empty. Someone had cleaned them out.

I was a widow with six behavioral placements. It never occurred to me that I couldn't do it. In fact, I suddenly realized I was not as busy. For years, the only time I had been able to sit down was to go to the bathroom.

Bert had moved back from Chicago before Auggie had his leg amputated. He was a huge help, taking his dad to appointments, therapy and so on. I was tremendously grateful he was living at home. Even though he was only there a couple of days a week, I was comforted to know he had a room there.

Auggie had managed to continue driving almost to the end. I was totally shocked when, after his death a W-2 arrived listing his wages for six months at $20 thousand. I had no idea he had earned that much from driving that last year. Bert found $700 that Auggie had hidden in his night stand. To my knowledge, every penny he had spent had come out of my checking account. We never found out what happened to the rest of the money he had earned. Before I moved out of the house, I pulled out every drawer and checked every possible hiding place but never found any more money.

Several years later, as I followed the moving van down the driveway, I realized I was a different person than I had been years earlier. When we had moved into that house, I had known that I had to do whatever it took to stay afloat and I had done it. I had watched a lot of boys come and go and been affected differently by each of them. Five months before I moved out of the home I had shared with Auggie and an endless stream of foster children, I had married Vince and was anxious to start a new chapter in my life. I had mixed feelings, wondering what I would do with my time and wishing I had not gotten rid of nearly everything I owned.

Throughout the years, I had always been waiting for something to happen to bring happiness such as for me to finish school, my first husband to graduate from college, getting out of that troubled marriage, for my second husband to quit drinking, and for me to find a job so I could pay the bills, etc.

This day, as I followed the moving van to my new home and new life, I realized I no longer have to foster disturbed children and I'm no longer waiting. I've found peace, contentment and happiness.

It is an honor to be asked to help someone in need.
—My Dad

2

RYDER
The Foster Kid Who Wasn't

Ryder, who lived with his single mother, discovered a stack of girlie magazines in a makeshift fort in the wooded area behind the subdivision. This was a huge find for a six-year-old boy and, being unselfish, he decided to share. The next morning, with the magazines tucked away in his backpack, he got on the St. John's Catholic school bus and sat down next to his friend, Erik, also six. Unable to keep his forbidden treasures to himself, he slipped half of the magazines into Erik's backpack and showed the rest of them to his other buddies.

One of the boys told the priest, "Father, Ryder has a lot of dirty magazines and everyone is looking at them." Ryder was summoned to the office and "confessed" with perfect eye contact. He said, "Father, Erik gave me the magazines. He has them in his backpack." Erik was shocked as he watched the priest pull the magazines from his backpack and swore he had been framed.

In the subdivision where we lived, there was an old barn filled with hay. It was a perfect place for little boys to play, but it burned to the ground one sunny afternoon. Neighbors gathered around the burning barn, watching copperheads slither out of the burning inferno and speculating that Ryder might have been responsible.

After spending an afternoon playing with Erik, Ryder was lying on the floor. He told his mom, Kristie, that he was worn out because he had been in an accident that afternoon. About that same time, Erik's parents found their car at the bottom of the hill. The boys had been playing in the car and had released the brake. The car had rolled down the hill with the boys in it. Ryder was known as the neighborhood troublemaker.

Auggie and I liked this spunky kid, who spent a lot of time at our house. Most weekends I took the kids to a movie. A natural-born con artist, Ryder would wait until the concession stand lines were long and then jump in and order candy and a soda. Slowly counting his money lying on the counter, he would choke back tears, explaining, "I don't have enough." The bored teenager, noticing the long line behind Ryder, would tell him to put the candy back. Ryder would whine saying, "I want the candy. You keep the soda." Ryder refused to move until the teenager told him he could have the soda or some kind soul stepped forward to pay for it. It worked every time!

By the time he was 12, Ryder was running wild, getting into trouble, and taking advantage of his single mother's absences. Kristie told Auggie, "Ryder is more than I can handle. I'm going to put him into foster care." Auggie replied, "No way! Don't do that. Just send him to us." That was the start of our journey as foster parents. The state was never involved in the arrangement and we were not paid.

Ryder was a likable kid and we had few problems with his behavior, but there were occasional incidents. Once, shortly after the boys got off the school bus, an angry mother came to the door. She was livid, yelling that Ryder had beaten the snot out of her son, Trent. Auggie said, "That's impossible. He came in the house as soon as he got off the bus." Trent's mom asked Ryder, "Is that true? You weren't the one who hit my boy?" As he shoved cookies into his mouth, Ryder said, "Nah, I beat him up. It didn't take long."

A neighbor, Andrew, who was a local television reporter, wanted to do a cover story about how easy it was for young children to buy cigarettes. Andrew picked Bert and Ryder to do the buying. The boys jumped at the chance to be on television. Andrew picked them up in the news van and dropped them off at convenience stores. The boys marched right up and told the clerks, "Gimme that pack of smokes," pointing to the cigarettes they wanted. Every time the clerk sold cigarettes to the youngsters. Then Andrew would go in the store accompanied by his camera crew and ask the flabbergasted clerk if he was aware it was illegal to sell cigarettes to children. After three successful stops, Andrew brought the boys home and they got to keep the cigarettes!

When Ryder was 14, Kristie insisted he move back in with her. He didn't want to go but, as we told him, we had no legal rights. Kristie had moved to another subdivision and she watched as Ryder got on the bus. However, after school, he rode the bus home with Bert to our house. We told him he couldn't stay with us—that he had to go back to his mother's house. We drove him home and went out to dinner. Later that evening, as we drove into our driveway, we saw Ryder sitting on the front steps with a big grin on his face. "I told her I was going to kill myself if I had to live with her," he said, adding, "She said I could stay here." Ryder lived with us another year, then returned to Kristie's home.

Ryder thought it was a brilliant idea to take nude pictures of his girl friend, who willingly posed for him. All was well until they got into a fight. He told her he would get even with her. He mailed the nude pictures to her father complete with his return address and a signed note. The enraged father called Ryder and said he was coming over to beat the crap out of him. Not to be intimidated, Ryder said, "Bring it on; I'll be waiting." He sat on the front step with a baseball bat. The father never showed up but talked to Kristie instead. Ryder was told he needed to return every picture and he did so, later musing to Bert, "What was I thinking? I should have kept a few!"

It wasn't long before Ryder got into real trouble. Out of boredom, he stole his sister Heidi's car and invited four of his buddies to go along. They headed to Wisconsin, a trip that landed him in juvenile detention.

After he was released, he returned to Kristie's house. Restless, he again had the urge to travel and, along with a buddy, headed to a convenience store intent on stealing transportation. They found a car with the keys left in it and jumped in. Discovering it was a stick shift, which they had no idea how to drive, they went on to another car. The second car also had the keys in the ignition, but there was a baby in the backseat. They found a third vehicle, a van with the engine running.

They hopped in and headed for California. Their journey ended in Colorado where they led officers on a high-speed chase until they encountered road spikes. Once more, Ryder found himself locked up in a juvenile facility, this one out of state. While he served his time, he earned a GED, making a nearly-perfect score. He was offered scholarships. He was released owing restitution, which he had no intention of paying. They told him to leave the state and warned him that he would go to the adult facility if he did it again.

Kristie told him he could come back home with the stipulation that there was to be no drinking, drugs or trouble. We no longer lived in the area, but our daughter, Caroline, did. She had a college degree, a good job and an apartment. Bert and Ryder decided to party in the city on a Saturday night and crash at Caroline's place.

In a drunken stupor, Ryder initiated a fight. He could barely stand up, much less fight. The next morning, he was overheard screaming in the bathroom, "What the fuck happened to my face? Shit like this doesn't happen to sober people." He refused to leave Caroline's apartment until after midnight. He was hoping Kristie would be asleep when he got home. He caught a break because she was asleep. But it took more than a day for the swelling and bruises to disappear so he got busted. Kristie kicked him out so he had to find different living arrangements. He went to live with his sister, Heidi, from whom he had earlier stolen the car.

He soon found himself in trouble again and I bailed him out of jail.

Heidi, 19, had moved in with a boyfriend, leaving Ryder on probation and homeless. He called Caroline and she brought him to our house. We didn't have an extra bed. Half the basement had been sectioned off to house emancipated boys who were no longer eligible for foster care. Ryder found a mattress and joined the gang in the basement.

Ryder stayed with us for four years. He worked at low-paying, dead-end jobs, but was always respectful to me and Auggie and caused no problems at home. However, he was drinking and doing drugs outside the home. He dated a minister's daughter and, when she enrolled in college, he moved with her to the college town. Soon after, he was doing 120 days shock time for showing up drunk at the probation office.

He left the area and the years rolled by. Being intelligent, he eventually found good jobs as a skilled machinist, but due to drug and alcohol abuse, was repeatedly fired. The good jobs became fewer and farther between.

Both he and Kristie attended my wedding to my new husband. Ryder was still making contact with Bert and Caroline from time to time. I got reports back from them. He usually called them while enveloped in a drug and alcohol-induced haze. Heroine and crystal meth had become his drugs of choice. He recently texted Bert that his left arm had been numb for three days and he couldn't hear to talk on the phone, so he had sent him text messages.

When Bert told Caroline, she was terribly distraught and called the drug hotline to see what these symptoms indicated. She was told, if he doesn't get to a hospital, he'll die. She called me, not knowing what to do. We didn't know where he was so there was nothing we could do. We didn't hear any more so we thought he must have cheated death one more time.

Then most recently, Heidi called Caroline with the news that Ryder had attempted to make his own drugs, something called "bath salt" and had either overdosed or poisoned himself. He's hospitalized. His brain is fried and he has lost all of his intelligence. He can't speak, only mumbles, and is now little more than a vegetable. They are unsure as to whether he will make any significant recovery.

3

ALISHA
Delivered in Handcuffs
Shared Her Mother's Boyfriend

I watched an attractive 15-year-old handcuffed girl get out of the back of a police car. I opened the door to let the officer bring her in and led them to the kitchen table. The officer took the girl's handcuffs off, commenting, "It sure is hot out there today."

She rubbed her wrists while scowling at the officer and said, "You had 'em on too freakin' tight, now my wrists hurt." He looked at me and said, "This is Alisha. Good luck. Sign these papers and I'll be on my way."

The officer left and I showed Alisha her room. She had nothing to put in it and asked if I would drive her numerous places to pick up her belongings. The social worker would be coming by in a bit with a clothing allowance of $100. I was thinking, "I'm in it now, better hang on for the ride."

Auggie and I had attended the required training sessions to be foster parents and had the newly-acquired license. I was apprehensive about having my life turned upside down with extra children in my home, and had been reluctant to take in my first placement. Children's welfare had already called a few times offering placements but I was having difficulty jumping in. The supervisor phoned. She reproached me, "You're not accepting any placements. Do you really want to be a foster parent? Is there a problem? Should we quit calling?" My goal was the big bucks from therapeutic placements so I could pay down our mountain of bills. I gave myself a pep talk so I could say, "Yes" to the next request. It wasn't long before they called to see if I would take Alisha. She hadn't been attending school, had no place she called home, and was running wild. I said, "I would love to have Alisha."

My training had been for traditional placements, not for those with behavioral problems. My introduction to fostering was in the form of a wild, handcuffed child, who hadn't been accepted in the experienced homes. I quickly learned how the system worked. When the caseworkers go down their list of properly-qualified foster homes and everyone turns the child down, they will then place that child in any available foster home. Frequently a therapeutic placement ends up in a traditional home with the state paying a lower maintenance fee—favorable for the state's budget, but bad for the unsuspecting under-qualified parent. Unfortunately, the foster parents are clueless and can't handle the child. The newly-trained foster parents then drop like flies.

When our 14-year-old son, Bert, came home from school and saw good-looking Alisha watching television, he said to himself, "Happy birthday, Bert." They were in the family room, talking and getting acquainted when I overheard Alisha ask, "Have you ever been stabbed?" The relationship went no further than Bert thinking she was cute. She was cut from different material than anyone he had known.

A few days later, Alisha's mother, Kari, was standing at our front door. She was a mirror image of her daughter. I was new at this game but knew she shouldn't be there and knew Alisha had given her directions to our home. At that time, parents were not allowed to know where their children were.

I said, "All visits are through children's welfare. You can't be here." They both glared at me. Alisha asked, "Can I at least sit in the car with her for a while?" I agreed to 30 minutes, convinced they would just drive away but they didn't.

Thirty minutes later, Alisha came back into the house, followed by Kari and her boyfriend, who was carrying their child. The boyfriend looked young enough to be a placement. Alisha stated, "I want you to see my baby brother." What could I do? I held the baby and made small talk with Kari and her boy-toy. After they left, Alisha told me her mother had seven children, including triplets, but the toddler was the only one she had custody of.

Alisha knew a girl in a neighboring subdivision and asked if I would take her there. I drove her, visualizing in my mind how I would meet the parents, get a phone number, and be happy that she had a friend living nearby.

When I pulled up in front of the house, Alisha pointed and said, "That's her mom on the steps." I saw an obese woman wearing a tank top and spandex pants, hanging onto a can of beer, with a cigarette dangling from the corner of her lips. Alisha bounced out of the car, shouting, "Hi, Trixie, where's Starla?" Blowing smoke out of her mouth, she responded, "I suppose she's in watchin' TV." Alisha motioned for me to follow her and we entered a foul-smelling, cluttered living room where the TV was blaring. I met 15-year-old Starla, noticing her stomach was swollen with pregnancy. Starla offered Alisha one of her cigarettes and they began chatting. Alisha asked me, "Can I stay here awhile and walk home?" I told her to be home in two hours.

Two hours later, she arrived with Starla and 15-year-old Ronnie, who had joined them in their walk. They had a brilliant plan. Alisha and Ronnie would raise Starla's baby. Starla was thrilled with the plan and agreed to give her baby to the two youngsters. I couldn't believe what I was hearing. I said, "What a fantastic idea. You'd better start making some plans," knowing this plan would fizzle out before the sun came up the next morning. The idea was never mentioned again.

Alisha asked if she could hang out with some friends at the mall. That sounded safe enough so I said, "Sure, I was planning on going to the mall anyway." When we arrived, I gave her instructions to meet me in the food court in a couple of hours. I was at the food court at the designated time and started the wait, checking my watch every five minutes. An hour later, she casually showed up, offering no explanation as to why she was late. When we got home, I overheard the phone conversation, in which she described in graphic detail her sexual encounter in the mall parking lot. I suspected she intended for me to overhear. I simply informed her I would not be taking her to the mall anymore.

By the time Alisha had been in my home three weeks, that tiny 15-year-old had given me an incredible number of fostering experiences. Because I was a rookie, I called the case manager frequently, asking for advice. She suggested I go through Alisha's room to check for drugs or anything that could be causing a problem. I didn't find any drugs, but found a notebook and started reading. I learned that being in my foster home was hampering her sex life. She wrote about the hot sex in the parking lot and how she and Ronnie "fucked in the bushes" on the walk home with Starla. Apparently Kari shared stories with her daughter, relating her own wild sex, and this was elaborated upon in the notebook as well.

When she returned from school that afternoon, she sweetly asked if she could get a soda with some friends. I gave her permission, adding that she should be home by 6:30 in time for dinner. We waited until 7:00 PM then ate without her. At midnight I reported her missing and went to bed.

Alisha was on the lam for several weeks before the police found her in a dilapidated old house with a group of runaways. She was then placed in Cheryl's therapeutic foster home in a neighboring subdivision. Cheryl had two pre-school foster boys for whom parental rights were in the process of being terminated. They were Alisha's cousins.

At the next foster parent training session, I sat by Cheryl and we chatted about Alisha. She had left my home with nothing but the clothes on her back. When she was placed with Cheryl, she had something else—crabs! Alisha had been in the bathroom and had calmly asked Cheryl to come in because she wanted to show her something. The "something" was little

6

66

Through Hell and Out the Other Side

things that were stuck on her eyelashes and eyebrows. To Cheryl's dismay, she recognized what could be crabs. She asked Alisha if she had them in her pubic area. Alisha responded, "Lots and lots".

I moved out of the area and lost contact with Alisha for several years. I ran into Cheryl and asked about her. Alisha had had a moment of fame on a TV network morning talk show. The theme had been mothers and daughters sharing boyfriends.

Where there is room in the heart, there is always room in the house.
—Sir Thomas Moore

16

4

ADRIELLE
The Drama Queen

Since Alisha was on the lam, I cleaned her room, packed her things and waited for the next placement. A few days later, a jolly social worker asked if I would take Adrielle, a 13-year-old girl. I agreed to do so, wondering if anyone bothered to check my contract that stated, "Two boys, ages 12 through 18." I was given a brief summary of Adrielle's background and how she came to be in foster care. The school had placed a hotline call, alleging the mother was abusive.

An hour later Adrielle, accompanied by a social worker, was at my door. I opened the door with a cheerful, welcoming smile, pleased to see she was not handcuffed. A quick glance revealed a slender girl with curly blond hair hanging to her waist. She had the deer-in-the-headlights look.

I took her to her room to unpack and sat on the bed to talk with her. She evaluated the room and said, "I would like a different bedspread with curtains to match. I don't care much for the color of the walls. I want a new color to match the curtains and bedspread." I thought, "That ain't going to happen." She wasted no time moving on to the next topic, explaining how mean her mother was.

I learned through Adrielle and the documentation from children's welfare that her mother, Sunny, was a kept woman, supported by a married man. Adrielle, her little brother and Sunny, were living in a new house provided by Sunny's man. It had to be kept in perfect condition at all times. All the picture on the walls, every piece of furniture, even every plant, had to be approved by the paramour. He planned to sell the house at some point. Together they had a six-year-old son. Sunny was not employed and was, therefore, available to him at all times. He paid tuition for Adrielle to attend a private school.

She settled in, spending hours drawing cartoon characters working toward her goal to have a career in animation. Occasionally I noticed tears slipping down her cheek as she looked at a picture of her little brother.

Maybe she was homesick.

I transported her daily so she could complete the school year and attend eighth grade graduation with her class. I discovered that a private school expected more than a public school. It seemed I was always running her somewhere or attending something. Fostering was intended to help out financially; however, I quickly found that with Adrielle, a traditional placement, I was "in the hole." I had to buy her a new dress for graduation. She had a birthday party and invited her entire class. After that, she gained so much weight that none of her clothes fit and the measly clothing allowance barely bought new underwear.

Mike arrived five weeks after Adrielle. She wanted to be included in everything Bert and Mike did, but they found her to be a nuisance and delighted in teasing her. It was a long summer. We moved from our large home to a smaller home in the country. I was so busy I didn't know if I was coming or going and was constantly listening to complaints about how mean the boys were, which was probably true.

We moved most of our belongings in the back of an old pickup Auggie bought for a couple hundred dollars. You could see the highway through the holes in the floorboard. We hired a moving van to deliver the larger items. My daughter, Caroline, had accumulated massive amounts of possessions when the money was rolling in. Adrielle brought her stuff in one trash bag along with the few new clothes I had been able to buy for her. At the end of the day, the van driver asked me, "What's Adrielle—the ugly sister, who doesn't get anything?" Even though it was none of his business, I knew it looked bad. I simply said, "I gave birth to Caroline 19 years ago. Children's welfare brought Adrielle 10 weeks ago," and walked away.

Adrielle loved attention and used exaggeration for effect. But it is possible there was a grain of truth in the stories she told. I doubt if she would have been placed in foster care today and probably should not have been back then. The family could have been monitored with in-home services such as counseling for Mom and the children to try to keep the family together.

She discovered the teachers lapped up every embellished story she fed them. The concerned principal made a hotline call one day to report that Sunny was an abusive mother. Based only on the information from Adrielle, the police were waiting on the parking lot when Sunny arrived to pick her up. They told her they were there to take custody of Adrielle due to reports of abuse.

The paramour saw this as an opportunity to take custody of their son. Sunny had been tagged as an unfit mother. The new house was sold and Sunny lost both of her children and her home. I was curious as to what the paramour's wife felt about his love child living with them.

I enrolled the three teenagers in schools near our new home. Bert and Mike were to attend a different school than Adrielle. Hoisington was a small town and Adrielle's class size would be comparable to her private school. She made a few friends and asked if they could come over. The girls took one look at the handsome, charismatic Mike and immediately lost their interest in being around Adrielle. She was furious. I suggested they hang out in Adrielle's room but the girls weren't about to leave Mike.

Needing a break, I tried to arrange a respite weekend which I never got. The first lady on my list declined when she realized I had Adrielle. She said it would be a conflict of interest for her to do respite because her husband had been one of the detectives who had worked with Adrielle. Sunny had been called in for questioning and had attacked him.

I recalled that a different detective had been brought in afterward because I had been asked to bring Adrielle to the police station for questioning. He took an active interest in Adrielle's welfare—I felt a little too active. After we moved, he thought nothing of driving 60 miles to take Adrielle to dinner to "discuss the case."

I was new and naïve so I assumed the detective knew what was in her best interest and that I should listen to his advice. Apparently he did not agree with the appointed guardian ad litem on what was in Adrielle's best interest. He suggested I write a letter to the court requesting a different guardian ad litem. I did.

When the court date arrived, I patiently sat outside of the courtroom. At that time, foster parents were not included in the court proceedings. Today the court encourages foster parents to participate in the hearings, realizing they have valuable input.

I waited on the hard bench all morning. The social worker finally approached me and said, "Adrielle will be admitted to a psychiatric hospital for evaluation. She won't be returning to your home. The judge feels you overstepped your boundaries by writing that letter. In the future, don't write any more letters."

I learned two things with Adrielle's placement. I would not be writing more letters and I would not accept another female placement. The years slipped by and, on my quest to find my former placements, I discovered Adrielle was traveling with a well-known musical, designing sets.

5

MIKE

The Cycle is Broken
Became One of the Family

I opened the door, staring at a skinny 15-year-old boy, covered with tomato soup. He was accompanied by a big burly police officer. An hour earlier I had agreed to take Mike as an emergency placement, making it clear I would only keep him over the weekend because I also had 14-year-old Adrielle. I was assured they'd find a new placement for him by Monday.

I led Mike and the officer to the kitchen table to hear the details of how the tomato soup ended up on the boy. The officer said, "There was an altercation between Mike, his mother, Marlene, and a neighbor, Harold, who lived on the other side of the duplex. Harold held Mike while Marlene hit him. She grabbed the soup off the stove and threw it at him." Mike had only the clothes on his back which were covered with soup. I asked Bert, who was two months younger, but larger, if he could find something for Mike to wear. The two boys headed to Bert's room. The officer remained seated and said, "I've seen Mike around. I think he's a decent kid. I hope he does well in your home."

Bert found a few changes of clothes for Mike. There were no behavioral problems that weekend. However, I was concerned that Mike and Adrielle were too chummy. Monday came and went with no word on moving Mike, and then Tuesday and Wednesday slipped by with no word. Thursday I made the call asking, "I was told Mike would only be here over the weekend. When can I expect you to pick him up? You know I have a teenage girl here, and I'm worried they are entirely too friendly." The overworked, stressed-out case manager let out a sigh and answered, "Truthfully, we don't have anyone willing to take a 15-year-old boy." I foolishly thought that was their problem, not mine. I said, "Well, I want him moved. I've got two teenagers in heat. This is not a good situation in my house. It's summer and they're together all the time."

They assured me they would find a placement soon. In the years that followed, I found this was common practice. Go down the list of foster parents, find someone willing to take the child and hope they don't complain. I never asked again to have Mike moved, and children's welfare never offered to move him. By the end of the first week whatever sparks had been ignited by teenage hormones were extinguished.

Bert wasn't sure what he thought about Mike, other than hoping he'd go away. The bored teenagers decided to play Monopoly™ on those long, hot summer afternoons. Adrielle was really gloating over the fact she was winning. Bert and Mike, not to be outdone by a girl, decided to merge and, of course, they turned the tables. Adrielle stormed off to her room, yelling how much she hated them, until the door slammed shut behind her. Bert decided Mike was fun to have around. I found Mike amusing and today, many years later, thank God for sending Mike to our home. I love him as my son.

Marlene loved Mike in her own way. She was an intelligent woman with mental illness. She was a dog groomer and, for extra income, she raised dogs in the tiny duplex. One bedroom was Marlene's and the other bedroom had crates of dogs stacked up.

Mike frequently brought home notes from school, citing disciplinary problems. Marlene was clueless how to make him behave. Out of desperation, she attended school with him, determined he would change his ways. Mike told me, "Do you know how embarrassing that was?" Marlene decided home schooling would solve two problems. One, he would stay out of trouble, and two, he could take care of the dogs while she was working. The home schooling consisted of handing Mike a stack of books after which he was on his own.

It was not in Mike's nature to sit home all day taking care of dogs, and doing schoolwork. The family next door had a son Mike's age, and he would venture over there at every opportunity. Marlene had an ongoing feud with the neighbor. She forbade Mike to be there. The man received disability checks that provided time on his hands to smoke his marijuana and figure out ways to annoy Marlene. She, in turn, did everything to antagonize him.

Everything was secretive years ago. I'd drive up to the back door of children's welfare to be greeted by the case manager, who whisked Mike away. Marlene entered by the front door and sat in the waiting room until she was called for the visit. Every effort was made to keep the foster family and biological family separated. I was informed what kind of car she drove and to keep an eye out for it. Marlene and I both attended the family meetings. She complained that Mike was completely out of control.

Mike was assigned to Dr. Mueller, a psychiatrist. Marlene was to attend the sessions with Mike, with the goal being reunification. During the first session I was sitting in the waiting room reading my book, when

Marlene came out with a smile on her face. She said, "Enjoy my son." A few minutes passed and I was summoned to join Dr. Mueller and Mike. Dr. Mueller said, "Mike, would you like to tell Ellen what took place?" Mike said, "Mom asked if I wanted to come home or stay where I am. I told her I wanted to stay put."

A month after Mike moved in I took the kids to the Fourth of July festivities, including the grand finale fireworks display. Mike asked, "Can I hang out with my friends? I haven't seen them in a long time." I said, "Sure. Meet us at the car at 10:30." We waited by the car, watching 10:30 slowly tick by, and then 11:00 came and went. I noticed the place was beginning to look deserted. At 11:15, I announced, "If he's not here in 10 minutes I'm leaving. I'll contact the police and children's welfare and report him missing." Ten minutes passed so we piled into the car with no sign of Mike. In the distance we spotted a young boy running toward us, hollering, "Wait, wait, I'm coming." As he approached he said, "Sorry. I'm sorry. I didn't realize what time it was." A few days later he admitted, "I was in the woods swapping spit with Bridgette."

The summer days were slipping away as we prepared to move. Arrangements were made for Mike to attend a camp for a few days. While he was gone, we hired a chimney sweep. When he completed the job, he presented us with a bill and a VHS tape, with a homemade version of a Christmas movie he had found in the fireplace. Auggie said, "Put it in the VCR. That's no Christmas tape." Well, he was right about that. The quality of the porn movie was so bad that you could barely make out the picture. I guess when you're 15, it's still a prize. Bert and I picked Mike up from camp. I asked, "Mike, did you have fun?" He went into detail about the great time and all the fun activities. I casually asked, "Have you watched any good Christmas tapes lately?" I heard him moan and watched in the rear view mirror as he slithered down in the back seat, listening to Bert sing about Santa Claus coming to town.

I made a trip to the discount store with three teenagers tagging along. They scattered, while I filled my shopping cart. The boys tracked me down so Mike could ask me, "Will you buy me this box of (24) condoms?" Laughing, Bert said, "I'll bet you'd be happy if you could use all of those." Mike responded, "I'd be happy if I could use just one."

Our home finally sold after sitting on the market for months. We bought a house in the country 65 miles away. It was a smaller home, for $60 thousand less money. It was a two-story house in the middle of a cow pasture. The first time Mike saw the house, the only comment he made was, "This kinda looks like a step down."

Mike was aware of the 'For Sale' sign in the front yard. He did not want to leave the area, so the plan was to search for a new foster home. With the closing date two weeks away, we asked Mike to have a seat at the kitchen table. I said, "We'll be moving in two weeks so it's time to contact your case manager to find you a new placement. If you'd like to move with us, you're welcome. We'd love to have you." He silently sat there for a few minutes then tears started to trickle down his cheeks. Before long, he was sobbing. I didn't have a clue what to say to this upset child other than, "Its your decision. No one can make it for you." He stood up, dried his tears with his sleeve, and said, "I'm goin' with you."

Auggie had grown fond of Mike, and was happy he would be moving with us. Later that evening he asked Bert and Mike if they would ride along to deliver his bills. On the way home Mike said, "I wanna stop for a hamburger." Auggie said, "No." Mike jokingly said "I swear to God, I'll start cryin' again." Auggie bought him a hamburger.

We worked hard packing up, making many trips to Hoisington in that piece of junk pick-up, unloading, and going back to reload, emptying our big house. The house had an attached three-car garage with an attic above it. The attic was large, high enough to walk around in, with a few boards over the unfinished floor. I was handing down the Christmas decorations to the boys, carefully walking on the boards. Somehow, I missed the board and the next thing I knew, my entire leg was hanging down into the garage. The boys thought that was the funniest thing they had ever seen. I guess it was quite a sight. After endless laughter, Mike managed to ask, "Are you all right? I thought it was the second coming." The belly laughter continued off and on for days. Auggie was not amused. There was a huge hole in the ceiling. Mike worked hard, never complaining, and turned the work into fun.

The first thing on the itinerary was to enroll the three teenagers in school. I discovered there was no high school in the rural area. The students could choose between five high schools to attend, and the district paid their tuition. I'd meet the bus at the end of their route and the boys would be transported the remainder of the trip. Bert and Mike didn't want to be in the same school as Adrielle, therefore I was on the road a lot.

The principal was a good old boy from the totally white area. He informed me, "We don't acknowledge MLK Day at this school and as long as we can get away with it, we never will." Bert and Mike thought they had stepped back into the sixties. They told me, "These country boys like to talk about how fast their tractors go," or, "That dang hawg kept gettin' outta his pen. I cracked him a good 'un on the head. Didn't mean to kill him." The aggravated bus driver told Mike, "I'll bet you'd kiss a nigger." Caroline was appalled and said, "You need to report him to the principal." Under the circumstances, I didn't see much point.

Mike made friends easily, happy to put the home schooling behind him. He did not want to be labeled, "foster kid". The students were curious about the relationship between Bert and Mike. The only explanation they ever gave was, "Bert's two months older; we have the same mother." I told the boys coming through my home not to go to school and tell everyone they were foster kids. It tends to label them, setting them apart. After a few years it was common knowledge that the big house a mile outside of Hoisington was a foster home. It was no secret. If you lived in that house, you were a foster kid. When I wrote checks with the address printed on the top, I'd often hear, "Oh, you're that woman right outside of town with all those kids."

Auggie enlisted the help of Bert and Mike to put up a fence for the dog. Normally, Auggie kidded around, but this day he was in no kidding mood. The boys were singing about working on the chain gang, referring to Auggie as Warden and Massa. They were relentless, singing, laughing, and Auggie was fuming, telling them, "Shut the fuck up." Finally he threw his shovel down and stomped off to the house. He told me, "Those boys are fuckin' out of control." I had to go outside so he wouldn't catch me laughing.

On a Saturday morning I was gathering the laundry, while the boys were sleeping late. I was going through Mike's pockets, cheerfully announcing every item I pulled out. When I pulled out glow-in-the-dark condoms, I said, "Well, this is a step-up from the generic brand in the discount store." I proceeded to read the label as I watched Mike pull the blankets over his head. When he came up for breakfast Auggie was singing about a little glowworm.

We allowed Mike to use our car after he got his driver's license. One night, long past curfew, I was nervously pacing the floor and Auggie was playing solitaire as we waited. Finally I saw the headlights coming up the driveway. Mike came in, all smiles, saying, "You won't believe this. I went through a sobriety check. They took the seats out, went through the trunk, searched everywhere, and it took a long, long time." I walked to the phone and dialed the sheriff's department. I said, "I'm curious about the sobriety check. My son was late getting home, because he said it took a long time to search the car." When the deputy quit laughing he said, "That's a good story, but there was no sobriety check." "All right, You're grounded. Good night."

Auggie and I were sitting at the kitchen table having a friendly chat with Matt, a neighbor. He said, "Well, time to head home." As he walked toward the door he spotted Mike sitting in the living room with his head in his hands. I heard Matt say, "You wrecked their car, didn't you?" I heard the answer, "Yes." Mike was going too fast on the gravel road, lost control, went into the ditch, taking out the fence and finally stopped when he hit a tree. Auggie drove him to the scene of the crime to assess the situation. In the ditch lay the license plate. The fence was down and there were cattle in the pasture. They came home and I was designated to find the farmer who owned the cattle, and Mike was to help fix the fence.

While driving, trying to figure out which farmer owned the cattle, I mentioned to Mike, "We'll probably find a farmer named Bubba, in bib overalls, carrying a shotgun, with a snarling skinny hound dog, and 'No Trespassing' signs posted everywhere. It didn't take long and we saw a tall, older man, out by a barn. He had on bib overalls with his faithful dog by his side. Mike told the farmer, "I ran off the road and tore your fence down. I'm sorry. I'll help fix it." The man stared at him a few long minutes, and said, "So, you're the one that tore down my fence." After another silence he said, "No need to help, but if it happens again, be sure n' lemme know."

There were no scheduled visits, but Marlene called Mike occasionally. She asked if she could bring Mike's dog, Koda, to our house. I agreed to it without contacting children's welfare to ask permission. I opened the front door to let her in, no more sneaking around to drop Mike off at the back entrance. She came several times, eating meals with us, and giving the dogs a bath in the bathtub. She told me, "I'm happy Mike lives with you. He attends a small school, there is a father in the home, and he lives in the country."

The boys were 16, and both landed a job at service stations, one across the road from the other. Mike would charge Bert for a candy bar, and Bert would carry out a case of beer to be enjoyed later with their buddies. One night liquor control was waiting in the parking lot. They charged Bert with a "minor in possession". They went into the station and asked Mike if he knew Bert. He denied knowing him and gave them a phony address. Mike was not charged with anything but he did get fired.

Mike, Hayden and Bert were about 30 minutes into a movie when Hayden (Chapter Seven) started playing with a paratrooper knife. Mike jumped up, grabbed the knife, and jumped on Bert, playing like he was going to stab him. He asked, "Are you scared?" Bert replied, "No." Then Bert moved his arm—the one upon which Mike was resting his hand with the knife. By doing so, his hand went down and the knife went into Bert's eyeball. Mike started laughing because he thought he got Bert in the nose. When he realized Bert's eyeball was deflated and he was holding the fluid in his hand, his laughter quickly became tears.

Bert didn't think it was that big of a deal. It didn't hurt. However, when he looked through his left eye, he could see a hole. He said it was like when you get your picture taken and you see that blue dot from the flash. Bert walked out of his room, into Auggie's office, sat down in the desk chair and rubbed his eye, thinking it would go away after a couple of minutes.

I was blissfully unaware as I prepared a dinner of chicken-fried steak, mashed potatoes, gravy, and peas; one of Bert's favorite meals. I hollered, "dinner's ready," and the crew made their way to the table.

I have trouble thinking or talking about the tragic accident. I recall Bert calmly walking into the kitchen with his hand over his eye, and I asked, "What's wrong?" He answered, "Nothing, Mike just stabbed me in the eyeball with a paratrooper knife." I looked at him in disbelief. "No he didn't. Everyone would be in a panic." He calmly answered, "No Mom, he really did. You wanna see the weapon?"

Thirty seconds later Mike came around the corner with tears in his eyes and the knife in his hand. That's when I believed him and my motherly instincts kicked in. I said, "You have to go to the hospital." He responded, "No, I wanna eat first. I'm hungry." About this time Matt came over. He took one look at Bert's eye and said, "You need to get to the emergency room. That doesn't look good"

We climbed into our hunk-of-junk car and made the 15-mile journey to the hospital. Halfway there, the magnitude of the accident sunk in, and Bert yelled, "Holy Shit! I have a hole in my eye." As we pulled into the parking lot he said, "I'm so glad Mike stabbed me and I didn't stab him. I can't imagine how he feels."

When we arrived at the ER, we were immediately led into an examining room. The ER doctor checked his eye and called in a specialist. I did not realize the extent of his injury until the emergency room doctor asked Bert, "When was the last time you ate?" It was then I realized he would be going into surgery. The doctor told the nurse, "Prepare Room 403 for emergency surgery." Bert started to freak out. They informed us it would be a little while before the surgeon got there. He was leaving the golf course right away. They hooked Bert up to a morphine drip which he happily accepted.

Auggie was in the city when he heard the news. He called, not a bit happy, and asked to talk to Bert saying, "Mike paged me and said he poked you in the eye and now you're in the emergency room. You two are always fuckin' around. I knew one of you would eventually hurt the other. Put your mother on the phone."

Bert was shocked because Auggie always encouraged the boys to act like boys, rough and kind of beating each other up. Bert handed me the phone and I gave Auggie the rundown. Now he was inconsolable and said, "Put Bert back on the phone."

In broken sobs, Auggie told Bert, "I'm sorry. I thought he gave you a ringer or somethin' like that. I didn't know it was so serious. I'm on my way."

Driving 60 miles, he walked into the hospital 25 minutes later, too late to see Bert before surgery. He was sobbing uncontrollably, overwhelmed with the thought that he had been the same age as Bert, 16, when a tragic accident had changed the course of his life. The doctor told him, "Your son will be alright," but there was no consoling him.

Caroline made the same mad dash to the hospital and joined us in the waiting room. She asked, "How's Mike?" No one had thought about Mike. She called and Mike answered the phone crying. She tried to calm him down saying, "Mike, it was an accident. We all know you didn't mean to do it."

Bert came through the surgery with four stitches in his eyeball and an eye that would cause him problems the rest of his life. He had a total of four eye surgeries. Bert never blamed Mike, even years later. No one blamed Mike. Every anniversary Bert mentions missing the chicken-fried steak.

When we were allowed to see Bert after the surgery, we found him livid. He yanked off his oxygen mask and tried to pull out the IVs. The doctor pushed the mask back down on his face so he retaliated by punching him in the stomach and kicking the nurses who ran up to stop his bizarre behavior.

Auggie and I stood over him begging him to stop, afraid he would hurt himself. He was screaming, "Get this shit off of me right now." They gave him a sedative to knock him out. I suspected the doctor was at the point he would have liked to use a baseball bat to knock him out. Later Bert woke up to find his concerned family at his bedside. He looked at Mike and said, "You're the asshole who did this to me." He was trying to make him smile. Instead, Mike began bawling. Years later Bert said, "To this day, I wish I could take back that comment but I'm not going to worry too much about it. I was on a lot of prescription drugs. He's still my brother."

We all sat in the room feeling upset but relieved to know he would be all right. It was late and we discussed where we could get a bite to eat. A nurse came in and asked Bert if he wanted anything. He said, "Yeah, I wanna go with my family to the restaurant and have fun." She said something to the effect there was a rule that you had to stay in the hospital for at least 24 hours with a punctured eyeball. Thirty minutes later he was asleep and we silently slipped away.

I arrived at the hospital early the next morning to be there when the doctor showed up. Bert checked out his eye patch in the mirror. He was thinking it would be a cool black one like a pirate would wear; however, much to his dismay, it was a clear piece of plastic with three holes with gauze behind it so he couldn't see out of it. It looked like a jock strap for a two-year-old. He said, "It's going to suck wearing this embarrassing jock strap to summer school."

The doctor arrived, checked the eye, and much to Bert's relief, said he would be released that day. Bert said, "This must be what it's like to be an inmate being released from jail." The doctor went over the lists. He was not to bend over past his waist, lift anything heavier than five pounds, do anything strenuous and absolutely no contact sports ever, or his eye could pop. He put the eye patch and the gauze back on, set up an appointment for Monday afternoon, late enough that Bert wouldn't have to miss school, which Bert referred to as a "dick move" in his opinion, and sent him home.

When we got home, he took his pain pills and lay in bed until the next morning. The next day he felt much better and wanted to do something. He yelled down to Mike in his bedroom, "Hey, want to play some football?" He answered back in a broken voice, "no."

Bert really felt sorry for him, knew it had been an accident, and didn't want him to beat himself up over it. Mike didn't emerge from the basement until the next morning when it was time to go to summer school. He wasn't a great student either. The day passed slowly.

The next morning I awakened Bert saying, "Get moving, time to go to school and we have to get back to the doctor this afternoon." He moaned, "This is not a 16-year-old's sumertime dream vacation."

We walked side by side into the school with the jock strap attached to Bert's face. I told the teacher what happened and explained that, after he put the eye drops in, he needed to keep his eyes closed for five minutes and, if he had a headache, he was to lay his head down and no one was to disturb him. The teacher, a very sweet lady, put her arm around Bert, told him how sorry she was and led him to his desk. Boy did he milk that! He probably was awake for a grand total of 45 minutes for the rest of summer school. Granted, he did fail, but he said it was the only time he got to sleep in class with the teacher telling everyone to be quiet so they wouldn't wake him.

The first day back, they woke Bert for lunch and he met Mike in the hallway and some other kids they had befriended. When one of the kids asked what had happened to his eye, he told him the story. He responded, "Wow, so if I slap you in the eye, it'll pop?" Mike glared at him, "Even if you accidentally come close to touching that eye, I'll kill you." Bert said everybody knew right away that he was serious so that was the last comment anyone made of that kind.

They all piled into a car and headed to meet some of the girls for lunch. After lunch, they raced back to the school. The girls, in a separate car, won. Bert related to me the only reason he remembered was because the girls were walking in front of them when one of them turned around, lifted her shirt and flashed them. The boys were all happy and a little dumbfounded. But Bert, thinking quickly, said, "Hey, I missed it. I only have one eye. Could you do that again?" She happily obliged. Bert said to all the boys walking with him that day, "You're welcome."

I was waiting in the parking lot after school and we headed to the doctor's office. The doctor entered the examining room, catching Bert playing with one of his medical instruments. After scolding him, he carefully removed the plastic eye patch and gauze covering the eye. He put Bert's head in some contraption that had a magnifying eyepiece and looked at the injured eye. He said the stitches in the eyeball looked good, then let me look at them. Like I knew what I was talking about, I agreed.

After that, he made some adjustments on the machine and checked the eye pressure. He told Bert not to move or blink until this little blue neon canister poked him in the eye and beeped, kind of like checking a tire. Good news. Eye pressure was fine. Then they moved on to the eye chart. Bad news. He couldn't read the giant "E" at the top.

The doctor said not to worry, that eye had not seen light for 48 hours. It would get better. After checking everything out, he put the plastic protective eye cover back, this time without a gauze covering. Bert was able to somewhat look through the clear plastic cover. The doctor gave Bert a list of more rules. The one rule that got his attention was no sex for two weeks. Bert blurted out, "I don't think that will be a problem, Doc. You got me wearin' this goofy eye patch for the next six weeks." The doctor said everything was looking good and he should be okay and sent us home. What he didn't mention was, after an eye hasn't seen daylight for 48 hours and you ride home in bright sunlight at 3:00 PM on a summer day, you will get one of the worst headaches you can imagine.

A few months earlier, Melanie, the case manager, had encouraged all of the foster parents to take out an insurance policy in case there was a problem with the foster kids. It was cheap so I signed up for it. I never gave it another thought until I attended a training session where they asked if there were any questions. I asked, "My son had an accident involving a foster child. Do you think that policy would help pay the huge medical bills piling up?" They had no idea, but suggested I contact the company. The company agreed to pay all of Bert's medical bills. After the four surgeries, a representative called asking if he could meet with us. Seated at our kitchen table, he announced, "We need to discuss a settlement for the accident." Oh my God! We didn't see that coming. He said, "We feel $40 thousand is a fair amount." I was happy to just have the medical bills paid. Auggie looked at him and said, "I'll tell you right now, I ain't gettin' no damn lawyer. Forty thousand ain't enough." We chatted for awhile, and walked outside to look at my garden. By the time he left, he had agreed to pay $80 thousand dollars. Shortly afterward, the company cancelled the policy for all foster parents.

Mike decided to locate his biological parents. Marlene had adopted him when he was 10. He remembered his grandmother was the editor of a newspaper in a neighboring state. Using the school computers he was able to find enough information to place a call to his grandmother. She exclaimed, "Mike, we've spent years looking for you." We arranged to meet at a halfway point for a reunion. We ate dinner together and then spent time in a park. Among the family pictures his grandmother brought were several of her with the U.S. President. Mike asked her about his brother, Jerrod, who was one year younger. His grandmother had raised Jerrod, but said he didn't come along as he had other plans. We found out later that his plans consisted of confinement in a residential facility.

Grandma told Mike, "I don't know where your father (her son) is, and haven't seen your mother in years." The visit ended with plans to keep in touch. A week later she called telling Mike, "I'm so sorry to tell you this, but your father is dead." Another week passed and she called to say, "Mike, your father isn't dead after all. We plan to drive to Hoisington next weekend to see you." Mike looked at me and said, "They'll never show up." He never heard from them again.

I had only received limited information from children's welfare pertaining to Mike's past. He had some recollection of his childhood and became an avid investigator searching out the unknown details. When the boys were two and three, his parents had left them with their grandmother. She took them to work with her, placing them on a blanket in the corner of the room where they remained all day. Eventually other employees complained, hotlining the situation to the state office. She was required to hire a sitter, and that is when Marlene entered the picture. She became lax on picking the boys up, occasionally just taking Jerrod. Eventually, she never went back for Mike. After several years Marlene left the state, and adopted Mike. Marlene found God and to show her dedication, she wore long brown robes. Harold lived on the other side of the duplex with a door linking the two apartments.

When Mike turned 18, we were summoned to appear in court for his emancipation from the system. He would no longer have health insurance and as far as the court was concerned, he no longer had a place to live. Mike and the guardian ad litem stood before the judge requesting he be allowed to remain in the system, stating he would like to attend community college. The stern judge said, "No! Someone else needs that bed more than you." He did not ask Mike if he had a place to go. Every day foster children are emancipated with no plan and nowhere to go. Many end up addicted to drugs, homeless, or incarcerated, without hope. I looked at Mike and said, "I'm going home. Where are you going?" He said, "I'm going with you," and he did. Mike continued to live with us for several years.

Bert's best friends were his 'brothers' who lived with us. What one didn't think of, the other ones did and they were all in it together. One of their escapades, "The Macyville Massacre," has become a legend.

It was a Saturday night and Ryder, Mike and Bert had plans to go to a dance in Macyville. Before they left, Auggie gave Ryder strict instructions, "Absolutely no drinking." It was a violation of Ryder's probation. After those few words of wisdom, we watched the Trouble Trio drive away, turning right at the end of the driveway, instead of heading left toward Macyville.

As the story later emerged, we learned they had taken a 15-mile detour to a gas station that would sell them alcohol for the evening. After that, they went a few miles further to pick up Mike's girlfriend and headed for the dance.

Their night started off great, hanging out with friends, playing drinking games and acting like teenage hotshots. They even had fun on the drive there. There was construction on the bridge and it was down to one lane. Ryder and Bert made the best of the delay by having a few beers and handing a few out to the road workers.

At the dance, Ryder was putting some moves on a pretty girl. He didn't take into consideration that she might be someone else's girlfriend and she sure wasn't acting like she was attached. All the fun came to a screeching halt when Bert looked over to see a big redneck pouring a beer over Ryder's head. Ryder kicked the guy in the nuts and got in a couple of sucker punches before the guy's friends rallied to his aid.

Ryder took off running to the car. This guy must have been president of the Macyville Rednecks because within seconds about 15 guys joined him in close pursuit.

Bert immediately sprinted after them, catching up with the gang, and managed to get into the car with Ryder. Mike was in the backseat with his girlfriend, having sex. That was not good timing. At this point, the crowd turned into a mob of about 40, and they were pissed.

Mike got dressed quickly but he couldn't find the key. As he looked for it, the hillbilly lynch mob was kicking the car, throwing bottles, and trying to pull the boys out. Ryder pulled out a small pocketknife and began to stab people who were trying to crawl through the window. Bert grabbed Auggie's tire iron and began swinging at anyone who was close.

Someone threw a full beer bottle, hitting Ryder's face. His nose exploded, spraying blood all over. Bert was angry because Ryder and Mike were both wearing his shirts. That's right, three shirts ruined with one beer bottle.

Right after the beer bottle incident, a girl climbed onto the hood and began jumping up and down on the windshield, completely shattering it. By this time, Mike found the key. Bert and Ryder said he started the car and, like a moron, stuck his head out of the window and announced, "Look out guys, we're leaving now." As they pulled away, the mob continued to throw anything they could pick up. When they reached the road, it was impossible to see through the windshield. Mike stuck his head out the driver-side window and Bert stuck his head out of the passenger-side window and off to the hospital they went.

In the ER, it was obvious Ryder was the one who needed to be treated. They got him in pretty quick and Bert called us. Mike's girlfriend called her mom, who had to drive 40 miles to pick her up. She wasn't happy, but she took it much better than we did.

Bert called, explaining, "We'll be a little late because Ryder is in the ER." I listened to Auggie scream, "You guys were drinking and got in a fight!" What could Bert say. He was right. Then Bert told him that his car got a little banged up. That was an understatement. There wasn't a straight panel left on the car. The windshield was shattered and spider-webbed. It was like one of those cars you pay to smash in with a bat at the carnival.

As the boys were sitting in the hospital, Ryder said, "OMG, that car's really fucked up. What are we going to tell your parents?" Bert suggested, "We'll park it up front, paint a panther paw on it with a note that says, "GO HOME, WHITEY. NOT WELCOME." Ryder looked at Bert and said, "I'm really not in the mood for your jokes." When they got home around 2:30 AM, we were wide awake and ready to yell. Bert walked in and said, "One day you guys will find the humor in this." I felt the wrath of Auggie, as he quickly responded, "Bullshit. Sit the fuck down." Auggie yelled at them for about an hour with me chiming in occasionally. Eventually the yelling was over and the boys wandered off to bed.

Bert knew Auggie was pissed. Ryder paid for a new windshield and they tried everything they could think of, but he wouldn't talk to them for a week. Finally Auggie broke the silence, "You two didn't even fight back or try to defend the car—you pussies." Ryder meekly said, "Auggie, we left part of the story out. I stabbed three people and Bert used your tire iron when people tried to get in." Bert told me he didn't know why he was surprised with Auggie's response, but he was. "Why didn't you say that to begin with? That makes all the difference in the world. Just don't tell your mother." After he heard the rest of the story, he was no longer mad and did find the humor in it. I was confronted in the grocery store by people asking, "I saw that car. Did anyone live through the accident?"

Mike had a good heart. After being out of Marlene's home for years, he agreed to spend the night with her. I dropped him off and told him I would pick him up in the morning. When I arrived he jumped in the car and said, "Just leave." For the first time as he talked I got a glimpse of his young life. He said, "The dogs had the bedroom. There was little food in the refrigerator—mostly the dogs' medicine and food. I slept on the couch, and never had a blanket. I used my coat." It reminded me of a movie when the big football player said he never had his own bed. Mike did not have a bed or even a blanket. Mike said, "Damn. I had Bert's coat and left it there." Bert returned the following day to retrieve his coat.

Marlene's feud with her neighbor continued for years. Her revenge against the neighbor was in the form of constant 911 calls for every real and imagined offense. The prosecuting attorney contacted Marlene and warned that if the calls did not stop she would spend 30 days in jail. She continued with the calls. The prosecuting attorney called me to discuss the case and explained that Marlene had been given every opportunity to avoid jail. I was asked to bring Mike in to get his view. Mike told them that the neighbor and his mother were both at fault. Marlene called me and said, "As a citizen, I got a right to be protected from my neighbor. I'll never back down. I might even look good in orange." She found out alright—because she did end up serving a 30-day jail sentence. When she was released she moved out of state.

Fun-loving, sweet-natured Mike became angry and defiant. He stole $700 from the restaurant where he worked. The consequence was a weekend in jail, probation, and a felony on his record. Auggie kicked him out. I knew things were not going well but I missed him. I prayed for him every Sunday in church. We didn't see him for a long time.

A year later, Mike showed up and, as we were sitting around the kitchen table, he said, "I really screwed up and I regret it." Auggie looked at him and said, "Get your shit and come on back home." He left and about 15 minutes later, returned with some of his things. Auggie said, "Is that all you have?" Mike said, "No, I was just in a hurry to come home."

Occasionally we were lucky to find respite and go away for the weekend leaving Bert and Mike at home. I always warned them, "Do not have a party." Returning one weekend, I took the trash from the car before I went into the house. When I opened the trash-can lid, I saw the can was full of empty beer cans. I was furious. I stormed into the house yelling, "Of all the stupid, idiotic stunts you two have pulled, I would think you'd be smarter than to leave the beer cans for me to find." They were 19. I was stupid for leaving them alone.

A few months later, we left again with the same warning. When we returned, the house was spotless and there were no empty cans or bottles. Those two weren't much for cleaning so that should have been a red flag. I stopped to chat with our neighbor, Amelia, and she asked, "How's Auggie? We haven't seen him for awhile, and were kind of worried. I told Noah he was probably all right because I knew you guys had a big party a few weeks ago." I walked away screaming, "Bert, Mike, I want to talk to you two right now." I could hear Amelia saying, "I didn't mean to tattle on anyone."

By this time the boys were 20 so it was not realistic to think they would go with us, so we left again, with the warning, "Don't you dare have another party." We usually arrived home late Sunday afternoon. However, we drove through the night and walked in around 6 AM. What a sight! Kids were sleeping everywhere. I went in the basement following the trail of a shirt, jeans, panties, a bra and discovered Ryder in his twin-size bed with some gal. I kicked the bed and told his friend to get dressed and go home. She popped up naked to inform me, "I didn't even fuck him." This story has escalated through the years. The story now has me going through the house yelling, "Whores everywhere—get these whores out of here." The truth is that I was mad. Auggie was not mad. He told Bert and Mike to let him know the next time so he could warn them when we were coming home.

Mike loved deviled eggs. No matter how many were on the table, he would eat every one. One afternoon, Auggie sat in front of the barbecue grill, cooking pork steaks. Mike sat beside him, consuming one deviled egg after another. Auggie later guessed Mike had eaten about 24. The next day while Mike was at his construction job, he realized the need to find a bathroom quickly. He drove his pickup next to a portable bathroom, jumped out, and dashed inside. Relieved, he came out, and looked at the empty spot where his pickup had been parked. He looked at the bottom of the hill and there it sat. As he made his way down to the pickup, he passed a gentleman who was checking out his mailbox that had been struck by the rolling pickup. Mike said, "Sorry, I'll pay for it." The gentleman shook his head, looking at the wrecked pickup at the bottom of the hill and said, "Son, this is the least of your problems."

Girls liked Mike but he settled on one girl in particular, Kierston. I told Mike, "You've got the cream of the crop and the pick of the litter with that girl. She is really special." Mike moved in with Kierston when she gave birth to a beautiful baby boy, Mikey. They planned a wedding, and as the wedding date approached, Mike got a surprise phone call from his biological aunt. They made arrangements to meet and the aunt drove the 100 miles to Mike's home. Mike called and invited me to meet the aunt from the past. She told him his mother was living in Texas and his grandfather was dying from cancer. It was his grandfather's wish to see Mike before he died.

When Mikey was three, Kierston and Mike married. Many members of Mike's biological family were at the wedding. His biological mother, adoptive mother, and foster mother were all present. My six-year-old grandson, Zander, thought that Kierston, in her wedding dress, was the most beautiful woman he had ever seen. He begged for dollars, so he could dance with her over and over for the dollar dance. One of the foster boys told his counselor he thought it was incredible that a foster kid would have such a nice wedding. Mike had lived for years with many of the boys in our home and several of them participated in the ceremony. I consider Mike to be my son and was happy for him.

Years later we were having a picnic in the park. I was sitting by my fiancé, Vince, and we were watching Mike play catch with his two sons. Vince stated, "The cycle is broken," and it truly was. Mike is a hands-on father and Kierston is a wonderful mother. Their boys are on the honor roll. Mikey is on the student council. They are both involved in scouts, sports, and the community and Mike is coaching Little League. Vince was not there during Mike's teenage years, but he has grown to love and respect Mike as much as I do. Mike told me he's lucky he ended up in my home, but I feel like I'm the lucky one.

Even if you don't have anything to do, you need to get up early and get a good start on it.
—Ellen Harlie

6

JORDAN
Charged With Making Bomb Threat

Judeen, the foster mom, finished peeling potatoes. Thinking it was too quiet, she realized she needed to check on eight-year-old Wylie and six-year-old Jordan. As she approached their bedroom door, she overheard, "Bend down more, I can't get it in." Fearing the worst, she charged into the room, seeing Jordan on his hands and knees, and Wylie trying to insert his penis into his half-brother's anus. Judeen grabbed Wylie, sat him on a chair in a different room and told the boys, "Don't even think about moving." Jordan sat in that room pondering how to get even with Judeen for yelling at him. Opportunity came knocking when he saw her heading down the stairs with a laundry basket. He snuck up behind her and pushed, causing Judeen and the laundry basket to crash to the bottom. That afternoon six-year-old Jordan became my fourth placement and first therapeutic placement.

The boys' fathers were basically sperm donors (absentee fathers). The state was in the process of terminating their birth mother's parental rights. A parent aide had been working with the mildly-retarded mother of four, teaching her skills of parenting and cleaning up the filthy house. The aide noted fetish porn magazines lying around the home, depicting adults in diapers. Mom supplemented her state aide income by selling X-rated movies at flea markets.

Jordan was a cute little boy with red hair, green eyes, and a million freckles. I wondered what the green eyes had seen to rob him of his innocence and turn him into a disturbed little boy. Innocence is precious. Once it's lost, you can't get it back. I was to find most of my placements had lost their innocence at an early age.

The problems began immediately. While I was busy attending my endless chores, I noticed the house was getting cold. Jordan felt a sense of power when he could turn the thermostat all the way down unnoticed, then deny touching it. He decorated the bathroom walls with feces.

Jordan was safely planted in front of the TV with a few toys while

I did laundry. Headed to the bedrooms with an armful of folded laundry, I stopped dead in my tracks, surveying the damage. He was in the process of pulling up the floor tiles in the entry hall.

I learned from Jordan to always carry house keys in my pocket. While I was outside, he locked every door. An hour later, he finally unlocked the door. The odor hit me as soon as I stepped in. I found feces artwork on more walls than in just the bathroom.

My first therapeutic placement also taught me never to leave matches around. We discovered a 12-inch hole burned in the side of an armchair covered with non-flammable material.

During his tantrums Jordan left a path of destruction. One of my prized possessions was a handcrafted grandfather clock that had been built by my brother, J. R. I explained to Jordan, "The clock is special, don't touch it." Big mistake, the clock became his primary target. Monitoring Jordan was a full time job. If he was out of my sight, there was a problem. There were sensors on the door and window of his room. At night, a remote alarm sounded in my room if either his window or the door to his room were opened.

Jordan exhibited behavioral problems in the home, at school and in the car. As I was driving he looked passively out the window. Out of nowhere an enraged boy emerged screaming and kicking the dashboard. He would attempt to open the car door to jump out. Fortunately he never thought to take off his seat belt, giving me time to pull over. My van spent a lot of time on the side of the road in Parish County as I tried to calm Jordan.

Shopping was a challenge because I had to hang on to Jordan or he would run out of the store. He rebelled by kicking and biting. I imagine it was quite a sight to see me dodging his kicking foot as I threw the groceries into the cart. I noticed people casually walking by, staring at this out-of-control, screaming, but adorable, redheaded little boy as he attacked me.

A very angry principal summoned me to the school informing me my worst nightmare had come true—Jordan was suspended for a week. When I arrived, I was escorted to the principal's office. Glaring at me with teeth clenched, she said, "Jordan is always hiding. His teacher realized he was missing while the class was at recess. She came back to the classroom to find Jordan under her desk. When class resumed, the teacher, who is soon to retire, sat down at her desk and the chair collapsed. Jordan had loosened all of the screws in the chair with his fingers." Jordan was brought to the office and I asked, "Jordan, what were you thinking?" He replied, "I was wishin' I had a screwdriver." I struggled to hold back a smile at his answer.

I had a small old steamer trunk full of dress-up clothes that my granddaughter, Coleen, liked to play with. Jordan loved to play dress up too. He'd parade around the house in the dresses and heels carrying a purse. His prized item was the pink-feathered boa. Jordan insisted on wearing the feminine attire in public. The foster boys had no problem with Jordan's transsexual tendencies as long as he didn't leave the house.

The local church sponsored a Christmas party for foster children, at which they served food, organized games, and allowed the children to make ornaments out of dog treats. Jordan was proud of his ornament and couldn't wait to hang it on the tree. "Hang it high so the dog can't eat it," I told him. Well, the dog did eat it. Jordan whined and carried on endlessly until Mike told him, "Go call a cop." Later the phone rang, and the sheriff asked, "What's going on? Who placed the 911 call?" I assured him that no one had made such a call from our house.

He said, "There most certainly was a 911 call, and I want to know who made it and what's going on." He had my attention, so I yelled, "Did anyone in this house call 911?" Mike laughed and said, "I told Jordan to go call a cop because the dog ate his decoration." I was reprimanded for not supervising the phone.

While I prepared dinner it was necessary for Jordan to be in the kitchen with me. It was a wonder that I ever got dinner on the table. He'd start by kicking the pantry doors. Then when asked to stop, he'd escalate to pulling out drawers and emptying the contents onto the floor. He'd throw more things before I got the first stuff picked up. My cabinets had cracks, the light was broken, and I had to replace two coffee pots. I spent more time restraining Jordan than I did cooking. I placed him in a restraining hold, talking calmly to him, silently praying he'd calm down. He tried to head-butt me or bite me, often succeeding, and called me names that most six-year-olds have never heard. Jordan was the first to break my glasses in a fit of rage, but not the last. His tantrums started again at bedtime. I thought Jordan liked to be restrained. He found the tight hold comforting but resisted being hugged.

One evening while I was preparing dinner, Jordan deliberately put his finger on the red-hot burner, leaving a nasty burn, but he didn't cry. For a moment I just stood there amazed at what had I witnessed. I mentioned this incident to Beverly, the consultant. She asked if he had put just one finger on the burner, instead of several fingers or his entire hand. She said, "He needs to feel something, even if what he feels is pain."

If I was lucky, I could put Jordan in time-out and he'd sit there for a few minutes before attacking me. Any time-outs had to be in my presence or I'd be paying the consequences of his revenge. While in a time-out, he'd glare at me with those green eyes and say, "I'm listening to the Devil. He wants you." I expected him to levitate at any minute. Other times, when his tantrums had left me exhausted, he'd focus those green eyes on me and say,

"Are you upset? Why don't you pray to your God? Go ahead, pray and see what happens." With this troubled child, I learned the art of disassociation.

I was faithfully writing reports about Jordan's extreme behaviors, to discuss at the staffing meetings. I realized there was no way I could express how serious these behaviors were, so I decided to tape him during one of his escapades. After dinner, knowing it was just a matter of time before show time, we set up the old-fashioned video camera. Right on schedule Jordan started the performance. Mike and Bert were helping me film, because I had to hang on to Jordan. I restrained him, speaking softly asking, "If I let go, will you be all right?" He went limp, lying in my arms, saying, "I'm all right." When I let go, he jumped up and started kicking me. He darted over to the dog, attacking, kicking and hitting. Again I held him, talking calmly until I could let go. This time he picked up a glass and threw it at Mike, hitting him in the forehead. Mike looked into the camera, pointing at the huge red bump on his forehead. This was a normal night and now I had it on tape.

I informed children's welfare I was bringing the tape to the next staffing. I heard gasps and moans as the group watched the video. I was right. There was no way I could express his behaviors on paper, but they sure understood the film. It was decided right then and there, this was a seriously-damaged child that needed to be placed in a residential facility for his safety and the safety of others.

I explained to Jordan that he would be moving to a residential facility. We had a handyman doing some work in the house at the time. He witnessed many tantrums, but understood Jordan was a damaged child. Being kind, he said, "Goodbye and good luck." Jordan looked at him, stuck up his middle finger and said; "Fuck you and fuck your mama."

Jordan was placed in a residential facility where he remained for a couple of years. The facility was a huge old building with large rooms that housed six to eight boys per room. Jordan was the exception. His room was tiny with just enough space for a bed and small dresser, it had formerly been a janitorial closet. The toys I sent along disappeared. The windows were large and tall. Jordan was caught several times standing on the windowsill naked.

Parental rights were terminated. The powers that be decided Jordan should be placed in a pre-adoptive home. The adoption profile was sent out with a picture of Jordan. The information said he needed a home with structure. Translated, a home with structure means the child has behavioral problems. Immediate interest was expressed in the adorable little boy, and he was placed with a family that had longed for a child. Tidbits of information trickled back to me. He wouldn't leave the thermostat alone. He smeared feces on the walls and had severe tantrums where he broke things.

It didn't take long for the pre-adoptive parents to admit defeat and want him out of their home. He was placed in residential care again. There was another attempt in a pre-adoptive home, which was also a dismal failure.

Jordan spent the remaining years until his eighteenth birthday in residential care. Years later, another placement told me, "I lived in the same residential as Jordan. That kid was an out-of-the closet, flamin' queer." I knew when Jordan was six, he was gay. On his eighteenth birthday he was released. He returned to his mother's home.

I didn't hear anything about Jordan for several years until I read the headlines in the local paper. A man who allegedly made terrorist threats at a local motel was charged in connection with the crime. The name, Jordan Parker, caught my eye as I read the following article.

MAN CHARGED WITH MAKING BOMB THREAT

Jordan Parker, 24, was charged in Parish County Circuit Court with making a terrorist threat, a Class C felony; and two counts of third-degree assault, both Class C misdemeanors.

According to an affidavit, Parker allegedly told the assistant manager that there was a C-4 bomb in the hotel.

According to the "probable cause warrant" from the Police Department, Parker said the bomb was on the second floor of the hotel and set with a two-minute timer. The hotel was evacuated and no explosive device was found.

In addition, Parker allegedly verbally threatened a woman at the hotel, telling her he would kill her.

Bond was set at $75,000.

There are consequences for stupidity—Too bad—So sad.
                                                                    —Ellen Harlie

7

HAYDEN

Change the Blinker Fluid

I yelled, "Bert, Mike, and Jordan, come on. I have to go to juvenile detention to pick up a kid. He's going to be living here." The boys sat in the
waiting room while I was escorted to a locked room that was furnished
with only a bed and a Bible. Sitting on the bed was 13-year-old Hayden. He
was a handsome boy, at least 6'2", and a little overweight. I told him my
name was Ellen and he was coming home with me. He followed me and I
introduced him to the boys. They all laughed and joked around on the way
home. He was not upset about going to a foster home.

Hayden had landed in detention because of a fire. He had struck a
match and held it to hair spray as it came out of the can. Some landed on a
throw rug, so he threw the smoldering rug into a dumpster. The dumpster
caught fire and spread to the surrounding field. This was not his first problem
with the juvenile office.

He lived with his grandmother, Neva, and a younger brother. His
mother, Tiffany, was in the Army, having left her six children with anyone
who was willing to take them. Children's welfare informed me Neva requested they take custody.

Hayden was a likeable boy. Of all the parental figures I worked with,
his grandmother was among the nicest. Her home was small, but clean. Neva
loved Hayden and Hayden loved her. He just could not stay out of trouble.

Hayden had never had a male authority figure in his life and he
didn't like Auggie setting rules for him. Fed up, he said, "Get off my back
you crippled old bastard." Auggie picked him up six inches off the floor and
sat him on the couch, saying, "This is my house and you will respect me."
Hayden's eyes were as big as saucers as he stared up at Auggie, shocked at
what had happened. His shock was soon replaced by anger. He bolted up
and said, "I'm callin' Grandma." Neva answered the phone and Hayden was
screaming, "Get me the fuck out of this crazy house. That old bastard threw

me on the couch. Come and get me right fuckin' now." Neva hung up on him. When he tried to call back, she had the phone off the hook. He stormed off to his room, slamming the door behind him. An hour later he came out as if nothing had happened. Eventually Neva called inquiring if Hayden had calmed down. I said "He's fine, would you like to talk to him?" They chatted for quite awhile. She called the next day and said, "Someone should have done that a long time ago. He sure was surprised to learn Auggie was strong enough to handle him." He was never disrespectful to Auggie or me again.

Auggie liked to shoot craps with the boys. I protested loudly that he could not gamble with foster kids. They didn't quit, but instead moved the game out of my sight. Auggie was still running his trucking company from a home office. His gambling change was in a coffee can he stashed in his desk. One day he discovered the can was empty. Both of us suspected Hayden, because none of the other three boys had a history of stealing. I checked young Jordan's room and he didn't have it. Auggie set the empty can on the table and asked, "Which one of you boys stole my money?" All of them said, "I didn't." We sat at the table staring at each other, wondering how we would determine the guilty party. Finally Auggie said, "Go outside and don't come in until someone admits to it." Mike and Bert knew they didn't do it and they were pissed. They told Hayden if he did not admit to the theft they were going to throw him in the pond. He said, "Fuck you." They grabbed him and dragged him to the pond, which was only waist deep. They struggled to pull that big, fighting boy across the yard. I heard him screaming and hollering so I went out and put a stop to it. He never did admit to the theft, but as long as he lived in our home, we never had anything missing again.

As soon as the grade school kids got off the bus, I headed four miles west to Mike's bus stop. Bert had chosen to attend a school in the opposite direction, so my next stop was eight miles east to Bert's bus stop. No one liked all the extra running. There was a hard driving rain as I pulled in to get Bert as he got off the bus. Bert made a mad dash to the car and just then, Hayden locked the doors. The result was what he anticipated—Bert got soaked and was mad as hell. I told Hayden to unlock the door and the fight was on. Sitting in the front, Hayden grabbed the umbrella, turned around, swinging full force to hit Bert. He missed, and nailed me in the side of the head. It hurt but I didn't say a word—just sat there with tears rolling down my cheeks. Hayden repeatedly told me how sorry he was that he had hit me instead of Bert. I didn't talk to him until we were home. I grounded him because his intent was to hurt someone.

On a bitter cold day, Hayden decided to go ice skating on the pond. I warned him that the ice might not be thick enough and told him to step cautiously around the edges before going out further. He came back into the house with his pants wet up to his hips and a silly grin on his face. He said, "Guess it wasn't solid enough."

Soon after this, I got my next placement placement, Simon. When I saw that the boys were spending time playing board games, I thought it was great. But when Hayden accused Simon of cheating him out of two dollars, the fight turned physical and Simon yelled, "Let's take this outside. I'm not tearing up their house." Although Hayden was a head taller than Simon, he realized Simon could beat him to a bloody pulp so he retreated to his room, whimpering.

After three tries, Bert had his driver's license. He was happy to drive everywhere we went. We all piled into the car headed to the next destination. As he pulled out of the driveway onto the highway, he complained, "Mom, the blinker doesn't work. I told you we need more blinker fluid." Mike joined in saying, "We're going right by an auto store. I call 'not going in to get it'." Bert yelled, "me either." Hayden shrugged and said, "I'll run in and pick it up." The conversation continued with Mike saying, "Get a gallon so we have extra." Bert pulled in front of the store and said, "Get the good stuff—not the cheapest." I handed Hayden ten dollars. Everyone was dead serious, playing this out to the fullest. We sat in the car watching Hayden talking to the clerk, followed by customers and employees who were all laughing. The clerk walked out with Hayden, asking, "Who sent this boy in here?" Hayden had a silly grin on his face.

Children's welfare contacted Hayden's mother, Tiffany, pressuring her to take her son. She agreed. She was stationed at a base in the south and living with a boyfriend. I made several trips to the nearest base to fill out the necessary paperwork. All went well and, after eight months in my home, he got on a plane to join his mother.

I guess there was a valid reason she didn't have custody of her six children. Hayden hated living with Tiffany, hated her boyfriend, and six weeks later, he was on a plane coming back. His spot in my home had been filled, so he was placed in a different foster home. Neva was an active part of his life, and soon he was living with her. He was never in the foster care system again. I lost track of him for many years, but decided to track him down, finding him hundreds of miles away. He has a family, a job, and is doing well. He wrote me a note, "You made a difference in my life."

8

SIMON

Sleep With One Eye Open

Simon found out his mother was not fooling around when she accused him of holding out on her share of the drug money. That was Simon's version of why he was brought to our house in the middle of the night. His mother contacted the authorities claiming Simon was using drugs and she was powerless to handle him. His social worker drove several hours to bring him to our door because other foster parents refused to accept him as a placement. Sixteen-year-old Simon was covered with tattoos and had a ponytail reaching to his butt. I found him to be a likeable kid.

I quickly learned that putting a group of teenage boys together results in havoc. School was out for the summer so when the boys came down for breakfast, I informed them that we had a new placement, 16-year-old Simon. They dug through the trunk of dress-up clothes and also found a pair of pink pants someone had worn for Halloween. When Simon finally crawled out of bed in time for lunch, they were sitting at the table ready to perform. They were winking at Simon, and throwing kisses at each other. Simon was convinced he had landed in a home of homosexual boys and he avoided them like the plague. Matt showed up that afternoon and caught on to what the boys were doing. As he was walking out the door, he quietly told Simon, "You'd better sleep with one eye open." Simon screamed, "I'll fuckin' kill anyone that touches me." By the end of the day, he realized he had been played. The rest of his short stay was uneventful and he got along well with my entourage.

Simon had one brother a couple of years older. Several years after Simon left our home, I heard that his brother had been killed in an automobile accident. Simon was shot and killed in an incident involving drugs.

9

KYLE

The Unfixable Child

Sitting on the deck, sipping a glass of iced tea, Dana watched her three young foster children playing in the yard. In the blink of an eye, five-year-old Kyle pulled down four-year-old Ethan's pants and bit his penis. Horrified, Dana bolted off the deck to stop the attack as Ethan's blood curdling screams penetrated through the peaceful neighborhood. Within the hour, she called children's welfare to have Kyle removed from her home.

With Kyle's background and the penis-biting incident, he had to be placed in a specialized home. Children's welfare was hoping I was that home because I had an opening. When Melanie called, I responded, "There's no way in hell I'm taking a five-year-old boy. I take teenagers." A few hours later, Melanie called begging, "Please, we can't find anyone to take this child. Would you consider keeping him for the weekend as an emergency placement?" I reluctantly agreed, making it very clear I wanted him picked up on Monday morning.

The following morning I met Dana, who was relieved that I was going to take Kyle home with me. An adorable, blue-eyed blond, a sad little boy with no front teeth got out of the car. He told his six-year-old sister, Clara good-bye. My heart went out to this vulnerable child. I loaded up his pitiful few possessions, which consisted of six cheap toys and two discount store bags of worn-out clothes. Dana handed me an envelope, and drove away. For the fourth time in his young life, he was headed to a new home with complete strangers. He had four older sisters in the foster care system. Very few homes are willing or able to take five placements so the children started to get separated. Initially the three youngest had been placed together, while the two oldest got split up into two different homes. By the time Kyle came to my home, the children were in five different homes and would never again live together. Now, years later they have lost contact with each other.

While Kyle was checking out his new environment, I read the disturbing letters in the envelope. The first letter was from the home previous to Dana. It read, "Four-year-old Kyle requires constant supervision. He destroys his toys, lies about everything, bites himself and bites his clothes that are now full of holes. Kyle will eat until he makes himself sick, so the amount of food he is allowed has to be closely monitored."

Dana's letter was equally upsetting. "He's destructive. He has been molested. He masturbates and has molested another boy, age four, and will most likely do so again. He's a very bad liar. He will whine, cry, get angry and do whatever he can to convince you he's telling the truth. When he says, 'But this time I am telling the truth,' it's a good sign that he's still lying. He hoards food, hiding it all over. He hits, kicks, and punches, spits on other kids, is extremely aggressive and requires constant supervision. He has ADHD and is taking Ritalin®." I read the letters and immediately called Melanie to remind her that Kyle had to be picked up first thing on Monday morning. She promised they would have a home for him. At that time she gave me the background information involving Kyle.

There were six children, all of whom had suffered horrendous abuse in this dysfunctional family. They left the area one step ahead of the law and settled 1200 miles away. The oldest daughter, Erica, made a hotline call accusing Dave, the father, of sexually abusing all the children. When Dave found out about the allegations, he started throwing things into the rattletrap old station wagon. He yelled at everyone, "Get in the fuckin' car now! That bitch, Erica, made up lies about me and I'll go to jail if we don't get the hell outta here." Within the hour they were on their way out of the state. Several of the children did not bother to put on shoes. Kyle was two years old. Erica was left behind.

The authorities caught up with Dave when he made it back home and charges were filed. The children told horrifying stories of sexual abuse and were placed in protective custody. Dave was a small man, undoubtedly suffering from short-man syndrome. Joyce, his wife, was mentally slow. She had had sex with numerous men and Dave, obviously, was not the father of all six children.

The family had un-neutered pets and Dave delighted in torturing and killing the endless supply of kittens and puppies. He would tell the children, "You'll do exactly as you're told or say good-bye to Rover." Also, "Don't think I won't do to you what you watched me do to Fluffy." The children were locked in a closet if they got on his nerves.

Dave was a drug dealer and user. He had the children stand guard at the windows watching for police when he did his drug deals. He told the young children, "Always be on the lookout for soldiers (police). They steal little kids and keep them in cages."

Kyle was rescued from one abusive situation and placed in another one. Sherry, the foster mom had a daughter, Kara, who was several years older than Kyle. Kyle innocently told his counselor, "Kara always wants to play with my wiener." He added, "Sherry has big tits and a nice pussy." He complained, "Grandpa doesn't like me and hits me with his cane." Children's welfare removed him and his two sisters from that home. The three were placed in another home and it didn't work out either. Dana had room for two so Clara and Kyle were moved there—until the penis biting incident.

A few hours after I picked up Kyle, we met Caroline for dinner. At the restaurant, we were getting acquainted, playing around with Kyle. I asked "How does a cow go?" and he said, "Moo." I asked him, "How does a pig go?" He let out a snort like I've never heard before. I don't know how that loud hideous sound came out of that small child. Everyone in the restaurant started laughing. Caroline said she was laughing at me because my red face gave away my embarrassment.

As the weekend progressed, we fell in love with that precious unloved child. Monday morning Melanie called and said, "We can't find a placement for Kyle. No one will take him with his history. We're doing our best." I responded, "Keep trying. I don't keep five-year-olds." On Wednesday she called and said, "Bring Kyle to children's welfare. We found a placement and the new foster mother will be here to pick him up."

Little did I know that three years later, I would have that foster mother's son, Gavin, in my home. Gavin hotlined his mother alleging she hit the little foster kids. The hotline was substantiated and Gavin was placed in my home.

I told Kyle, "You'll be moving today. We'll get your things together and take you to meet your new family." He crawled under a desk and refused to come out. He asked, "If I hide, will they find me?" Auggie pulled him out and held him. Kyle was begging, "Please don't let them take me away. I want to stay here. Please don't let them get me." I pried Kyle's arms off Auggie's leg as he screamed and begged. Tears were rolling down Auggie's check. I put that sobbing little boy into the car and drove to children's welfare.

When we arrived, Melanie introduced Kyle to his new foster mom, and explained, "She's a nice lady and you'll love it at your new home." Kyle let go of my hand and ran out the door. Melanie caught him, hanging on as he kicked, hit and bit her. Several social workers came to her assistance, hauling him off to a back room and telling me to leave. The floodgates opened when I got in the car. This little boy touched my heart and I couldn't let him go. When I got home, between my sobs I asked Auggie if it would be all right if we kept Kyle. He said, "That poor kid—Yeah it's OK."

I called Melanie, and asked if we could have Kyle back. She said yes, but we would have to sign an agreement to commit for one year. I was given the following letter:

Ellen and Auggie,

As you are well aware, Kyle has exhibited very aggressive sexual behavior. One of the reasons that I feel very optimistic about the prospect of Kyle coming to live with you is that his sexually acting-out behavior does not seem to frighten or appear to intimidate you. I also appreciate the fact that you have experience in working with this type of behavior due to another child you fostered, Jordan. I am also appreciative of the fact that you currently do not have any small children in your home whose safety we would have to be concerned about with regards to Kyle sexually assaulting them. Kyle will be in your home for at least one year. I am anticipating that it will take that long to terminate the parental rights with regards to a trial and any appeal there might be. I also want to remind you that not only does Kyle have problems with sexual activity; he has a host of other behavioral problems. Kyle has been known to lie, engage in sneaky behavior and throw temper tantrums. By nature, he is a physically-aggressive young man, who can engage in rough play.

I am only aware of one act of property destruction. He and his sister hit an expensive car with an iron skillet at a garage sale. Kyle is also on medication for hyperactivity.

It may appear to you that I am attempting to change your mind about fostering Kyle. That is not the case. I am just concerned that once Kyle is in your home, you will tire of the responsibility and request that Kyle be moved. I saw firsthand how attached Kyle got to you in such a short time. I don't want him to be hurt any more than he already has been in his short life. Kyle desperately wants to have a mommy and daddy and to belong in a family.

If after reading this letter you would still like to provide a foster home for Kyle, please contact me and we can discuss plans for how to protect Kyle and schedule a time for Kyle to return to your home.

—Melanie

I immediately called Melanie, agreeing to commit for the one-year period. She informed me, "I'm covered with bruises. He's such a sad, scared little boy reacting the only way he knows how." We decided to bring him back into our home when we returned from attending a family reunion 500 miles away. I called Kyle every day so he knew we cared and were looking forward to having him back. In one conversation he told me he threw a rock at a chicken. He said, "I didn't mean to hurt it but it got dead anyway."

Kyle moved into our home with all kinds of services. He was seeing a counselor whose name was Darrena, twice a week. Melanie made regular visits to our home to monitor his progress. He saw a psychiatrist for medication management and had a monthly visit with a consultant at the children's division. The consultant, Beverly, was an amazing woman who could come in at every angle to target what needed to be done. The first time I took Kyle to meet her she put her hands on his shoulders. He doubled up his fists and started swinging. I was horrified, but she reassured me these were the behaviors she wanted to see so she could deal with them. Kyle was wired with a primitive response to danger. He did not like to be touched. He had lost the ability to trust and feel safe with adults. When Kyle got home, he told Auggie (speaking of Beverly), "She has black skin and a lot of it." It was requested that Kyle have a psych evaluation. The evaluation said he would be better off in a residential facility. We never considered it. All the services were given a copy of the psych-eval. At that point it was decided Kyle would be assigned a case manager from the mental health facility, in addition to a mentor who would spend an hour a week with Kyle—all of these services for a five-year-old child.

At the time Kyle moved in I didn't have a room for him. Caroline lived on campus while attending college, but still had her room at home. I let Kyle sleep in Caroline's bed, but he was not allowed in her room during the day. To my horror, when I was ready to tuck him in one night, I discovered that he had found a pair of scissors and cut up the sheets, blankets, and pillow slips. When Caroline came home for a weekend, she told him, "If you ever touch anything of mine again, I'll destroy your things." He never again touched any of her possessions; however, if the scissors were not securely locked up, he left a path of destruction. He cut up bathroom curtains and bedroom curtains and even cut out chunks of his hair.

I frequently had my grandchildren, Colleen and Jimmy, for the weekend. Colleen was the same age as Kyle. Strangers would approach me to admire the twins. Oddly enough they looked like twins, same size, blond hair, blue eyes, and adorable.

When it was time to enroll Kyle in kindergarten, we discussed the new adventure and I explained to him what to expect in school. The first day, I watched him get on the bus as I waved good-bye, and off he went. When the bus pulled up in front of the school, he refused to get out. The principal finally carried him off. He went into the classroom and crawled under a table. Every day Kyle would get off the bus, walk into the classroom, and crawl under the table. He refused to leave the safety of his table for several weeks. Little by little, he ventured out. As the time passed, they were wishing he was back under that table. Within a short time they hired a personal aide to be with Kyle all day, every day.

I was washing breakfast dishes while listening to a morning radio show. My interest peaked when I heard, "Do you have a naughty kid? Call us. We'll put the fear of Santa Claus into them." Five-year-old Kyle certainly could use the fear of Santa Claus. This delightful boy, whose favorite word was "fuck," had been in my home for four months.

Beverly said, "It's not realistic to tell Kyle he can't say 'fuck' in your home. Make a chart, starting with, if you say fuck three times or less a day you will get a reward. A few days later, move it to two times a day and so on." He was doing a great job, but I thought it wouldn't hurt to get a little help from the fat man in the red suit.

I called the radio station, and explained that Kyle loved to use the "F" word. They said, "Put him on—we'll get the bleeper ready." Kyle was charming and funny talking with Santa, and the radio hosts had him on the air a long time. Beverly called me, "I was on my way to work and I heard Kyle talking to Santa. It was cute beyond words."

Later, Caroline called, "Mom, I'm coming home this weekend and we're going on a Christmas outing." That sounded fantastic. However, my heart sank as I thought, "How will I ever keep track of Kyle? I can't even keep track of him when I go after a gallon of milk much less on crowded streets," but I couldn't disappoint my daughter so I'd have to be creative.

The big day came and we were off for a fun-filled good time, or so I hoped. On the way it hit me—a solution. I sweetly said, "Kyle, we're going to have a fun day and I want you to be safe. There'll be a lot of people and some of them are bad. Bad people always wear red shirts. If I holler 'red shirt', that means you need to get right back to me immediately." As we mingled in the crowd, if Kyle ventured very far, I'd yell, "Red shirt!" and he'd come running back. Problem solved.

Santa Claus was there, going up and down the street in a sleigh pulled by horses. We got in line and finally it was our turn. We climbed into the sleigh, with Santa helping Kyle, saying, "Ho-Ho-Ho! Have you been a good little boy?" In all of his five-year-old innocence he said, "Yes sir, I haven't said 'fuck you' in two weeks."

Kyle knew Santa was jolly. Now he realized just how jolly he was. For the entire sleigh ride Santa and Caroline laughed hysterically. When one would gain control, the other one would start all over again. I alternated between being embarrassed, and seeing the humor of it all.

Ryder was dating the preacher's daughter, which meant one more plate at the dinner table. The preacher died unexpectedly, so I set aside time to attend the visitation. I doubted if Kyle had ever been to a funeral or had any idea about the mystery of death. So I explained to him that the body was in the casket, but Jesus took the preacher's soul to heaven. We arrived and the place was packed. I took Kyle by the hand and led him to the casket. He stared at the body for a few minutes, and then in his loud booming six-year-old voice he said, "I'll bet Jesus is pullin' the soul outta him right now. Will he take the casket too?" The preacher's wife gasped in horror as laughter erupted all a-round us. I grabbed his hand and escaped through the crowd.

My mother called to say, "Dad and I are coming for a visit this week-end." I always felt a little apprehensive with these visits. They had never wit-nessed the behaviors the boys exhibited on a daily basis. Bad language was never acceptable and would not be tolerated. We decided to take them for a scenic drive and were checking out the massive locks and dams on the river. Auggie was playing the part of tour guide, explaining how the locks and dams worked. Kyle innocently asked, "If you can say 'dam' in the river can you say 'fuck' in the river?" Mom and Dad ignored the question. Auggie couldn't stop laughing and I slithered down in my seat.

Kyle was running and playing with the boys when he tumbled down the hill. He cried for a few minutes then joined right back in the fun. A few days later he fell off his bicycle on the same arm. He never complained and it didn't swell. I noticed he used his left hand to support his right hand, so I asked him if it hurt. When I touched it, he let out a painful gasp. I took him to the emergency room and X-rays proved it was broken. As soon as they put the cast on his arm, he started banging it on his head. I had to physically stop him with the doctor telling me, "Don't let him do that." I don't know what that doctor was thinking but I was thinking, "Oh shit!" Kyle had bruises on his head the entire time the cast was on his arm.

Kyle would never sleep in a room with the windows open. Every night I had to go through the ritual of showing him the windows were down and locked securely. He was afraid soldiers would come in during the night and take him. Kyle would frequently wake up screaming from nightmares, and claim it was because his knee hurt. Bert was often awakened by the screaming and he would rub petroleum jelly on Kyle's knee, which had magi-cal powers and instantly the knee would feel better.

Kyle and his sister, Clara, had back-to-back counseling appointments so they could see each other. Kyle looked forward to spending time with his sister. Being separated from Clara was a huge loss in Kyle's young life. The visits ended when Clara's foster family requested to have her moved. She frequently masturbated and the situation was progressively getting worse. Her foster mother complained, "Clara's finger is always in her vagina and the odor is nauseating." The foster family couldn't tolerate this behavior but, they were helpless to stop it.

Clara was a pretty little seven-year-old girl. Children's welfare placed her in what they hoped would be a pre-adoptive home. The prospective parents were horrified by Clara's behaviors. She masturbated with a vengeance, rubbing her bottom on every male she had contact with and explained to them she needed to have sex. I don't think she was in that home a week. Eventually Clara was adopted by a family with two children just a little older. A couple of years passed and Sophia, the adoptive mother, called me. She asked how Kyle was doing. I said, "Truthfully, not so good." She responded, "Clara cost me my marriage. I was happily married for 18 years. Clara chipped away at the very core of my family's existence until my kids ended up in counseling, and my husband and I ended up hating each other."

Kyle would get mad, screaming, "I'm runnin' away. I hate you and everybody that lives in this stupid ol' house." I always told him, "Good bye, I sure will miss you." This particular day he found a suitcase and threw a few things in it and headed out the door. He walked down the driveway and just sat there. I casually started working in the garden so I could keep an eye on him. He started yelling at me, "If you weren't so mean, I wouldn't have to live on this ol' dirt road." I ignored him. Pretty soon Mike wandered by, sat down and talked to Kyle. I had that warm, fuzzy feeling as I watched Mike put Kyle on his shoulders and walk off. Life was good again.

Another time he decided to run away and Bert told him he would help him pack. They packed his suitcase and headed down the stairs to the front door. Bert shook Kyle's hand and said, "Good-bye." It was just starting to get dark, and Bert said, "Sure is dark out there, maybe you should wait un-til morning to leave." Kyle thought that would be a good idea. He went back to his room to play and forgot all about running away.

Anytime Kyle thought about his father, pure hatred spewed out of his mouth, claiming, "When I grow up I'm gonna kill my dad." This was addressed in the counseling sessions. Darrena told me, "Chances are he'll never run into his father; however, he may run into someone who reminds him of his father. He may react without even realizing why."

I mentioned to Darrena that Kyle believed his mother to be sick. Sometimes when he got mad he would say, "As soon as she gets better she'll come and get me." Darrena tackled that situation with a straight forward, no-nonsense session, explaining truthfully, "Your mother is not sick. She did not keep you safe and it was her choice to not have you in her life." Kyle listened without emotion and didn't have much to say. Never again did he mention his mother was coming back to get him.

During the therapy sessions, Darrena would attempt to regress Kyle to the toddler stage to get the nurturing and cuddling he was deprived of in early childhood. Even when he was five and six, I would hold him, and if he wanted, he could have a bottle and a blanket during the sessions.

When we decided to be foster parents, we never planned on adopting children, never discussed it or even thought about it. Kyle was seven when children's welfare informed us parental rights had been terminated for Joyce and Dave. They were not permitted to suggest to the foster parents that they adopt the children; however, some mighty strong hints were dropped. Kyle felt this was his home, and children's welfare knew we completely accepted this little boy with all his baggage. It was going to be extremely hard to send him away. We procrastinated, putting off what would be a painful decision. Finally, Bert said, "You can't send him away." We didn't. We adopted him.

Kyle handled the court hearing just like any other day. He knew he was going home with us. Nothing was changing for him in his mind. On this special day, his main interest was the candy machine located in the court-house. When we arrived home, a large balloon arrangement was on the table. A thoughtful teacher had brought it.

Kyle was the cutest little boy. His teeth had to be extracted when he was three due to sugar drinks in his bottle and his permanent teeth did not come in until he was ten. The missing teeth just added to the mischievous, animated facial expressions. His behaviors were disturbing, the tantrums frequent, but if you could catch him in between, he was delightful. I decided to take him to an agent just to test the waters. They loved him. Everything he said was cute and funny. They put him on a big screen monitor and more and more people showed up to watch this amazing child. He did everything right and the agent was blown away by him. I was told he would be the next child star. They scheduled Kyle to come back and were very excited to have him. I was excited. When we returned, he was like a different boy. He had shut down, wouldn't talk, and looked like a zombie—so much for his show biz career. I was told, "Don't bring him back."

In a therapy session I witnessed Kyle regress to a toddler, reliving the despicable acts his father had performed on his children. In a trance-like state he said, "My daddy has my sisters on the bed. He's kneeling over them with his wiener in one hand, and the other hand is where my sister pees. No one has any clothes on. My sisters are crying saying, 'No, Daddy, please let us up.' I was sitting on the floor, rolling a ball, wanting him to leave my sisters alone. All of a sudden he peed (ejaculated) on them. He told them he was done--they could get up." Kyle was sobbing while reliving the horror. He was gently told, "Kyle, you are here, you are safe, look at your mother (I was crying). She loves you. Look around the room. Rub the material on the chair. You're here—not in that bedroom. This is now. Let the memories go. It's over."

I was told by children's welfare that he was too young, that he could not remember the abuse. After this disturbing incident, Darrena said,

"There's no doubt he remembered. He recalled small details. He's young and couldn't have made that up." He was not hypnotized, his mind simply slipped back. The principal had a little talk with me to say, "Kyle has to stop telling everyone his dad peed on his sisters." I told her, "He's working with a counselor and both of us are doing all we can. He's a little boy who, through no fault of his own has been through hell." Parents did not want their children around Kyle.

Kyle fell off the swing at school causing a big bump on his head, so I had to pick him up. When he got home, Mike teased him, calling him a swinger. Kyle grabbed Mike by both ears, pulled his head down to his level, doubled up his fists, and started swinging, yelling, "I'll show you what a swinger is."

Attending school was becoming a challenge for Kyle. His behaviors became more and more erratic, bizarre, and difficult to deal with. He was disruptive to the point where the teachers wanted him out of their classroom. The school district psychologist had Educational Services give Kyle intensive testing to evaluate behavioral learning problems, which included evaluation of interpersonal difficulties, inappropriate behavior, unhappiness-depression, physical symptoms and fears. Each of the headings was loaded with a long list of symptoms. After that, Kyle spent most of his time in a resource room with a personal aide and special education teachers. Most of their day was spent trying to control his behaviors and maintain a peaceful atmosphere which rarely happened. Kyle did not receive much of an education due to his behavioral problems and as time went on, the situation only grew worse.

There were few dentists who would accept Medicaid. The closest participating dentist was 45 miles away. During Kyle's appointment, I sat in the waiting room until the receptionist called my name, telling me the dentist would like to speak to me. The no-nonsense dentist said, "I refuse to treat your child. We quit in the middle of the procedure. He started swinging, hitting me and my assistant. Don't bring him back." Kyle had post-traumatic stress disorder. They had a mask over his nose, his eyes were closed, and when he opened them, he saw two strange adults leaning over him. Kyle reacted, believing they were going to harm him. After many phone calls I found a dentist 80 miles from home and had no choice but to take him there. This time he did just fine.

When Kyle was ten, he refused to eat, including his favorite foods, ice cream, or candy. It seemed like his body had shut down. I got notes from school saying he would not eat his lunch. He was skin and bones. The kids called him 'Lollipop' because his head was too large for his emaciated body. His face was gray, the color of death. Nothing I tried would make him eat and I was scared. When it was time for my monthly meeting at children's welfare, I took him along because I needed help. Kyle was adopted and no longer under their jurisdiction, but they had assured me they would always be there to help. Beverly was alarmed when she saw Kyle's condition. She calmly talked to him and finally asked what his favorite food was. He responded, "Chicken wings." She made him a deal. If he worked very hard, she would buy him some chicken wings. For whatever reason, Kyle started eating and Beverly gave me money to buy Kyle his chicken wings.

Kyle's eating habits were horrible. Because of this and the medications he was taking, he was often constipated. He constantly clogged up the toilet. I heard him screaming from the bathroom, "Call an ambulance, call 911." He was constipated and in excruciating pain. He screamed over and over to call 911. I called the doctor, and was instructed to bring him in immediately.

Kyle thought he was going to die. In the elevator on the way to the doctor's office he started saying the Lord's Prayer and Hail Mary. He was crying, "Mommy, I love you. Please pray for me," repeating it over and over. I tried to comfort him, noticing the curious stares of the fellow passengers on the elevator. We went into the waiting room and sat down. The praying continued, begging me to pray for him, and telling me he loved me. He sat there about five minutes, got up, and raced down the various examining rooms until he found Dr. Larned. He grabbed hold of his arm, while the stunned doctor, patient, and patient's mommy stared at this terrified child. Kyle was chanting and pleading, "Help me, please, please help me." Because he was making such a scene, we were immediately escorted into an examining room with Dr. Larned right behind us. The doctor told the nurse to prepare an adult enema and bring in a large portable potty. Kyle ran to the bathroom to attempt one more time to have a bowel movement. It worked. It was alarming to see the huge bloody feces in the stool. I don't know how he ever pushed it out. The doctor lectured him about how important it was to eat fruits and vegetables.

I was relieved Kyle was all right. We got on the elevator and I noticed two of the same people from the earlier ride. Kyle was perfectly calm, the chanting and praying forgotten. The lady sympathetically asked, "Does your child have to be hospitalized?" I responded simply, "No, he's fine."

Although Kyle went through a period of time during which he quit eating, he never stopped hoarding food. This was not an unusual behavior in my home. Darrena suggested I leave a container of food in his room so he would know it was available. I filled a container with individually-wrapped snacks and put it in his drawer. It did not make one bit of difference. Every nook and cranny in his room had food saved from his dinner and confiscated from the pantry. I found a cake mix and can of frosting hidden in the garage.

Kyle's temper tantrums were legendary, so severe he would go into seizures. As he got older, the tantrums became more frequent. Shopping was a challenge. Kyle would scream obscenities, crying loudly, attempting to hit and kick me while I hung onto him so he could not run away. One sweet sympathetic clerk told me if she could, she would give me my stuff. I learned to disassociate, not to take anything personal, and to just hope no one would get hurt.

Kyle was only hit on one occasion. It was Christmas Eve and we had a lot of company. Kyle had one tantrum after another all day long. Auggie and I were both fed up and exhausted from trying to deal with Kyle's behaviors while trying to entertain guests and have a nice Christmas for the boys. We heard Gabriel screaming, "Kyle took my toy and pushed me down." Auggie smacked Kyle. Everyone cheered! Auggie was called "Smack Daddy" for several months. Amazingly, Kyle calmed down and the Christmas festivities continued without further incident.

I was always vigilant, keeping an eye on the boys. Kyle was not the only child with severe behavioral problems. If I was not on top of the situations that were always popping up, someone would be hurt. I always had many children, so the majority ruled when trying to get to the bottom of what happened.

Two things to be remembered at all times were do not take anything away from Kyle and do not touch him. The school had informed everyone who worked with him not to put their hand on his shoulder or touch him in any way, because he would start swinging at them. Kyle did allow me to touch him and I did so at every opportunity. I started when he moved in, by reading him a book every night before bedtime with my arm around him and the book in front of us. This became a nightly ritual he was comfortable with. I suspected the tantrums were his way of being held. When I talked to him, I put my hand on his shoulder, or when I put something into his hand, I used both hands so he had human touch. He was like a wild animal.

When the children in my home were fighting over something, I took it away and put it in time out. If they did not keep their things picked up, I took a bag and cleaned their rooms and they did not get back their belongings unless they managed to keep their room clean for a week. This did not work with Kyle. When I took his radio, his fist aimed for me, missed, and put a big crack in the wooden door. The boys were outside playing with a remote control Ferrari®. They were fighting over it and it was getting out of hand. My son-in-law, Jack, decided to take care of it by going out and taking the Ferrari® away. That was one of the tantrums when Kyle left the planet. It was scary, as if he was possessed, screaming, "Give me my fuckin' Ferrari®." I didn't give in to his tantrums. I maintained my control over him.

When I caught Kyle shoplifting I asked the manager to call the police. Kyle was not the least bit concerned what the consequences might be as he stood waiting defiantly. When the police arrived, Kyle glared at them, saying, "You think you're bad asses, but you don't scare me. Fuck you." The officer pulled me aside and asked, "What is Kyle's diagnosis and what meds is he on?" I answered their questions, and was informed, "We are not going to take responsibility for Kyle. It would require a private nurse to monitor him at the detention center. The center would call you to pick him up as soon as he arrived. He was caught shoplifting several times and there was never a consequence. That sent a loud and clear message to him.

The small rural school he attended informed me Kyle would not be allowed to attend any extra-curricular activities or be on school property if school was not in session unless I was with him. There were times he was not allowed on school property even when school was in session. He was sometimes home-bound, with a teacher coming to our home two or three hours a week. If Kyle and I were the only two in the house, he was fairly easy to handle, but as soon as the other boys got off the bus, all hell broke loose, and usually Kyle was the instigator.

There were instances when Kyle became angry and said that he was going to call children's welfare, and tell them he wanted to be moved. I always told him, "go ahead," calling his bluff. He then screamed, "I'm really gonna call children's fuckin' welfare. Goddamn it, I want outta here!"

I received a call from the school counselor, "I'm concerned about Kyle. He insists he was a German shepherd before he was a little boy. I carefully explained to him that he was never a dog, but he didn't believe me." I mentioned this while we were eating dinner, and the teenage boys started laughing. Bert said, "We told Kyle everyone was a dog before they were human. He said he remembered being a German shepherd."

While the boys were in school, I attended a training session. I came home and threw the material on the table, which included a bright SEND HELP sign. It was suggested we keep it in the car in case of emergency (before cell phones). Kyle saw the sign and asked if he could have it. I said, "Sure." Not too long after this, a sheriff's deputy came to the house to make out a report on a runaway. He inquired about the sign. I laughed and explained, "Kyle thought it would be funny to put it in his window." He continued making out his report and when he finished, he asked, "Do you mind if I check out your house?" I said, "Go ahead," and thought, "That dang sign."

I walked into the kitchen with my rowdy bunch of boys being unusually quiet, and keeping an eye on me. I ignored them and went about the business of fixing lunch. I turned on the water and got a blast of cold water sprayed on me. Laughter erupted from the boys. Kyle had put a rubber band on the handle of the dish-rinsing spray nozzle. This prank was repeated numerous times over the years, and I fell for it every time.

The Fourth of July was always celebrated in a big way at our house. It was legal to shoot fireworks in the country so all the city folks came to our place for a day of barbeque, swimming, and noisy firecrackers. Damien, who was a black foster child, complained, "Tell Kyle to quit calling the fireworks, 'nigger chasers'. One more time and I'll take him down and beat his fuckin' brains in." I told Kyle, "Knock it off. You know the "N" word is inappropriate and very offensive to Damien." It wasn't long and the boys were screaming, "Fight! Fight!" as they cheered on Damien and Kyle. A good fight was always a source of entertainment. I broke up the fight and confiscated the offensive fireworks from their stash.

On a hot summer afternoon, I watched Kyle walk toward me, staggering as if he were drunk. When he started talking, his speech was slurred. I thought he was playing around. I kept an eye on him for about 10 minutes and decided he was not playing. Something was wrong. I took him to the emergency room. When the doctor checked him out, he jokingly asked Kyle if he had been to the wine cellar. His medication had caused the problem. I am not sure what the doctor gave him but he snapped out of it.

Kyle's mental health was rapidly deteriorating and we were helpless to do anything about it. He was frequently in a manic state, his eyes darting back and forth, and his body in constant motion. Justin, his case manager from the mental health center, said Kyle had rapid mood swings in the time he spent with him. We tried many medications and cocktails of medications. Nothing worked. He was in and out of psychiatric hospitals for years. The psychiatric hospitalizations did nothing to help Kyle. The psychiatrist told me it did help because it gave me a break while he was hospitalized.

Information that trickled back to us about Kyle's siblings was not positive. Becky, his 15-year-old sister, was excited about the vacation her foster parents planned. The car was packed with luggage, the children's favorite toys, and all the information to complete an upcoming seminar. Becky left with the car during the night to meet her boyfriend when everyone was sound asleep. Her boyfriend was waiting in his car and, in their infinite wisdom, they decided to torch the foster parents' car. Becky was placed in a different home.

By the time Kyle was 14, the situation appeared hopeless and we were worn out. Auggie had had enough and told me, "Either Kyle goes, or I go." I admitted Kyle to the psych unit, and told them, "Kyle is more than we can handle. It's time for him to go to a residential facility." The doctor agreed. A long list of medications had been tried by the hospital and none of them were effective. They moved on to a new drug by injection. After a few weeks they found a residential facility 60 miles from our home that was willing to take him. I did not see Kyle for two weeks after the first injection. I was stunned. The results were amazing. For the first time, I saw Kyle as a normal boy. The mood swings were gone. The anxiety, agitation, paranoia, all gone. It was a miracle.

Kyle was in residential about a month before they managed to get the records transferred for him to attend school. He started school in the city, in totally unfamiliar surroundings. He didn't know anyone and was having a hard time adjusting. He begged me to let him come home. I was called in for a meeting, with teachers, staff, principal, counselors, and so on. Kyle was overwhelmed and it broke my heart to see tears running down his cheeks. He had to make the adjustment. There was no choice. I mentioned to him that he had a relative attending that school. Suddenly I had everyone's attention, asking who the relative was. The kids that came to this school from the residential facility came with a lot of baggage and a troubled background. When I said, "Jake Conner," you could watch the jaws drop all around the table. Jake was a popular kid. His mother, my cousin, Kelly, was a respected volunteer involved with many aspects of the school. The revelation seemed to change the course of the meeting. There was now a determination to help Kyle with his adjustment to the new school.

I had frequent visits with Kyle, and started to bring him home on the weekends. He would beg me not to take him back. I talked to his counselor pointing out he was a changed boy and I would like to have him home when the school year was over. It was approved. He continued doing well so I asked if he could come home in time for Christmas. It was approved. The weekend visits continued with Kyle begging to come home. I talked to his counselor again and asked if I could bring him home for good at Thanksgiving. The counselor said, "Why don't you just take him home this weekend." I told Kyle, "Pack your stuff. You're coming home for good." Kyle was a happy boy.

He wasn't home very long when his mental illness started showing signs of returning. Slowly the magical miracle drug was losing its effectiveness. Kyle was rapidly declining to his previous state even though he was still getting the injections. To make matters worse, the medication had caused him to gain 50 pounds, which added to his misery. Since then, no other medication has been found that could help him.

On the Saturday morning before Father's Day, Auggie died of a heart attack. Todd's girlfriend, Sadie, picked Kyle up and took him to the hospital. I believe he was grieving in his own way but there was no outward sign of it. Kyle was the only adopted child who went on the 500-mile-drive to the burial. I can't explain why, but I felt it was the right thing to do. Auggie and

Kyle could not be in the same room together without conflict. I always tried to be present when the two were together in order to prevent an angry outburst. It was exhausting.

I was wondering how I'd be able to manage all the troubled boys in my care and make sure that I could get them to all their appointments. After Auggie's death, Kyle put him on a pedestal, forgetting the fact that the two constantly butted heads. Kyle told everyone I killed Auggie by poisoning the chicken soup we had for dinner the night before.

I found I could do it all. I was no longer taking care of Auggie and could not believe how much extra time I had every day. I talked to Kyle about the accusation. He would only say, "My dad was fine before he ate that soup."

The summer Kyle was 15, he got a job working at the concession stand at the community swimming pool. He was excited and wanted to work full time to get a big paycheck. I convinced him to start part-time to see how he liked it. That job turned out to be one of the few successes in his life. He didn't work many hours, but he did manage to keep the job.

I signed up for Kyle and two other foster children to attend a two-week summer camp about 100 miles from home. There were several camps to choose from but the boys all agreed on the wilderness training camp. It consisted of sleeping under the stars, cooking over a campfire, bathing in the river, learning what plants are poisonous, and being one with nature. Kyle was there a few days, and in typical Kyle-fashion, was horsing around. He was swinging from a tree when he slipped and cut his leg on a rock. He was transported to the nurse's station at the camp headquarters. The nurse evaluated the situation, and called me, "Kyle fell out of a tree and cut his leg. I put antiseptic on the cut and he will go back to the camp." That sounded logical to me.

A few days later the director called and asked me to pick up Kyle. They were not going to tolerate his behaviors and he refused to cooperate on any level. I was totally aggravated. I had won a night at a bed-and-breakfast across the street from Kathleen and was looking forward to using it that night. Steaming mad, I made the 100-mile-drive to pick up Kyle.

Driving out of the camp, Kyle showed me his leg. He said, "I deliberately got kicked out. There's no place to take a shower and they wouldn't let me get in the river because of the sore. I was hot and miserable." My anger was immediately redirected to the camp. The sore looked horrible. Our first stop was the emergency room. The ER doctor was appalled. He said the wound needed stitches, but too much time had passed. There would be a large scar. Kyle was put on antibiotics and I was given strict instructions on how to treat the wound. The doctor's parting words were, "I should hotline that camp." I did call the camp director to voice my anger and concern.

I discovered Kyle missing when I called the boys to the kitchen for their bedtime snack. I asked, "Does anyone know where Kyle is?" One of them said, "Yeah, he found some condoms. He's on his bike headed to Kaylee's house to use them." Kaylee, a cute girl with a bit of a reputation, lived on a farm about two miles away. I ran to the car, hoping Kyle had not made it to his sexual encounter. I spotted him pedaling down the highway in the dark and thanked God that no one had hit him. I told him "Get in the van and throw your bike in the back. What are you thinking, being out this late? No one can see you on the highway in the dark." He came right back at me, "You never want me to have any fun." A couple of hours later everyone was in bed for the night. I decided to crawl out of my cozy bed to check on Kyle. His window was open and he was gone.

This time I called the sheriff's department. Kathleen was staying with me and she offered to look for him. She found him nearing Kaylee's house. He initially refused to get in the car with her, but she managed to convince him it would be in his best interest. The deputy, on a power trip, shouted at Kyle when he walked in, "What is your major malfunction, young man?" Kyle stared at him and defiantly answered, "Fuck you." The deputy's face turned bright red, and he screamed at Kyle, "You're nothing but a punk kid that needs to be taught to have respect for authority." Unimpressed, Kyle simply responded, "Fuck you." I thought that puny deputy was going to have a heart attack. With shaking fingers he made out his report while Kyle stared at him. I asked the deputy what I could do to prevent Kyle from leaving again. The answer was. "If you call five more times tonight to report he's missing, a deputy will never do anything except show up. If he's out at two in the morning and gets hurt or in trouble, you're responsible for him." Now I wanted to say, "Fuck you."

During this time period, another foster boy we had adopted, Connor, was living with us again. The two boys kept me on my toes. If one wasn't in trouble, the other one was. When Colleen was visiting, a part of Kyle emerged that was surprising. He warned Colleen, "Don't ever be alone with Connor. He will hurt you." Kyle was never far from her, observing, ready to do battle to protect her.

By the time Kyle was 16, there was not much I could do with him. Like so many of the boys who have been in my home, consequence and reward charts had no effect. He was sinking further and further into the firm grasp of mental illness. His behaviors were becoming bizarre and unpredictable.

Kyle had his room in the basement away from the other boys. Each boy had his own baggage and Kyle knew which buttons to push to create havoc. One evening while I was preparing dinner, Kyle came bouncing into the kitchen in a manic state. He had sewn his right fingers to his left fingers. I don't know how he accomplished this, but he was proud of himself. It was a gruesome sight.

Kyle managed to get jobs at fast-food restaurants, but he could not keep them. One of the restaurants served chicken and he was allowed to bring a generous amount home. He was proud to share it with the group of hungry boys. That job lasted about two months. I suspected he found pleasure giving the boys something they liked, and he put forth an effort to keep the job.

I was thrilled when Kyle announced he wanted to go out for the high school football team. He dropped out after a couple of weeks when he discovered the coach expected him to shape up or ship out. He was spiraling further and further into the nightmare world of mental illness. There was no way to reach him or reason with him. I suspected he smoked marijuana every chance he got. He was self-medicating. There was no consequence that could stop him from doing something that gave him relief.

Kyle was no longer taking his prescription medication. I gave it to him every morning, watched as he put it in his mouth, but he was cheeking it. He'd then go around the corner and take it out of his mouth so he could sell it at school. I always had the medication in a locked closet and personally handed out the meds. When I insisted he take his meds in front of me and let me check his mouth, he refused.

A couple of months before he was 17, he went to a high school football game. I told him to call if he could not find a ride home. He never called and he never came home. The next morning I called the school to see if he was there, explaining that he had not come home the night before. He was not in class. The school officer spotted Kyle on the campus and gave chase. He called the city police to help him catch Kyle. After they had him in custody, he was transported to the juvenile detention center and, as usual, they called me to pick him up as soon as he walked in. The staff at the detention center told Kyle if he waited until he was 17, I wouldn't be able to do anything about it. By the time he reached his seventeenth birthday he was totally out of control, skipping school, staying out all night, and shoplifting, while I watched helplessly. I was responsible for Kyle until he was 18. I watched the calendar, marking off the days, like a prisoner marking off the days while sitting in a cell.

Justin, from the mental health center, called one morning and said he spotted Kyle sleeping on a bench outside of a store. He just drove on. I had taken the boys to the movies. Kyle decided he did not want to go and asked if I could pick him up after the movie at a prearranged spot. He wasn't there, and I didn't see him for a couple of days.

John was Kyle's case manager from children's welfare. I complained to him, I was completely worn out from dealing with Kyle. John told me he was off the clock and would help me find Kyle and take him to the psychiatric hospital. Our plan was to get Kyle into my minivan, hit the locks, and take off to the hospital. We found Kyle at his friend Mark's house. John said, "Get in the car, and we'll talk." Kyle immediately walked around the van peering through the windows, to see if there were any clothes packed for him. He knew if there was a bag, he would be going to a psychiatric hospital. Satisfied there was no bag, Kyle got in the van. John got in the back with him, I locked the doors and we took off along with the three foster boys who were with me. The hospital had been alerted we were on our way with Kyle and there was a good possibility he would run when we arrived. We were informed they would do nothing until we managed to get him in the door at the hospital. Throughout the 65-mile drive, Kyle told us he intended to take off the minute we got there.

Most of the trip was through hilly, curvy, wooded country. Caroline called about 30 miles into our trip, crying and upset. She was on the same road and had hit a deer. She was all right. There was quite a bit of damage to her car but it was still drivable. John wanted to know the exact location so he could pick up the deer on the way home and butcher it.

When we arrived, I pulled up to the main door to let John and Kyle out. Good to his word, Kyle took off running. I went to the admitting desk to inform them Kyle jumped out of the van and ran. John took my van to track Kyle. The three foster boys were still in the van. It turned out the hospital was willing to help after all. They called the police. Several police cars showed up and a helicopter with a spotlight. John was keeping in touch by cell phone while Kyle was walking down the highway, heading back to Georgetown. When the police closed in on him, he took off running. He headed down into a ditch, trying to get away in the dark. With the spotlights from the helicopter, he didn't have a chance. They cuffed him, put him in the back of the patrol car, and delivered him to the hospital. The password for Kyle's hospitalization was 'Runner'.

After we completed the admission procedure, we headed to where the excited boys were waiting. They had a great time claiming it was like living through an episode of *Cops*. We stopped at a service station, bought some plastic bags and proceeded to retrieve the deer. John was kind enough to share the meat with me.

After 10 days Kyle was released and my vacation was over. There was no change in Kyle's behavior.

Mark was a friend Kyle occasionally hung around with. His mother,

Shelly, called one morning to inform me that when her husband left for work, he had discovered Kyle sleeping on their porch swing. He stormed back in the house yelling, "Call the police. Get that worthless kid out of here." Shelly convinced him not to, stating, "Mark and Kyle have been friends since kindergarten. I'll call his mother." I told Shelly, "I really appreciate your thoughtfulness. Kyle's out of control. Half the time I don't even know where he is. Do me a favor. If this happens again, call the police." My experience proved it was a waste of time to call the police in Georgetown, which was a large neighboring city. There never seemed to be a consequence for anything Kyle did with the exception of school suspension. That was a consequence for me, not Kyle!

A few weeks before Kyle turned 18, I asked Justin to help me get a court order to have Kyle admitted to a psych hospital. He agreed. Anything was worth a try. So, with two signatures and $70, I had my court order.

The Georgetown police called to arrange a plan to pick up Kyle. We agreed to meet at a gas station on the way to school. I pulled in and noticed two patrol cars waiting. As soon as I stopped, they walked to the car. All the boys knew something was up but they were clueless as to what. The officer opened the door to the passenger side and said, "Which one of you is Kyle?" Kyle looked at me and said, "You fucking bitch, I hate you and I hope you die." He got out of the car. They cuffed him, and put him in the back of the patrol car. I could hear him screaming "Fuck you bitch," as they drove away.

The boys sat in the car shocked as they watched the entire scene unfold. I always told the boys, "Never underestimate me." Finally, Miguel said "Wow, Ellen, I'm sure never gonna underestimate you."

Kyle was admitted to a state psychiatric hospital. He was uncooperative and refused a meeting with me. I told the staff I would show up anyway. When I got there, Kyle attended the meeting with me present and was surprisingly agreeable. The bottom line was Kyle would be 18 in a few days and would be free to do whatever he wanted. He was released and came back home. His birthday was in November and he was still attending school. He had few credits. When school started that year, he decided to enroll in the tech school welding program which he seemed excited about. He found out they actually expected him to work and follow rules, which he was incapable of doing. I bought all the expensive equipment required for the class. He lasted less than two weeks. He spent most of his time in the resource room sleeping, when he even managed to get to school.

There was a fair in our small town which all my boys eagerly anticipated. Tony, the local police officer, called me about 1:00 AM and said, "There's a very upset father whose 13-year-old daughter hasn't come home. The last time she was seen, she was with Kyle." I told Tony, "Kyle isn't here.

You know I try to keep him out of trouble, but it doesn't seem like there's anything I can do. If you find him, put the fear of God in him." The police in that small town always went the extra mile for me. An hour or so later, Tony called back and said, "I found Kyle walking home. I hope the father doesn't press charges, but he said he intends to. I told Kyle in explicit language what happens if he messes around with a 13-year-old girl." The father did not file charges and, once again, Kyle "got away with it."

After Auggie died, Kyle received death benefits from Social Security. From November until school was out in May, he could have had a sizable check each month for doing nothing but being a warm body in school. He managed to stay long enough to get three checks. Most of the money went for drugs. He spent $400 for a golden retriever puppy. He took care of it for three days and disappeared. I gave it away. I begged him to stay in school and spent hours trying to set up on-line classes by working with the public school, and also tried to help him get a job.

In desperation, I approached Alexandra's husband, Curt, about hiring Kyle. A foster parent and friend, he owned a custom-made furniture business. I offered to pay half of Kyle's salary if he could work with Curt a few days a week. It was a wonderful opportunity for Kyle to learn a trade. Curt was a likable guy who had dealt with many teenage foster children. Kyle blew it. He would show up high, or not show up at all.

After his eighteenth birthday he discovered that, as an adult, he would go to jail if he was caught breaking the law—something new to him.

One morning I got up early to go shopping before the boys woke up. On my way home I got a frantic phone call from Johnny saying, "Kyle has a knife. He's threatening to kill me. He won't get out of my room." Johnny sounded more annoyed than scared. I told Johnny to give the phone to Kyle, and to my surprise Kyle actually took the phone. I told Kyle, "Get out of that room right now."

Johnny took the phone back and I told him, "As soon as Kyle leaves the room, lock the door, and don't let him back in. I'll be home in about 10 minutes."

When I arrived, one glance at Kyle, and I knew this was a serious situation. He looked like a wild animal ready to attack. He was pacing, agitated, picking arguments about everything. He had made me a wine cabinet in a shop class and it was hanging on the wall. Kyle went toward the cabinet to yank it down, telling me I could no longer have it. I stepped in front of the cabinet, trying to stop Kyle from destroying the cabinet, the wall and the glasses. Kyle pinned me to the wall with one hand on me and the other hand holding a knife to my throat screaming, "This is the day you die, Bitch." I managed to get the cell phone out of my pocket and push the numbers 911.

Relieved I heard, "911, what is your emergency?" I yelled, "He has a knife, he's going to kill me." With that response, Kyle let go and ran outside. In a very short time there were three patrol cars pulling into my driveway with Paxton, a former foster child who had been emancipated, right behind them. Paxton had no way of knowing what was going on, but said he had a feeling they were headed to my house.

The deputies went out in the yard searching for the knife. As they searched, I watched a deputy doing the get-this-catshit-off-my-shoe dance. The knife was found. Amazed, I watched as they put cuffs on Kyle and read him his rights. Finally he was getting a legal consequence but he didn't seem to care. Paxton told the deputies it was a good thing they got there before he did. The deputy told Paxton, "That's your mom. You can do whatever you need to do to protect her."

Twenty-four hours later Kyle called, "They let me out. Can you come and get me?" I said, "After what you did, now you think I should just come and pick you up like nothing happened? I'm not doing it." After a while, I started worrying, I still loved this boy and, even to this day, I love him. I drove the 30 miles to the county jail to pick up my wayward son. When I got there, I couldn't find him. I drove around for about an hour but he was nowhere to be found. Three days later he came home like nothing happened.

Kyle said, "A bunch of guys are renting a house. I'm moving in with them." Two days later he was back home. They had asked him to leave.

It wasn't long before he was a guest of the county jail again. He had stolen a cell phone. Kyle spent 24 hours in jail and was required to pay court costs and restitution. His life was spiraling out of control.

A few weeks passed and Kyle was picked up again. The police officer called and said to come get Kyle. He was being held in a cell. They had received several reports that a young man was acting suspiciously, sitting in front of a bush with his hands behind him doing something. When the police arrived, they discovered Kyle was going through a stolen purse. They did not think Kyle stole the purse but happened to find it in the bush. Kyle did have marijuana on him. I asked if I had to pick him up. They said no, they could hold him for 24 hours. I refused to take him home; however, I did pick him up at the end of the 24 hours.

I had several thousand dollars in savings accounts for Kyle. I met him at the police station with $2,000, to pay court costs. I told him, "Pack your stuff and get out. I'm done." He called someone to pick him up and left without a good-bye.

He realized there was more money in the account and called five or six times a day demanding, I give him his fucking money. There was no doubt it would be spent on drugs; however, I withdrew the money and handed it all over to him.

The police in Georgetown must have had my number on speed dial. This time he was not locked up, they were keeping me informed of his activities. The officer told me, "Kyle is sleeping in the attic of an apartment complex. We didn't arrest him, but he can't stay there."

A few weeks passed and there was another phone call. "An informant gave us an address where we could find the stolen items from some recent burglaries. We checked it out, and found not only the stolen items, but heroin. Kyle was in the apartment but there wasn't enough evidence to charge him." I inquired if Kyle was using heroin. The answer was "Definitely yes. We offered him a bus ticket to a homeless shelter but he wouldn't go." I told the officer, "Don't call me anymore. I have a foster home, and with Kyle being in and out of jail and using heroin, he can't be around the foster children."

Kyle called occasionally. He stayed with anyone that would let him, moving from place to place. He hid his belongings in an alley. He left home with a truck full of stuff, years of accumulated possessions. I seldom saw Kyle. When I did, his hair was matted and filthy, and he stank. I suggested he contact the mental health facility that had worked with him for so many years. He did and they found an apartment for him to be shared with a young lady. The building was new, the apartment was completely furnished—sheets, dishes, everything.

Kyle called, telling me, "The apartment is really nice. I need cereal bowls, extra towels, and any movies you can spare." I gathered the requested items, happy that Kyle had a place to live. Before I could get the stuff to him, he was gone. With the apartment came rules--rules he could not follow. Two weeks after he moved in, he walked out to live on the streets.

Kyle, obviously high, would call to say, "Hello Mom, how are you? I think you are a whore. Dad's only been dead three years and you have a fiancé. What kind of slut are you?" I would answer, "I'm not going to listen to this." and hang up. I spotted Kyle walking down the street so I pulled over and he got in. He was dirty. His flip-flops were held together with duct tape and his clothes hung on his skinny body. I wanted to cry. He proudly told me he beat up a big guy so bad he was in intensive care. He added he spent a few days in jail. Kyle told me all of the items hidden in the alley were missing. I bought him lunch, took him shopping at a thrift store and gave him $25. I hoped he wouldn't spend it on drugs.

Kyle begged to come back home saying, "Can't you give me just one more chance?" Would one more chance have made a difference? I'll never know because, even though I'll always have a deep love for that boy, I couldn't chance bringing him home while I had other troubled foster boys to protect.

He eventually left the Georgetown area with his fellow heroin addicts, moving 50 miles away. The last time I saw Kyle was on his birthday. I bought lunch for him and another young man. He was high and in such a manic state it was exhausting to be with him. I gave him money and drove Kyle and his friend back to the drug house. Kyle called a few times, telling me he was living with a girl and her mother and having sex with both of them. The calls eventually ceased completely and I have not seen or heard from him for years. I still take the local newspapers just to keep up on my past wards. I saw Kyle's name on the docket. He was charged with domestic abuse. Later it was on the docket again for violating a restraining order.

Raising children is like making biscuits; it is as easy to raise a big batch as one, while you have your hands in the dough.

—E.W. Howe

10

TODD

The Brotherhood

In spite of the fact that Todd came with a lot of baggage as a therapeutic placement, he was a good fit in our home. He was downgraded to behavioral after six months. Another six months passed and he was downgraded to traditional. At the end of the first year, Beverly said everyone was waiting for the other shoe to drop but it never did.

According to Melanie, who had dropped him off at our house, he had been on house arrest and that was not successful. Two foster homes had not been successful. The next step was residential and when he was released from there, we got him.

The first time I saw him, he was 14, cute and a little chubby. In the year Mike had been with us, he and Bert had formed a tight brotherly bond. Todd was quickly accepted into the brotherhood.

There were a few parallels with Todd and the typical foster placements, such as his previous involvement with the juvenile system and having a single mother. The biggest difference was that Mom had a good job, did not use illegal drugs, did not drink or smoke, had an immaculate home, and loved her son. She paid child support for Todd to remain in our home, because it seemed to be working.

We had not lived in the country home long when Todd joined our family. It still looked like a house plopped down in the middle of a pasture. A creek separated the acreage, with the house positioned toward the back of the property. The front section, facing the highway, was partially wooded and completely overgrown with brush, weeds, and poison ivy. Todd was like a ball of fire, chopping his way through the tangled mess. We gave him free access to the riding lawnmower and that boy would hardly quit for a meal. He was on a mission and did one hell of a good job. I enjoyed working alongside of him, and the two of us spent hours chopping, clearing, and in my case, itching. While we were working, a car pulled up and the driver inquired if he could buy the property. Todd's face fell as he asked, "You're not going to sell this, are you?" Today, many years later, it looks like a park.

I arranged respite and made plans to go to the city, have brunch and see a movie. At midnight the respite provider called, jarring me awake. I answered to an angry man saying, "You need to come get Todd right now. That little son-of-a-bitch ran away." Auggie overheard and said, "I'll go get him." He liked Todd and was not upset. When Todd got home, he told us, "I didn't run away. I walked down the road with the other kid that lives there. We came right back." I said, "Well Todd, looks like you get to go to brunch and see a movie tomorrow." We never sent him to respite again. Where we went, Todd and Mike went also. We weren't playing favorites, the fact was that many placements were so severe, I needed a break.

The boys were outside playing with water guns on a hot summer evening. I was in the kitchen, listening to the hollering and laughter, until it ended with Todd coming in with a bloody knee. The doctor stitched it up. The summer fun continued, until five-year-old Kyle hit Todd in the knee with a bat, so it was back to the doctor, to be re-stitched. I was reprimanded for not supervising Kyle.

The long summer days passed slowly and when Todd wasn't clearing brush, he was hanging out with Bert and Mike. Occasionally they played Ouija® board with fingers on a plastic disc, flying across the board, spelling out things from the spirit world. The three boys decided to play a trick on Colton, who was another foster child. They synchronized their watches, so at exactly 9:00, Bert and Mike would turn off the lights in Todd's room at the downstairs breaker box. Todd innocently asked Colton, "Hey Man, let's play that board game." Colton quickly agreed, with José following as they headed upstairs to Todd's room. At the designated time, Todd asked, "Mr. Ouija®, if you're real, make the lights go out." The room went dark. José's and Colton's chairs were pushed to the floor in their haste to get out of the room. I heard them running down the stairs, their feet touching every third step, as they darted out the front door. I jumped up, following them, asking, "What in the blue blazes is going on?" Hyperventilating, they pointed up the stairs. Todd was already in the basement with his partners. Suspecting foul play, I went down for an explanation. Through the laughter they explained their prank. They said, "Don't tell." I didn't. I told Colton and José, "It's nothing to worry about. Maybe there's just electricity in the air."

Todd was attending the rural grade school and, like a good little boy, completed his homework. Like naughty little boys, Mike and Bert wrote obscenities on the paper, unbeknownst to Todd. Totally oblivious to what was coming, he turned in the paper. He came home furious, saying, "I almost got expelled because of you fuckers." I never got a phone call, so I imagine Todd's bewildered look proved his innocence. Bert and Mike swore they thought he would look at it before he handed it in.

I was going from room to room, gathering sheets, with Todd close behind me. I pulled the sheets from José's bed, and out fell all the lingerie pages from a mail-order catalog. Todd stood there for a moment and then said, "Oh, this is good," as he fled out of the room, hollering, "Hey guys, guess what José had hidden under his sheets." I discovered years later that all the pictures of Caroline, from age 12 to 18, were missing from the photograph albums.

Todd did well in school, made friends, was invited to activities, and was a constant companion to Bert and Mike. If Todd wasn't with them, he was with Auggie. Auggie took Todd to the city to help deliver bills, partly because of his declining health, but mostly because he loved that kid. Todd blossomed under Auggie's supervision, only God knows why. Auggie had no fear when it came to fighting, and very little common sense.

Todd witnessed this many times, especially Auggie's uncontrollable road rage. One late night, bills delivered, they were headed home when a little sports car cut Auggie off. He blew the horn and obscenities began to fly. As it turned out, the guy in the sports car also had road rage. He began yelling back, motioning for them to pull into the next parking lot.

Auggie didn't hesitate for a second. He whipped into the fast food parking lot in close pursuit of the little sports car. The man jumped out of his car. Auggie had one of his gimpy legs hanging out when the man ran up to the van. He began pushing the van door shut on Auggie's handicapped leg, punching him through the window and yelling at Todd, "You need to tell your dad to watch his mouth." Todd replied, "That's not my dad."

Auggie chimed in, "Suck my dick, jack-off." Auggie realized he wasn't going to be able to get out of the van, and didn't want to hurt his leg more. As the guy was punching him through the window, Auggie put the old rundown van into drive and headed straight for the guy's new car. The man stopped throwing punches immediately and started pulling back on the van screaming, "What are you doing? That's my brand new car." Auggie calmly told him, "Like I give a shit. I got insurance."

The man quickly left, sprinting to his car as Auggie was inching his way toward it. By the time he got in his car, the only way to avoid being hit was to go over a two-foot embankment, which he did. As he drove over it, you could hear the metal and fiberglass scraping all the way across. Auggie felt satisfied that he had proved his point as they watched him drive away. He looked at Todd and said, "While we're here, we might as well get something to eat."

The next day Auggie was sitting at the kitchen table with a black eye telling the events of the night before. When Todd left the kitchen, Auggie told Bert, "Todd coulda' done something. Even if it was just gettin' out of the van and throwin' something at the guy so I could at least get out of the van."

A little later Mike walked in, took one look at Auggie's battered face and asked, "What the hell happened to you? You finally fall off your high horse?"

By the next summer, Todd was no longer a chubby little boy. He grew six inches, slimmed down and was a good-looking kid. We were outside working on a project when his juvenile officer showed up unannounced. He stood by me, and said, "My God, is that Todd?" I motioned for Todd to come over. He did so and briefly answered the officer's questions then asked if he could get back to work. As he walked away the officer said, "You know, I don't think I need to come back. I heard that boy was doing great and I believe he is." That was the end of court supervision.

Auggie's employee, Russ, was making 1-900 sex calls on a customer's phone. By the time the company figured out Russ was doing it and notified Auggie of the situation, the charges were close to a thousand dollars. Auggie paid the bill and lost the account. He was furious. He learned Russ was working as a rodeo clown, so we went to the next rodeo. We sat in the front row where Russ couldn't miss Auggie motioning for him to meet him outside. They stepped out and Auggie told him, "I want my fucking thousand dollars." Russ responded, "I ain't got a thousand dollars or even ten dollars." Auggie came back with, "Is that your wife sitting in the stands over there? Does she know about your obsession with the dirty fuck calls?" Russ, looking like one scared clown said, "Hey, don't tell my wife. I really don't have any money. I'll give you my pickup." Auggie drove the pickup home and I drove the car. The old pickup was turquoise with brush marks clearly showing. It was rusted through in several places and the passenger door was wired shut. When we got home, Auggie said, "Hey Todd, you want a pickup?" Looking at it, I told Todd, "Look at the bright side; you'll never lose it in a parking lot."

During Todd's rebellious period, he missed a lot of school and was held back several grades. He was 16 years old in the eighth grade and had a driver's license. It was decided to send him to a vocational boarding school. It seemed like a logical choice as he was Auggie's right-hand man and a whiz at repairing things. The application was filled out and he was accepted. He continued to attend grade school while waiting for an opening. Finally the letter arrived, informing him to get on the bus and be there by Monday. I told the principal Todd would not be returning as he would be attending a vocational school. She was appalled. She gasped, "He doesn't even have a grade school education. You can't take him out." I replied, "There's an opening in the school. If he doesn't take it, he'll lose it. It's not realistic to think he'll finish high school, and this is an opportunity for him to learn an employable skill." He left that school in the middle of the semester with a certificate stating that he had graduated from the eighth grade.

Through the years, I had several placements attend the vocational school. Todd was the only one who graduated. He earned a certificate as a welder and continued to attend the school, learning additional skills. While he was going to that school, Auggie drove about 200 miles to bring him home for visits. On one such trip home, they encountered a panhandler on an exit ramp. Auggie refused to give her money. She responded by lifting her shirt to expose her bare, sagging breasts and said, "Fuck you."

Caroline thought of Mike and Todd as extra little brothers. She was attending college not too far from the vocational school and thought nothing of Todd hanging out in her apartment for the weekend.

Todd completed the school when he was seventeen. He had the certificates and skills; however, he wasn't old enough to get a job in his field. We were happy to have him back in our home. Shortly after his eighteenth birthday, we were summoned to court for his emancipation from the system. While we were in the waiting room, I was describing how he had looked when he came to our home more than four years ago. When our case was called, the judge called me forward, and the juvenile officer proceeded to question me. "Ellen, please describe what Todd looked like when he came to your home four years ago." I giggled and answered, "He was about this tall," holding my hand up, "chubby, and so darn cute." Everyone chuckled and the judge continued, "I understand Todd is going to remain in your home. Will that create a hardship for you?" I answered, "No, we're happy to have him." He stayed a couple of years and there was never a moment I wished he wasn't there.

Eventually Ryder bought a condo in the city. Bert and Todd moved in with him. They were both employed at an aluminum siding company. After Todd worked there a short while, he asked why they didn't use a forklift that was sitting in the corner. The manager, Willie, said because no one can get it to work. Todd fiddled around with it and soon had it working, employing a rubber band and a paper clip. It continued to work for as long as the boys held their jobs. The company had lavish Christmas parties for their customers and employees. Kind-hearted Willie sent the leftovers home with Todd and Bert. When the boxes of food were brought in and laid out on our ten-foot kitchen table, the boys were like a pack of hungry wolves devouring the wonderful party food.

The condo thing wasn't working. Ryder was heavily into abusing drugs so the boys moved on. Todd was a country boy at heart so he moved back to the area. He was dating Sadie, a cute, slender blonde. No one knew Sadie well until Auggie died and she came to the hospital. Bert and the little group of foster boys stood there numb, not able to grasp that Auggie was gone. Sadie couldn't do enough to help. She drove the 15 miles to Hoisington and picked up Kyle, bringing him to the hospital so he would be included in the goodbyes. She did not go on the 500-mile trip for the burial, but remained to take care of the pets and water the plants and garden.

Eventually they married and finally I had another granddaughter.

11

JOSÉ

That's Not Sibling Love

C losing my eyes I forced the word "Yes" from my mouth. I amazed myself at what I would do to pay down the mountain of debt we owed. Accepting 16-year-old José, who had been suspended from school for a month, would be difficult. I must have been a glutton for punishment, accepting a child who had already been suspended, but I needed the money. Fleeting memories of an affluent lifestyle darted through my mind when asked if I would take José.

Fostering a teenage behavioral placement is a stressful job with the only relief being while the child attends school. José's current placement demanded he be moved due to the suspension. My goal was to make life miserable for boys who were suspended so they would be anxious to go back to school and avoid getting kicked out again. I was determined that suspensions were not to entail sitting in front of the TV and doing nothing. This rarely worked, but at least it was not a vacation for them.

José and his 14-year-old sister, Danielle, landed in state custody when Mom landed in a mental institution. José did not recall ever meeting his Hispanic sperm-donor dad, meaning that was the only role the father had played in his life. Danielle had a different sperm-donor father. He was white.

It turned out that José and I were from the same small town. What were the chances I would get a foster child from that small town 500 miles away? Why they were there and why they left are still mysteries.

Two hours after accepting the placement, we watched Melanie pull into our long gravel driveway with a dark-complexioned boy. I walked out to greet them and helped carry in two black trash bags containing José's meager possessions. I showed José to his room and let him get unpacked. Later, when he came downstairs, I sat at the table with him to get acquainted.

I explained to him, "The rules are posted on the kitchen wall, including the rule pertaining to suspension. You need to read it and sign the bottom. The rule I posted for suspension was:

OUT-OF-SCHOOL SUSPENSIONS

FROM THE TIME THE BUS PICKS UP THE OTHER BOYS IN FRONT OF THE HOUSE UNTIL THEY RETURN IN THE AFTERNOON, YOU WILL EITHER BE WORKING OR SITTING AT THE KITCHEN TABLE DOING HOMEWORK. YOU WILL BE ALLOWED A 30-MINUTE LUNCH BREAK.

In my house "work" meant spreading a load of gravel over the driveway with a shovel. The man who delivered the gravel knew the routine. He used to ask if I wanted him to spread the gravel with his dump truck, but I told him, "No, we have shovels."

The next morning the other boys went off to school and José was handed his shovel. Pretending to work requires at least some effort. It didn't take long to realize José wasn't much interested in work. You had to draw a circle around him to see if he was moving.

After a couple of hours, José came limping into the house. He claimed he had twisted his ankle and could not possibly shovel gravel. I knew darn well he wasn't hurt, but I had no choice but to take him to the doctor. The X-rays showed no injuries or damage. José was given crutches and the doctor told him to take it easy for a few days and then return to normal activity. Now I was really screwed. I struggled to invent chores he could do while incapacitated with the make-believe injury. Finally the days passed and once more he could go outside and pretend to shovel.

Nope, he hurt his ankle again. I called the doctor's office and told them I knew his ankle was not hurt. They explained he would have to be X-rayed again anyway. New X-rays proved what everyone already knew. His ankle was fine. The doctor and his nurse played the game. They wrapped his foot and told him to continue using the crutches.

I was determined José was not going to sit around doing nothing but there was little I could do about the situation. I gave him books in hopes they would keep him occupied. He sat in a chair with the books but he didn't read. You can lead a horse to water but you can't make him drink. About that time I considered doing some serious drinking myself.

Finally, José was cleared to go back to school and the pile of gravel was still sitting intact. He was just a warm body in school, taking up space. José was only 16, but he had been using drugs for years. He had either fried his brain on drugs or he was just dumb. Within a few weeks, he was suspended again. He picked up a desk and threw it in a fit of rage. Melanie said, "He's deliberately getting suspended. Enroll him in a GED class." The situation went from bad to worse. Now there was no hope he would be back in school. GED classes meant I had to drive him the 15 miles to Georgetown every dang day.

He was not a good fit in our home. The boys did everything they could to irritate him. I sent Bert and Mike to pick him up on an icy, cold day. They made sure they were late. Every time they stopped for him to get in the car, they would pull away and drive around the block.

José's sister lived in a foster home in Georgetown. I was asked to supervise the sibling visits so I arranged visits in a park and in my home. José decided to teach Danielle karate so she could defend herself. As José was showing her various moves, their bodies were smashed up against one another and his hands traveled to inappropriate areas as they gazed into each other's eyes. I would yell at them to keep a distance and they would, but only for a few minutes. Finally I told them I did not think the karate thing was a good idea. There was cause for concern regarding the relationship between José and his sister. She wrote on her books and arms, "Danielle loves José." This was definitely more than sibling love. They acted like two lovesick puppies around each other.

José was required to go to Narcotics Anonymous weekly. I suspect the meetings were similar to school and suspension; he was there, but did not participate. José had no friends at school and no friends in our home. He did have a friend from his previous foster home. They both attended the meetings. Bert and Mike gladly drove José to the NA meetings in Hoisington. They had just gotten their driver's licenses and were happy to go cruising while José attended the NA meeting for an hour.

One particular night, Auggie told the boys to stay in the parking lot after they dropped him off. He had a hunch José was going to run. Bert and Mike had no intention of sitting in a dark parking lot for an hour watching for José. When they went back to pick him up, he was gone. I called the sheriff's department and reported José missing. They eventually found him with his friend from NA. When they asked if I would take him back, I said, "No." José's presence in my home has caused too much grief.

A couple of weeks later, the boys were playing by the creek when they noticed two trash bags hidden in the weeds. I assumed José had put them there, planning to come back and retrieve them, but had been unable to find a ride. I emptied the bags as the boys watched. Every few minutes, they were claiming, "That's mine. He took my things." I took all the stolen items out and set the bags on the porch to take with me on my next trip to children's welfare. I found out later the boys had taken that opportunity to pee into the bags of José's belongings. Vengeance is mine, saith the Lord . . . and the boys in my home.

José was moved to a different foster home and after a while, there was no more contact or information. A few years slipped by and I noticed his name on the court docket on two occasions. The first charge was drug possession and the second was credit card fraud.

If you're going through hell, keep going.

—Winston Churchill

12

COLTON

His Father Believed Himself to be God

S itting at my kitchen table, I was in the presence of God. Also known as Fred, "God" was the father of Colton, who was my thirteenth place-ment. Most of my boys came from dysfunctional family backgrounds. Colton's background would be better described as bizarre. Colton had been living with his mother, Jannine, and his 13-year-old sister, Megan. Fred and Jannine were separated as far as living circumstances, but always seemed to be together during the day. They were the perfect couple, both very strange. Fred's permanent address was with his sister, Carlie, although I am inclined to think it was really La-La-Land. Fred had an older son from a previous relationship, also named Colton. The Colton in my home had been named after his half-brother!

Jannine and Fred were both mentally ill and low functioning. There had been a time when Jannine thought there was an unseen conspiracy to poison her. She was to the point of starvation when someone finally recog-nized she needed help. Fortunately, she was able to get the counseling and medication she needed to save her life.

When a child is taken into custody, within 48 hours there is a man-datory meeting with a support team to devise a plan to get the child back into the home. In order for Colton to return home, Jannine had to spend several hours a day as an outpatient at a mental health facility. Counselors worked with the clients, teaching skills, monitoring behavior, and evaluating their mental illnesses. Lunch was provided, prepared by the clients. The clients ran a resale shop to finance outings. Jannine reluctantly participated in these sessions and often made up excuses to skip.

The first supervised visit was at Jannine's trailer, with Fred present. Fred attended every visit. As Melanie, from children's welfare, and I pulled up in front of the trailer, I had second thoughts about going inside. The trailer was run down, with weeds growing out various places where the metal had separated. The front door was accessed by three steps to a small platform where the wood was completely rotted out. I had to carefully step onto the frame and jump to the front door. Inside, it was a cluttered mess. With a Chihuahua tucked under her arm, Megan was making a huge chocolate chip cookie in the cramped little kitchen. We cleared off a couple of chairs to sit by the table. I put my purse on the floor beside the chair. Melanie looked at me and then at my purse, making gestures. I wasn't getting her signals so she bent toward me and whispered, "Pick up your purse. Roaches will crawl in." As soon as Megan finished with the cookie, she put on her red-knit gloves which never came off again. During the course of the visit, her little Chihuahua kept yelping. Melanie looked to see what was bothering the dog, only to discover Megan was chewing on it! About every 10 minutes the dog would yelp and Melanie would remind Megan to quit chewing on the dog.

At this first visit, Fred shared with me that Megan had been raped. Her cousin, Jaxon, had brought a couple of friends to the trailer and they had raped Megan. Jaxon didn't participate but he didn't try to stop them either. Colton couldn't stop them. He was only 12 at the time.

Colton was a little odd but didn't cause much trouble in our home. I enrolled him in the eighth grade at the country school. When he came home the first day I asked him, "Well, Colton, how do you like your new school?" He said, "I love it because I like the color of the cafeteria." His behaviors in school were adequate. He didn't participate in class work or complete the homework. He was just another warm body taking up space.

Colton let the boys in my home walk all over him. If he was watching TV, they would walk in and say, "Colton, give me the remote," and he would hand it to them. Colton was sleeping on the couch when Mike decided it would be hilarious to crack an egg on his head. Colton jumped up and his fist went flying through the wall, leaving a huge hole. Colton had no friends, which was the case with almost all of the boys in my home. He did think his cousin, Jaxon, was the smartest person he had ever met. At least up until he went home for a visit and found all of his belongings missing. Jannine told him, "Jaxon just came in and took it all."

I watched from the kitchen window as Colton did some sort of wild dance. After every few steps he would hit himself with a stick. When I went outside to stop him, I saw the stick was sharp and Colton had several bloody gashes on his arms. I felt bad as I looked at his bloody arms and realized this was exactly what they had been talking about in the endless training sessions.

On another occasion, I noticed Colton doing something strange in the yard. He was crawling on the ground stalking something. When he came

84

in, I asked him what he had been doing. He showed me a bite mark on his finger and said, "I caught a snake and it bit me." Colton spent most of his time by the pond and wet-weather creek trying to catch lizards. The lizards would bite his earlobes and hang on forever. Lizards make unique earrings. I had to downplay their ability to shock me, knowing they would torment me with crawly creatures if they sensed I feared them. I pretended to be nonchalant. I was hanging up the laundry as three giggling shirtless boys approached me, each with lizards hanging from their nipples. In the distance I overheard the howls of pain as they attempted to dislodge the lizards. The fun never ended.

Sometimes I wrote chores on paper, including nonsense chores, and let the boys draw them out of a bowl. Colton drew, "Dig half a hole." He asked where he should dig it and I said, "behind the garage". An hour later, a sweaty Colton came in and asked, "How big is half a hole?"

It seemed like we were always in my minivan headed to some kind of appointment. All those rides in the van led to some very interesting conversations. One such conversation consisted of random thoughts of what the boys would do if they won the lottery. Colton said, "I would buy a large pond and charge everyone $5 to get in to fish." He continued, bragging, "I have relatives so rich they own a double-wide. It took two trucks to deliver their home."

There was another support meeting and I sat in the waiting room with the odd little family and witnessed just how bizarre Fred really was. Suddenly Fred put his hands out in front of him as though he was parting the Red Sea and he violently stomped his feet. He was in his own world, alternating between chanting and singing. Fred was not having a religious epiphany. He actually believed he was God. Jannine sat there as though this was typical behavior and Colton buried his head in his arms.

We finally made it into the meeting room and gathered around the table. Colton had a quarter in his hand tapping it on the table in an annoying manner. Melanie told him to stop. Glaring at her, he continued to tap. The counselor, Darrena, politely asked him to stop. He ignored her. In her whiny voice, Jannine asked him to stop. He would not. Finally I raised my voice, and yelled, "Colton, stop it right now! That's enough." He put the quarter in his pocket. I secretly wanted to gloat and to point out to everyone that I had accomplished what they couldn't. The emotionless group continued on with the business at hand. I agreed to allow supervised family visits in my home. What an experience!

Fred, Jannine, and Megan usually arrived on time, frequently in different dilapidated old cars. They were always trading one old piece of junk for another. During many of the visits, Jannine would say, "I need to talk to you alone. I have some really bad news for Colton. His father has only two weeks to live. How do you think I should tell him?" The first time, I was blown away and not sure how to respond. I observed Colton as she told him the devastating news. He didn't seem to have much of a reaction, which I thought peculiar. When she told him the same story week after week, I realized why he didn't have much of a reaction.

On one visit they showed up with a shiny new bicycle for Colton. When they came for their next visit, they loaded up the bicycle to take it back to the store. They told Colton they were sorry but they were out of cigarettes. I asked Colton how he felt about Fred and Jannine taking back his present. "I expected it. It happens all the time," he said.

One afternoon Jannine informed me, "I've been out of sorts for several days. My belly button's out of place again." My reaction was simply, "What?" Jannine said, "Yeah, when someone's just out of sorts, it's because their belly button's out of place. To fix it you take a votive candle and stick it on your belly button. Then you take wet bread and put it around the candle and light the candle. That'll pull your belly button back in place and make you feel better."

For the summertime visits, Fred showed up wearing shorts and nothing else, not even shoes. The shorts hung below his huge belly on his nearly-naked, 350-pound body. His first stop was always the bathroom and Jannine's was the pantry. She carefully went through everything and picked out what she wanted. If cheese crackers were available, it didn't take her long to choose. Then she'd ask me if she could buy them as she held out her cupped hands which contained her total wealth, a few coins, mostly pennies. I never took her money.

During almost every visit, Fred would raise his hands, indicating we were in God's presence. He would chant, talk to himself, and carry on. It was quite a scene. During one visit, he disappeared. I asked Megan where her dad went. She said, "He told me you were all goin' to hell, so he'd just wait in the car."

I tried to encourage the family to go out into the yard, sit on the porch, whatever, just to spend some quality time together. They were perfectly content sitting around the table—Jannine eating whatever she could get from the pantry, Fred being God, and Megan sitting there in her red-knit gloves.

Jannine loved fountain sodas! When it was time for them to leave, she would always ask to borrow money for a soda. At children's welfare they had a Jannine fountain soda fund.

On one occasion, they ran out of gas on the way to my house. Some kind soul stopped to help them and gave them a ride to get gas. When they got to the station, they revealed to the man that they didn't have any money. He paid for a full can of gas, bought Jannine a fountain soda and took them back to their car. One of my boys worked at that quick mart at the time and witnessed the entire scene.

On one particular visit, Fred was a little more scary than usual. The bizarre crew came in, followed by another man, who was introduced as Fred's friend, Fran. Everyone did their usual ritual and was seated around the table with the box of cheese crackers. Fran was chatting away, telling me that he and Fred had been friends for years. There had been five guys who had been buddies but now they were the only two left. Fred laughed and said, "One of them died a few years ago. Maybe you knew him." Then, he told me the man's name. I replied, "No, I don't recall knowing anyone by that name." He said, "Yeah, he was the guy that was executed."

As it turned out, Fred and Fran's friend had murdered an old woman who lived alone in an isolated area of Green County. I visited the old state penitentiary on a bus tour. It is now a museum and has been replaced by a new facility. As we toured the small separate building containing the gas chamber, the tour guide gave the name of the last prisoner to be executed in the old facility. OMG! It was their friend.

The family visits at my home were supposed to last one hour, but often stretched to two or more hours. When their hour was up, I would tell them it was time for them to leave. They always said OK, but the visits just lingered on and on. They weren't going anywhere until the cheese crackers ran out. At the next support meeting, I told children's welfare the home visits were not working out. It was decided Colton could start having longer unsupervised visits with his family in their home. Thank God! . . . and I didn't mean Fred.

One hot summer day Jannine called to inquire if she could borrow some clothespins. She said Fred was sweating like a mule so she took a sheet of plastic and made a little room just big enough for Fred's chair. She had a fan set up to blow air on him. I gave her the clothespins the next morning when I dropped Colton off for his visit. Fred was taking advantage of the morning air before retreating to his plastic room. He was sitting outside at the picnic table with a sorry-looking group of five or six men and women, enjoying their breakfast—beer. Most of them appeared as though they had been at the breakfast table a long time. A couple of dirty, scroungy, little kids were also running around.

Fred's counseling sessions were in the trailer until his counselor, Rodney, refused to go back. Fred had been put on oxygen part-time. With the oxygen machine running, he puffed away on his cigarettes. Next to Fred's chair in that tiny cramped room was a portable toilet that was rarely emptied and never cleaned. He always had a package of bologna next to him. The bologna sometimes had been out for a while and was coated with a greasy residue. Jannine whined, "Fred can't live without his bologna."

Colton was transitioning to move back home. He lived at my house Monday through Thursday, and then went home for a long weekend. It was summer and the day finally came when he could return home full time. I arrived with Colton at the agreed-upon time. There was no homecoming celebration. As a matter of fact, there was no one home. Colton was disappointed and angry. We left and wandered around a discount store to kill time then went back to the trailer and found them home.

Colton did not go back into foster care. For a year or so, Jannine contacted me occasionally, telling me she loved me and bringing me up to date on their lives. Researching the case recently, I discovered Fred has ascended back into heaven. Jannine is being Jannine. Colton has been arrested several times. The surprise was Megan. She is apparently doing all right. She is with an older man, has a child, and is managing just fine.

13

ERIC

I Am Not Dead

There is no Eric story, not from when he was in my home. He was there eight weeks, causing no problems in home or school. The story comes from before his placement and after he returned home. When I opened the door to catch my first glimpse of Eric, I saw a tall, thin 16-year-old boy, with kinky red hair and ears that stuck straight out.

I was enlightened as to the details of why he was in state custody before he arrived. When there is a stepparent involved, the teen often resents his or her presence. In Eric's case, it was the stepfather. His idea of quality time with Eric was playacting a popular interactive video game. Stepdaddy either became entranced in the game or deliberately intended to hurt Eric. For whatever reason, Eric carried the bruises.

A few houses down from Eric's home, in a peaceful subdivision, a statue of the Blessed Virgin sat in the front yard. In the silence of the night while the neighborhood slept, Eric slipped out of his bed on a mission to vandalize the statue. The first time, he knocked it over then crept back to his bed, thinking mission accomplished. The second time he wrote obscenities on it. The third time, he spray-painted it. The fourth time, the neighbor was waiting. The police arrived and Eric was taken into custody. Out of curiosity, I asked Eric, "Why? Was it because it represented religion?" He truthfully answered, "No reason. I messed with it because it was there, and I wanted to see how much I could get away with."

Eric smoked a lot of marijuana. It was suspected he smoked with his mom and stepdaddy. With Eric out of the house, the stepdaddy left also. I'm not sure whether mom kicked him out, or if he left because he lost his play-mate. Mom had a steady job and a nice house. With family counseling, Eric was returned home in record time.

Mom stepped up to the plate, determined to do what was best for her son. She encouraged him to get his driver's license. He was doing a great job, following the rules and showing responsibility. He was rewarded by being allowed to keep the car, under the condition that he make the seven-mile trip to pick her up after work. One day snow came down in sheets, mixed with sleet. On their way home, the car slid off the highway into the ditch. She died instantly.

Since he had been in my home recently, the word went out that I was the one killed. Obviously it didn't take long to prove that was false. An uncle in the city came forward to take custody of Eric and that was the last word on him.

14

NATHAN
Look Under the Manure

Devastated, Bert sat on the floor in his closet, looking at the empty jar. My heart broke as I realized what happened. My being a foster parent had caused my child pain. Bert accepted the foster boys in our home, never complaining about the change in our lifestyle. Three of the boys became brothers for life; however, many of them got on his nerves and stole his possessions.

He had an antique jar with $600 worth of dimes in it. Now there was only ninety cents left in the bottom of the jar. He had been complaining that he couldn't find his clothes. I didn't pay much attention because his closet was a mess. Nathan had his clothes and his dimes.

At the age of 16, Nathan had been released after spending two years in a residential treatment center. He was a small boy with blonde hair and a bad case of acne. Across his chest was a tattoo, depicting a huge devil stretched out of shape. Nathan's body had grown since he got the tattoo at age 11.

His mother, Joanna, was clueless or didn't care. Nathan had no rules or boundaries in her care. She showed up every other weekend for the visits, wearing skin-tight, revealing clothes and a thick coat of makeup that gave her an appearance of a cross between a clown and a hooker. She was married to a man 30 years older. As soon as Joanna sat down at the kitchen table, Old Man began rubbing her bare legs. Nathan stood behind her, running his fingers through her long hair and rubbing it on his face. Nathan and Parker, another foster child, worked at the local fast food restaurant. Parker would come home with tales of Nathan's hair fetish. Some girls told him to, "Leave me the fuck alone," and some didn't mind his fingers playing with their hair. Occasionally Joanna showed up without Old Man, explaining, "I'm due for some real fun. I'm hitting the bars by myself."

The boys in my home referred to Nathan as "Weirdo". They complained, "Every time I watch TV, Weirdo stares at me. He gives me the creeps." They were playing ball in the backyard, when Bert noticed Nathan staring at them out of the upstairs bathroom window. He shouted, "I'm telling Mom you're smoking." He had no idea Nathan was smoking. Nathan pleaded, "Please don't tell on me." I came out the back door, yelling, "Too late. You're grounded. You know better than to smoke in the house."

Nathan saw an ad in the back of a magazine, "Work from home, earn thousands of dollars." That got his attention. He saved $70 from his paycheck, and sent in a money order, preparing to be rich. It was a pyramid scheme. To make his thousands, he needed to place ads to find suckers to send him money just as he had done.

Nathan decided living in the country next to a cow pasture was an opportunity too good to pass up. He recognized dollar signs when he saw them. He carefully examined all the manure, searching for mushrooms growing on them. He dried them and sold them at school as a psychedelic drug. After he was gone, I was informed of his budding drug dealer activity.

Bert, Mike, and Todd, always being the practical jokers, made Nathan their target on April Fools' Day. They told him, "Someone entered your name for the bicycle giveaway at the radio station. They called here asking for Nathan, and said you had won." He was thrilled. The boys generously agreed to drive him to Georgetown. They waited in the car while he proudly strutted in to claim his prize. He walked out looking like a deflated balloon and said, "Very fucking funny, Guys."

Melanie was a regular fixture around our kitchen table. We were going over Nathan's charts discussing how he could improve. It wasn't going well. He was not interested in making improvements. He calmly stared at Auggie and said, "Fuck you." Thank God Melanie was there or Nathan would have gone to the hospital and Auggie would have been in jail. Auggie glared at him and asked, "What did you say?" Nathan cupped his hands around his mouth, and repeated it. Auggie jumped up, every fiber in his being wanting to lash out at Nathan. I thought, "Uh oh, this is it. This is the day they take all the boys out of my house, and I lose my license." He was so mad, his face was red and he was breathing heavily. I don't know how Melanie did it, but she managed to defuse the situation.

After she left, Auggie told Bert, "I'll give you fifty dollars to pop that punk," and Bert did it. Nathan came crying to me and, when I found out the details, I was furious. A few weeks later while we were sitting around the table, Nathan told Melanie about Bert. She ignored it, putting it off as boys being boys. Auggie told Bert, "I didn't mean for you to do it like that." Bert didn't get his fifty bucks.

Parker told me, "Nathan came in the restaurant with his mom and that old man. Nathan paid for the entire order with dimes." I complained to Melanie pointing out, "Nathan paid for the entire meal for three with dimes. The evidence is clear." She pointed out, "You can't prove where he got the dimes." I said, "Get him out of my house." The next weekend his mother came for a visit. Nathan did not come back. I packed up all of his possessions and delivered them to children's welfare. I didn't want anything there to remind me of him.

I had encouraged him to open a savings account and had been depositing a portion of his paycheck each week. My name was on the account since he was a minor. He had stolen $600 from Bert. I struggled, knowing I had to draw his savings out and hand it over. Melanie told me three times to get the money, and then Brooke, her supervisor, called and said, "You have to give him the money. You cannot keep it because he stole from you." He blatantly got away with stealing.

A few years later, on Fathers' Day, Nathan gallantly marched up to the front door and rang the doorbell. Todd opened the door, and without hesitation, shouted at the unwelcome visitor, "Get the fuck off this property and don't ever come back," and slammed the door in his face. Ryder heard the yelling. He was not sure what it was about but was always ready for a fight. He grabbed his shoes and headed for the door. He stood on the porch with one shoe on and the other in his hand, watching the car disappear down the driveway. Nathan will never know how lucky he was.

15

JACOB
Addiction Runs in the Family

Everyone in Hoisington knew to stay clear of Ace. His trailer, with old tires and car parts strewn across the yard, was down by the river. I suspected the home was full of mosquitoes because there were no screens on the windows and the tattered curtains flapped inside and out. It was rumored he could supply any kind of drug anyone wanted. I thought, "Thank goodness he doesn't have kids because I would probably get them and have to deal with him." Turns out I did have to deal with him. His nephew, Jacob, was placed in my home.

On one of Melanie's visits, she said, "There's a 12-year-old boy named Jacob that we're going to take custody of. He lives with his grandma, and we have had several hotline calls about the situation. Will you take him?" I had an opening and said, "Tell me more." Melanie went on, "His mother, Tammy, has six children and Grandma's raising three of them. She has Jacob, a younger sister, Lori Ann, and a brother, Caleb. Jacob is her target child. They live in a small trailer with a tiny fenced-in yard. If there is no school, Jacob goes to the yard after breakfast and stays there until bedtime. He isn't allowed to go in to use the bathroom. Even the dogs are allowed in, but Jacob isn't. In the heat of the day he lies under the trailer." The school and neighbors registered complaints of child neglect.

The family was originally from Hoisington so I knew the history. The grandma and grandpa had divorced and gone separate ways, leaving the small town. Tammy had a well-earned reputation as a wild child. Ace was still there in his palace by the river. Shelly, the third child, was raising Tammy's oldest daughter. Tammy and her two youngest children lived with Lamont, their father, in a violent environment. All of her front teeth had been knocked out by Lamont. She was an addict and a prostitute, grateful her abusive boyfriend allowed her to live with him.

Melanie brought Jacob to my home with the usual few trash bags filled with his belongings. He was a cute 12-year-old with dark eyes. Due to his background, I expected problems and that's what I got. He was defiant and resisted my efforts to get him to conform to rules.

One fall afternoon the boys and I were raking leaves and cleaning up the yard. Jacob worked for 15 minutes, and then said, "I'm not your fuckin' slave. I'm goin' in to play video games." I came back with my favorite phrase, "I can't make you do it but I can make you wish you had." It worked every time but in the back of my mind I always thought, "What am I going to do if he flat out refuses. I can't stand there with a whip and make him work." He had me but didn't realize it. I said, "I'm not going to argue with you. You have until six o'clock to complete the chore." He threw the rake across the yard, glared at me and walked to the house.

Several hours later Jacob asked Mike, "What'll happen if I don't rake those fuckin' leaves?" Mike shook his head and said, "Boy, don't even take the chance. You will live to regret it." About 5:30, I noticed Jacob completing his chore without another word. Mike came in the kitchen laughing, repeating what he had told him.

Mike was my golden child, causing no problems in the home. He was neither antagonizing nor aggressive. Jacob relentlessly provoked him, trying to get a reaction. Mike ignored the crude remarks until Jacob said, "You look like a child molester." Mike jumped up, preparing to beat the crap out of him. Jacob had the good sense to start running. Mike grabbed him halfway up the stairs and started pummeling him. I ran to the stairs screaming at the boys to stop, but I was thinking, "Maybe I should just walk away."

Jacob was either serving an in-school suspension, or more frequently, an out-of-school suspension. I was always ordering a load of gravel for him to spread on the driveway. The gravel haulers knew if I ordered gravel, someone was in trouble. It got to the point that they would come lumbering up the driveway in their big dump trucks, wondering what the kid did to get suspended, and ask, "Where do you want me to dump it, Lady?"

I sat through hour after hour of training sessions while they tried to pound into my head ways to stay sane and help the children. The topic for one endless session was, "Pick your Battles—Let Natural Consequences Do the Work". When the smug principal called to report Jacob was not wearing a coat at the bus stop, I foolishly thought, "This is a no-brainer. If he doesn't wear a coat, he'll be cold. At least he didn't hit anyone." I politely said, "I pick my battles. This isn't one I choose to deal with. A natural consequence is that he'll be cold." In her syrupy-sweet voice she said, "If he doesn't have a coat on at the bus stop, I'll hotline you." Before I could respond, I heard a click followed by dial tone. I told Jacob, "I don't care if you ever wear a coat the rest of your life, but just humor me and when you see that bus coming, put your coat on."

Jacob asked if he could take his classmate, Hannah, to the movies with us. I said, "That'll be fine. I guess we can squeeze one more into the van." Saturday, Hannah's parents were knocking on my door an hour early so they could get acquainted with Jacob. I led them to my kitchen table and listened to Jacob weave a tale of deceit. "Your daughter will be safe with me. I'll take care of her. I would never dream of kissing her, but would like your permission to hold her hand." The parents were bobbing their heads up and down as Jacob continued. "You can trust me." I was thinking, "No, you can't trust him, but what could possibly happen during a matinee movie." The boys took their usual seats in the front while Jacob and Hannah stayed in the back of the theatre. While the aliens were at war with the earth on screen, I made my way into the dark theatre to check on the young couple. There was enough light to see the two kids in heat, kissing, and that he had his hand in her pants. I tapped him on the shoulder and said, "Knock it off. See that seat behind you? I'm going to be in it."

The high school boys wondered what Jacob would do for money. They said, "Do you think you can drink a cup of syrup?" He answered, "Shit, I can drink two cups." This was looking interesting, so they added, "Two cups, and eat five bullion cubes in 15 minutes on camera and we'll give you $5." They got the old-fashioned video camera out and someone yelled, "Action." He grimaced and groaned, and 15 minutes later he was smiling into the camera proudly displaying a $5 bill. I came into the house to find my high school boys laughing by the bathroom door as I heard sounds of puking.

Jacob had problems following the rules of the house. I was consistent, telling him, "Until you do this, you don't get that." He would be furious, and yell, "I'm out of here; you and your stupid fucking rules," followed by the door slamming. He needed some alone time, and would return when he settled down. One day, Curt, our friend who was also a foster father, was driving down the highway when he spotted Jacob. He stopped. Jacob, still steaming mad, got in his pickup, telling him, "I ain't never going back to that crazy woman and all her stupid-ass rules." Curt listened to him rant and rave, and asked if he would like to go to his house and play pool. He called me and said, "Jacob is fine, I'll bring him home soon." Sure enough, Jacob came home as though he had never had a blow up. Thank you, Curt.

It was a rainy, dismal day and the boys were feeling trapped in the house. Everyone was irritable and the situation was escalating. Jacob announced, "I don't have to take this shit," followed by the familiar sound of the door slamming. Once outside the door, he realized that the rain was cold and he wasn't about to go for his usual cool-down walk. He ran to the neighboring house, pounding on their door. He told Amelia, "I hate those boys and

I ain't going back." Amelia called, "This has got to be your worst nightmare, a rain-soaked boy, running away, and seeking shelter at my home." I said, "It is a nightmare. The kids have been fighting all day. I wish I could run away. Tell Jacob to come home." A few minutes later, the door opened and I heard him go to his room. He put on dry clothes and went to the basement to continue the arguing.

Eventually the sun came out again but Jacob's disposition did not improve. The long summer days were filled with Jacob antagonizing his foster brothers. One warm night he decided this trip out the door would be his last. He filled his duffle bag, threw his guitar over his shoulder and took off. He was 14. By midnight I was driving all over trying to find the elusive runaway. Mike called me at 2:00 AM, saying he had spotted Jacob in George-town. I called the police and to my amazement they said, "Yeah, we stopped him walking down the street. He was so polite we let him go." What the hell? A 14-year-old boy, at 2:00 AM, carrying all his possessions and they let him go, without so much as a phone call to me. Jacob must have decided walking the streets half the night wasn't fun, so he knocked on the door of a boy he vaguely knew. The stunned father called me and said, "It's 3:00 AM and Jacob is telling me he needs a place to stay." I replied, "I am so sorry for the incon-venience. I'll be there in 30 minutes to pick him up." As soon as I drove up, the man waiting outside with Jacob went back in his house, closing the door behind him. Jacob got in the car, and I said, "Hi Jacob." And we drove home.

Grandma made no effort to contact Jacob in the years he was a placement. It was hinted that when I had an opening, they would like to place Caleb with me. A few times I had been willing to sit in Ace's palace down by the river so Jacob could feel some connection to his family. I found Ace not half as scary as he looked, but I sure did not want to cross him. Children's welfare tracked down his grandpa a few counties over to see if he had any interest in the boy. Grandpa contacted me saying, "If I had any idea that Jacob needed help, I would've been right there taking care of it. No one both-ered to call me." I said, "I'm sure it would help Jacob to have a relationship with you." However, I thought, "That's your grandson you cast aside years ago. You should've been concerned since the day he was born." Grandpa had remarried and I was amazed to discover his wife worked for children's welfare. It's never too late to attempt to help a child and they were stepping up to the plate, determined to do the right thing. Within a few weeks they had committed to adopt Jacob. This was Jacob's chance for a family, just like a feel-good movie where they all live happily ever after. They picked him up for weekend visits, to get acquainted. Jacob was a charmer, and everyone was giddy with happiness. The plan was for him to move into their home after six weekend visits. I could see cracks in the relationship on both sides before the end of the sixth visit. Besides being a charmer, he was a manipulator. He moved to their home on schedule, but five months later he was back in my home and he never saw them again.

We received word that his grandma had been diagnosed with cancer. Both of her hands were amputated and she was failing fast. Even near death, she had no interest in seeing her grandson, but Jacob requested one final visit with her. The visit went well, and she died a few weeks later.

I accompanied Jacob to the visitation. Ace was standing by the casket, shackled, in an orange jumpsuit, accompanied by two Parish County deputies. It wasn't long and a toothless woman was hugging Jacob. She said to me, "I'm Tammy." He had been angry with his mother and had spewed his hatred frequently. He had not seen her in years. But now it was obvious that Mommy's hug felt good. She had left her abusive boyfriend and was moving back to the area.

Once a year, there was a foster parent appreciation banquet. I noticed the aunt and uncle who had custody of the older sister were in the crowd. Later, Shelly approached me intending to give me a little insight into "Who's the daddy?" Tammy gave a list of three men to children's welfare so that they could establish paternity in order to collect child support. Much to the men's relief, all three failed. She gave them three more names; they failed too! She told them she couldn't remember for sure. However, she could probably come up with some married men she had been sleeping with. That was the end of the testing.

Jacob did his best to instigate fights. One afternoon he came into the kitchen with his hand over his eye and blood streaming down his cheek. Paxton followed him, saying, "He asked for it. He was standing out there saying, 'Come on. Hit me! You too big of a pussy to fight? Come on little girl, let's fight.' I popped him a good one." I turned my attention to cleaning up the bloody mess, and said, "Jacob, what's your story?" He said, "It happened exactly like Paxton said it did." I sure didn't expect that answer. In time, the gash healed but it left a scar running through his eyebrow.

I am known as the Queen of Cheap. Six boys meant six trips to the barber shop every six weeks, which adds up to a lot of money. The answer was to buy clippers. The boys didn't complain and cut each other's hair. Jacob was by far the most talented barber to pass through my house. He was amazing with the clippers. There was a time it was the in-thing to cut designs in their hair. Somehow or other Jacob managed to cut a target which covered the entire back of his own head, and it was perfect. Amazing!

Jacob shared a room with Zane, who was older, sickly, and didn't give a shit. Jacob was the alpha male and as long as he got his way, it was reasonably calm. One morning Zane crawled out of his bed and said, "I pissed in the bed." This was news Jacob could sink his teeth in. He teased him and ran out of the room screaming, "Zane wet the bed." I watched Jacob fly through the kitchen, laughing and teasing, followed by Zane who headed to the workshop. He came back in with a hammer in his hand, and determination in his eyes. With his body weak from the cystic fibrosis, Zane didn't stand a chance of catching Jacob; but he chased him anyway, swinging the hammer and yelling, "I'm gonna kill you, you son-of-a-bitch." Jacob ran down the driveway, jumped on the school bus, and disappeared. Luckily, Zane had a doctor's appointment, so the killing was postponed.

During the examination, Zane told the doctor, "I refuse to go back to that house. Jacob made fun of me because I wet the bed. Now all the boys'll tease me. If I go back, I'll kill him." I was thinking, "As soon as Jacob goes to sleep tonight, Zane is going to bash his head in with that hammer." I said, "I'm concerned about the safety of the boys." Much to my relief, he was admitted to a psychiatric hospital for three weeks. Due to the fact no one else would take him, he was released again to my custody. Life returned to normal with the usual arguing and bickering. There's no doubt in my mind Zane's intention was to kill Jacob.

Jacob blew the happily-ever-after chance with his grandparents, so children's welfare was determined to find him a new forever home. An older retired couple, Aggie and Bernie, seemed likely candidates. Bernie was a retired prison guard, and Aggie was an obese woman with health problems. The transition started with Jacob going on weekend visits. Guido, who would soon live in my home, was living in their home as a foster child, and it was clear they were not fond of the bi-racial boy. It was also clear that Bernie didn't like my boys, probably because Jacob weaved embellished stories about our foster home. Bernie came into my home, expecting the boys to bow down to him because he had been a prison guard. Jacob stood by his side, looking smug. Bernie told them, "I'd like one month with you worthless bunch of kids, and I'd straighten your asses out." He underestimated my boys. Never using foul language, the boys goaded him, making snide remarks until his face was red and he was just sputtering, "I'll have you bums all thrown in jail. That'll teach ya." He had barged into my home and was sticking his nose in things that weren't his business. I made myself scarce and turned the boys loose on him.

Bernie and Jacob had similar personalities, and I thought, "Possibly this is the perfect placement. They'll feed off each other and nothing'll stop them, or this placement will be doomed because they are too much alike." Sixteen-year-old Jacob moved to Bernie and Aggie's home. Immediately, news began to trickle back that there were problems. He was not the charming little boy he had portrayed himself to be. In desperation, six months later, Aggie called saying, "We don't know what to do. We always have stuff missing. I guess Jacob is stealing from us. He openly smokes pot and comes home hours past curfew dead drunk." I thought, "You're having more problems than I did. What's up with that, Bernie?" She went on, "The adoption process isn't going well because they claim they need more information." Translated, that meant children's welfare had changed their mind. A few weeks later Aggie called again and said, "That child is ruining my life. We are no longer interested in adopting him. For some reason children's welfare lies to us and misleads us." I knew the relationship between them and children's welfare was fragile. I'm not sure why as the institution and I had an excellent relationship.

One afternoon Jacob walked into their home smoking a joint and threw a note toward Aggie. He had been expelled for smoking marijuana on the bus. Bernie stuffed Jacob's possessions in bags and said, "Come on, let's go." He drove directly to children's welfare and announced, "I ain't taking that boy back home with me," and stormed out of the office. Consequently they lost their license.

Jacob was almost 18 and no one would accept him as a foster placement. He was emancipated by the court and moved in with his mother. His name appeared on the docket frequently for drug-related charges. Eventually, he served several years in prison.

16

GAVIN
His Parents Were Foster Parents!

"The strangest thing about Gavin was that his parents were foster parents. Kyle had been a foster child in their home. They belonged to a religious sect that encouraged disciplining children by spanking. Foster children are never to be spanked. Gavin told me, "I'm the one who hotlined my parents. I was tired of getting beat on. I told them if they didn't quit spanking those little kids, I was going to turn them in." Children's welfare investigated the home, the hotline call was substantiated, and their license was pulled. All children, foster and biological, were taken out of the home.

Parental rights had been terminated on two of the pre-school foster children. They were placed with Oliver and Judy who were anxious to adopt. Gavin's mom, Stacey, struggled with the loss of the children and called daily, begging to speak to the little ones. She was not allowed to have any contact. After a couple of months slipped by, the social worker dropped by for her monthly visit and found Oliver intoxicated and obnoxious. When she left, she took the children with her. Judy filed for divorce the next day.

Stacey did visit Gavin occasionally but never called. Gavin told me, "My mom is a whore. She was having sex with my uncle with all of us kids in the house. She said she felt sorry for him, and that was her way of cheering him up. Dad knew but didn't give a shit."

Gavin was only at our home two months when Grandpa stepped up to the plate and took the boy. Some years later I saw Stacey working at the concession stand at a local amusement park. She smiled brightly when she recognized me and said, "I have the greatest news. Gavin will be released from prison soon." Well, I guess that is great news.

17

ZANE
A Love Story Cut Short

Oh my God, what was I thinking? I agreed to take two 15-year-old boys, Zane and Aaron. It was apparent the older couple that had been fostering the boys was more interested in supplementing their Social Security than in the welfare of the boys. Mr. and Mrs. Hayes lived in the country a few miles from our home. They continued to eat out and visit with friends but the boys stayed home, eating what they could find. Aaron complained bitterly to Melanie that Mrs. Hayes would not allow them to go anywhere, not even to school activities.

Melanie asked, "Would you please take both boys? We know you encourage your boys to participate and keep them socially active. We are going to pull the license of Mr. and Mrs. Hayes. Aaron will be an emergency placement, staying only until we find an available traditional home for him. Zane has cystic fibrosis (CF), which qualifies him as a medical placement. However, his behaviors justify placing him as a therapeutic placement (which paid double)." I said, "Yes, I'll take them." Melanie continued, "You'll need to come to the office, so we can give you Zane's history."

I went to children's welfare for the meeting with Melanie. As we sat at a table, she took a deep breath and said, "You will be Zane's twenty-third foster home. Almost everyone has requested he be moved. When Zane was about 10, he was diagnosed with CF. His mother has multiple sclerosis (MS) and is in a nursing home. You'll have to drive to the city and meet with the team at the hospital to be educated on CF and how it affects Zane." I made the appointment.

I was seated at a table with the hospital team, ready to be educated. I was told, "Zane is so used to feeling bad, he doesn't know what it's like to feel good. You need to get as many calories into him as possible, extra desserts, double helpings, as much as you can get him to eat. His spleen is enlarged, which gives him a protruding belly, on his thin body. It's understandable that he's depressed. He'll need to be checked out monthly at this hospital."

I had done my part, learning everything I could about CF, and the two boys were moved to our home. I helped them carry their bags and boxes upstairs to the room they would be sharing. While they were unpacking their clothes, I noticed cockroaches crawling around in their belongings. I yelled, "Put everything back in the boxes, and take it outside." I went through their stuff, piece by piece, shaking the bugs out, and then dumped the clothes into the washer.

While I was folding their laundry, I noticed Zane wore girls' shorts. I asked him why. He said, "They were Mrs. Hayes' daughter's hand-me-downs and they fit me." He didn't seem to mind but I was appalled. I said, "Zane, I can't afford to buy you new shorts; however, I will take you to a resale shop and you can get enough to last the summer. The girls' shorts have to go."

The boys settled in and a home was found for Aaron three months later. He had little tolerance for Zane, but was easy to get along with and caused no problems. I took Aaron to visit his elderly mother several times. She was mentally ill and lived in a group home. I was impressed by the fact that he treated her with great respect.

Zane was an only child. His mother, Marta, was diagnosed with MS either while pregnant, or shortly after she gave birth. She entered, and never left, a local nursing home when Zane was about six. Marta tried to keep him at home with her for as long as possible. But, it was Zane who started taking care of her at a very young age. According to Zane, his mother had a dog that babysat him.

His father's background is sketchy. Over the years Marta gave him several different stories when he asked about his father. In one story, she claimed to have been raped by an unknown man, which resulted in Zane's birth. In another, his biological father turned his back on them before he was born. After he left my home, Marta told Zane who his father was and roughly where he was. I don't know if they ever made contact.

When Marta was placed in the nursing home, every member of the extended family gave reasons why they would not be responsible for Zane. He was placed in the foster care system. A couple in one of Zane's first foster homes was interested in adopting him. Marta refused to sign away her parental rights, fearing they would not allow him to visit her.

Zane was small for his age and always seemed to have a chronic cough that was treated as a cold. Eventually, testing proved he had CF. Other children in the foster homes would taunt and tease Zane, leading to behavioral problems. He was bounced from placement to placement. Zane learned his life expectancy was short and that he would die young, before any of his dreams could be realized. The emotional trauma Zane felt when he was diagnosed and condemned plunged him into a mixture of apathy and anger. This defined his social interactions for the next several years.

Hygiene was a problem with many of the children who came through our home and Zane was no exception. Zane had been in our home several weeks when I noticed his teeth were so dirty, it made me want to puke. I told Zane, "You need to brush your teeth." He replied, "I don't have a toothbrush." I said, "Zane, you have been here a long time. Why didn't you ask for one?" He answered, "The subject never came up." I gave him a toothbrush; however, it was a struggle to get him to use it. His room was a disaster. I used charts to encourage the boys to keep their rooms clean. I had hours and hours of training on rewards and consequences, what works and what will not. With Zane nothing worked because he didn't care. Rewards and consequences will only work if the child wants a reward or doesn't want a consequence. There was no reward that interested Zane and he could care less about a consequence.

Periodically, I dropped Zane off to visit with his mother for a couple of hours. I'd return to find him cuddled up next to her in the bed. Because Mrs. Hayes had a problem with Zane's need for this closeness with his mother, she refused to drive him to the visits. Marta's speech was impaired and I could not understand one word. Zane understood a little and would translate. The disease had ravaged her body and the only working part was her brain. She wore a bright red wig, which looked ridiculous, but obviously made her feel better.

In the three years Zane lived in my home he attended two family Thanksgiving dinners. His uncle picked him up and drove him to the city where his aunt hosted the meal. That was the extent of family visits, and no one ever called him.

Zane had a grandfather living in Georgetown. The grandfather's wife, Reba, was younger than Marta. The new young step-grandmother ran an ice cream shop, Reba's Reveries. For Zane's birthday, I thought it would be nice to go in, introduce myself, and order an ice cream cake. Reba was not nice. She said, "I'll be closed the day before you need it, and I certainly won't come in on my day off to make a cake." I said, "I expect to pay full price for the cake. Can I come in and pick it up the day before you're closed?" Grandpa was washing off the counters, listening to Reba's mouth run, never saying a word. Reba said, "I don't believe I'll be able to make that cake for you. Have a nice day." I had never been in that store and damn sure will not go in it again. Zane had told me, "My grandpa said if I had never been born, my mom would not have MS."

Zane was kind of weird, but the boys in our home tolerated him. He was content to watch TV all day. I attended the IEP meetings at school. There wasn't a thing anyone could do to motivate Zane. He sat through the meetings totally uninterested, bored to death. His average in school was low. In one class, it was only three percent. Zane did not care. He didn't care if he lived or died, so how could he care if he did all right in school, made friends, or accomplished anything in his life?

When possible, I scheduled Zane's appointments to fall while the boys were in school. There were times when the entire group accompanied us. On one such occasion, we arrived and sat in various chairs scattered throughout the crowded waiting room. Jacob plopped down next to Zane, who shot out of his chair like a bullet, screaming, "Get away from me; I'm homophobic. Don't touch me; don't come near me; you know I'm homophobic." I could not have been more shocked if I had seen monkeys fly across the room. Where that came from, I don't have a clue. Zane was in close contact with the boys most of the time. Jacob, for once, was stunned into silence. I simply said, "Knock it off Zane, and sit down." He did.

A side effect of CF was cirrhosis of the liver; a possible contributor could have been the high regimen of antibiotics he had received shortly after being diagnosed. I sat with Zane in the examining room and listened as the doctor explained to him that he had developed cirrhosis. Zane accepted the statement with no reaction. When Zane left the room to have further testing, I asked the doctor, "What is the life expectancy for Zane?" He replied, "Possibly five years." While we were eating dinner that night, Zane announced, "I have cirrhosis of the liver." Paxton stared at him and said, "Man, you're going to die. My dad had cirrhosis." Zane didn't respond, but left the table. He came back in a few minutes and said, "I looked up cirrhosis in the encyclopedia. You're right. I'm going to die. Pass the chicken." He added, "I don't fear death. I know it's coming." I looked at the boys sitting around the table, noticing not one showed any emotion.

Zane did have a temper. Often he would explode, slamming the door behind him and heading down the driveway toward the highway. Normally I paid no attention to a teen who decided to run. Zane was different. I knew he did not have a friend in this world to run to and had nowhere to go. I also realized he was a sick boy who needed his medications. Normally, I reported the runaways, and a deputy was dispatched to take down the information. Looking for runaway teens was not high on their list of priorities. Zane was the exception due to his medical condition. They would usually find him sitting in the park, put him in the patrol car, and bring him back.

Sometimes Zane could be a little rebellious and do something that

would surprise me. Once he dyed his hair white and bought a pack of cigarettes. Zane knew the consequences of smoking with CF. However, a part of
him wanted to be one of the guys and be normal. He told the boys he would
like to have sex. One of his rebellious acts was to save the tiny ketchup
packet from his meal and place it behind the wheel of a car. He thought it
was funny when they backed out and there would be a tiny little splatter.

Zane coughed all the time. He coughed up phlegm, letting it fly, even
onto the table. It was disgusting. He wanted to be a disc jockey, which the
boys found hilarious. While we were sitting around the dinner table, this 16-
year-old boy said, "I have seen the real Santa Claus. I heard something in the
living room and sneaked around the corner. There he was. I swear to God,
it was really him--the real Santa Claus. I saw him with my own two eyes."
The boys thought Zane was an idiot. No matter how much they teased him
or how cruel they were, Zane didn't back down. He was convinced he had
really seen Santa.

Zane's health was poor and he was frequently hospitalized in medical and psychiatric hospitals. These hospitals for children put forth every
effort to pamper the sick youngsters, keeping them comfortable and entertained. Zane loved to be in the hospital. When he was released, I was given
instructions on how to take care of his IV. The perpetually jolly nurse said,
"It's easy, and it only has to be done four times a day." That dang IV was
almost a deal breaker for me. Yeah, it was easy, but consumed six hours of
the day. I had to start the IV. The first bag would run forty-five minutes, to be
replaced by a second bag which ran forty-five minutes. That is an hour and a
half, four times a day. I was already seriously sleep deprived and now I had
to set the alarm to get out of my warm bed to take care of the IV.

Zane had a vibrating vest he was supposed to use every day for the
rest of his life. Its function was to break up the mucous in his chest. He used
it a few times but claimed he was claustrophobic, and it suffocated him.

As a terminally ill child, he was granted a wish through a special
program. He wanted a computer. Wonderful volunteers delivered his wish
complete with a beautiful cabinet to put it in. Within days Zane complained
his computer didn't work. Jacob informed me, "Zane's computer doesn't
work because he likes the pretty colors on the screen when he runs that huge
magnet across it." Someone was sent to repair the computer, but it never
worked again.

Zane told tall tales, possibly trying to impress the boys, when in reality, it made the situation worse. He insisted he had a special gift. He could
walk by a house and an electronic jolt would go through his body if the oc-
cupants had their TV on. The boys, in unison, said, "Zane, that's the stupid-
est thing I ever heard of." Poor Zane stuck to his story saying, "I swear I can

feel it." They answered, "Prove it. Go stand down by the bridge. When we turn the TV on, you raise your arm." He said, "You'll see", and walked to the bridge. He turned around and stood still for a moment as if waiting for the jolt. Then he raised his arm. He put it down in a minute and the arm would fly back up. He repeated this again and again. The boys stood by the window laughing since they had never touched any dial on the TV. Another story was the foster home that owned the tiny sports car that held eleven people. He also told the tale of the foster father who sat him on the ceiling fan blades, letting him twirl around.

When Zane turned 18 in February, he became eligible for disability. He was in no position to take responsibility for himself, so I was appointed his guardian. It was clear he had no interest in school, so a few months later, he quit and the mental health facility furnished an apartment for him.

I found myself responsible for Zane, only now I had to drive 44 miles round trip, and received zero payment. Everything was furnished in the apartment, except food and hygiene products. Out of his check I gave him an allowance to buy groceries and told him the importance of keeping receipts for everything he bought. I was the one who had to answer for the money.

As I opened his apartment door to visit, the stench hit me. Zane was on the couch eating peanut butter out of a jar. His hair was matted; his clothes were filthy. The coffee table was covered with food in varying degrees of decay. The kitchen was worse. The trash hadn't been emptied, dishes were piled all over, and there was barely a path to the sink. I guess the charts worked better than I had suspected because his room had never been quite this bad. There was no way I had time to take care of a disabled husband, six foster children, plus the emancipated boys, and clean Zane's apartment. My way out was a lady named Fern.

Fern was a friend of Marta's, who visited her occasionally. She lived alone in an apartment, and her paycheck barely paid the bills. She asked Zane if he would move in with her and share expenses. He told me that was what he wanted to do. It sounded like an answer to a prayer. I happily turned over guardianship to the sweet middle-aged woman who had his best interest at heart, or so I thought.

Several years passed with no word from Zane. I was beginning to wonder if he had died. The mystery was solved when he called me. He said, "I had to get away from Fern. She was stealing my disability checks. I left the state with my friend, David." He went on, "David lived in the same apartment complex with us. He does have some mental problems but he took good care of me. We lived in another state for several years."

I inquired about his health and he told me he felt good, adding,

"Guess what? I'm married. We decided to live in this area for a while." We ended the call, vowing to keep in touch. A few weeks later, I was waiting in a parking lot for Brandon to come out after his appointment. I saw Zane and his wife walking down the street laughing. It was a joy to see. I thought, "As soon as Brandon comes out, I'll drive down the street and see if I can find Zane and talk to him." I looked, but couldn't find him and never saw him again. Several months later, I learned from the internet that he was deceased. I contacted his wife, Kitty, and she brought me up to date.

David had mental health issues, but on a lucid day, he could remember quite a bit. David was about 14 years older than Zane, and he had a mission. It was to pull Zane out of his funk. He pestered him into eating healthier and forced him into believing that he cared about him. At times Zane's depression would swallow him. David would scoff, and relate stories of his—"visions" and "voices", which never failed to crack Zane up. He forcibly pulled Zane out every time he started to sink. David was concerned about his mom, who lived in a neighboring state. She was in an abusive relationship. He packed up his few possessions and moved closer. Zane went with him, trying to close the door on his past, pretending he was healthy, and looking forward to a new start with a friend. He underwent a temporary metamorphosis.

Zane met Kitty. As it turned out, David's mom and Kitty's mom had gone to college together. Zane avoided telling Kitty he was terminally ill with CF. He wanted to be normal. She stopped by their apartment one day and David explained to her that Zane had CF and he was hospitalized. She had very little knowledge of the disease but it didn't faze her. Zane was Zane, whatever disease might be synonymous with him. She didn't run away or judge him as many others had.

When he was discharged, Kitty and Zane had a long talk, discussing the disease and his life up to that point. In his mind he thought the doctors were trying to kill him, so in defiance he refused to do the treatments. He rarely used the vibrating vest. Kitty asked to see the vest and inquired if she could use it. She found the pressure on her (healthy) lungs and chest was unbelievable. She understood why the doctors wanted him to use it, but also understood the vest made him feel suffocated. Kitty quickly learned how to do the physical therapy by hand.

She spent the next six months meeting his doctors and nurses, and researching CF from every angle, asking as many questions as she could think of. She studied the cocktail of medications he had been prescribed. Zane and Kitty weren't together yet; she was just curious. Respecting his feelings, they discussed her growing knowledge of the reasoning for the medications, and he grew to resent the meds less. At first they were just friends. They talked about everything else too, not just medicine and the disease.

Around that time, Kitty acquired a stalker. He was a man she had thought of as a father figure, or an uncle, a man she trusted. He twisted everything out of perspective, and attempted to rape her. Looking for a safe haven, she found herself on Zane's doorstep, scared to death. He and David had a three-bedroom apartment, and Kitty was allowed to rent a room.

Zane and Kitty realized they were falling in love. Their romance blossomed as naturally as their friendship had. She didn't care that people were telling her she was crazy. Several years after dealing with the grief of losing him, she told me, "I'd do it again. Despite all the nights of worry, the questions, the endless coughing, and the debilitating grief, I'd do it all again. He was worth it."

During one of our telephone conversations, Zane had told me, "I don't talk to my mother anymore. She did a horrible thing to me." I couldn't imagine what that helpless woman could have done to make Zane so upset, and I didn't ask.

While he was living in my home, I hadn't been privy to Zane's true feelings regarding the missed opportunity for adoption as a young boy. It was never discussed. Kitty claimed, later in life, that Zane carried a deep resentment that Marta had refused to allow him to be adopted. Kitty also said she knew Zane loved his mother, but felt helpless and angry as he watched her disease progress. His feelings of helplessness might have contributed to their emotional distancing as he grew older. Zane called the nursing home several times a year to ask about his mother. At one point, it was revealed that she'd sustained infected bedsores and that, of all people, it was Reba who signed the papers to have Marta's leg amputated. I find it bizarre that Reba, who was not a blood relative, was allowed to authorize the amputation. After that, it seemed that Marta had given up. She died about six weeks before Zane and Kitty moved to the area. Her body had been donated to science. Kitty explored the possibility of spreading some of Zane's ashes with those of his mother, but it doesn't look like it will happen.

After spending most of his life not caring if he lived or died, he finally had a reason to live. He found acceptance, love, and happiness. Unfortunately, the euphoria was short-lived as the disease increased its grip on him and took his life. Kitty shared her memories of his remaining years with me. She said as Zane lay dying in the ICU, she met the doctor who originally diagnosed him. She found him to be highly professional and extremely intelligent, obviously with an exceptional mind for medicine. She could see that he understood aspects of the disease she could never hope to grasp. He took her into a conference room and flatly said there was no hope. There was nothing they could do, that she should give up then and there and allow nature to run its course. She had no problem picturing the doctor using the same tone and lack of emotion to tell a pre-adolescent little boy that he would die soon. Through the rush of intense grief, she felt a scrap of the anger Zane had experienced when he was diagnosed and condemned. Now Zane's wish was to live, and he fought death to no avail.

Theirs was a love story cut short.

18

BECKETT
Physically Misshapen

"There are trolls under the bridge. If they catch you, they will boil you for dinner." I overheard the boys playing in the yard warning Beckett about the danger of the trolls that lived under the bridge. The driveway bridge spanned the wet weather creek that crossed our property and connected the front and back sections of the property. I watched as Beckett went the long way around to avoid crossing the bridge because he was afraid of the trolls. I had carefully explained to Beckett that the boys were messing with him and that there were no trolls. He watched at a distance as I went under the bridge to check for trolls. "No trolls," I yelled. I walked back to Beckett, and said, "See, I proved there are no trolls. Give me your hand and I will go under the bridge with you." Backing away, he stared at me with those pale blue unblinking eyes, saying "No, the trolls will boil me." He never got over his fear of trolls enough to go near the bridge.

Nine-year-old Beckett was placed in my home due to lack of supervision in the previous foster home. The day he arrived, I opened the door to see a strange-looking child, with a large misshapen head and unblinking pale blue eyes. He headed straight to the piano and said, "Is that a piano?" Caroline whispered, "Oh my God, it's Forrest Gump!" Two hundred miles away, Beckett had lived in a foster home with four children and the foster mother, Mabel, who was an elderly lady. Although she was a sweet old gal, who made sure the kids said their prayers and ate their vegetables, she was oblivious to the behaviors in her home. The teenage girls entrusted to her care thought nothing of spending the night with various guys, leaving poor Mabel pacing and praying.

The teenager glued to the window, yelled, "Mabel, come quick. Beckett is giving Tyrone a blow job." In the back yard, Beckett was giving oral sex to a young teenage boy. A hotline call was placed and the investigation revealed that this had been going on for months. If Tyrone wanted oral sex while he was playing video games, watching TV, or hanging out in the

113

backyard, all he had to do was snap his fingers, point down and Beckett was willing to accommodate him. Both boys were moved that day. I accepted Beckett as a therapeutic placement.

Melanie gave me a brief history of Beckett's life. His father had never been part of his life and was in prison. His mother, Carrie, was mildly retarded. She had a knack for picking pedophiles for boyfriends. According to the case history, Carrie taught Beckett how to give her boyfriend oral sex when he was just a toddler. The state was in the process of terminating parental rights; however, until that happened, Carrie had visitation rights. I occasionally supervised their visits. The visits were held at children's welfare in a small room with chairs and toys. Mother and son were always happy to see each other and interacted during the visits. I was instructed to monitor their conversations. It was suspected Beckett had been sexually abused in ways too horrible to think about. The behaviors he displayed in my home left no doubt.

Beckett was taking showers, but his hair looked dirty and smelled awful. I asked if he was using shampoo. He stared at me with those unblinking eyes and said, "Yes." The situation continued to get worse. Finally, I told Beckett to put on swim trunks because I was going to observe how he showered. He appeared to do an adequate job until I handed him the shampoo. He looked at me and asked, "What am I supposed to do with this?" Problem solved.

Beckett was strange looking. His forehead was huge, giving him a deformed look. Also, his mouth wasn't quite right. When he ate, the food tumbled out of his open mouth. There was always food smeared on his face and clothing. Reminding Beckett to chew with his mouth closed was a waste of time. Observing Beckett eat spaghetti was so nauseating that after listening to and watching him slurp up spaghetti, to this day I am not able to eat spaghetti with tomato sauce.

While the boys were in the basement playroom, Beckett watched Jacob pull a sheet over his head and walk toward him. Beckett raced up the stairs screaming hysterically. "The monster is after me. He's going to get me."

Beckett had an innocent quality about him. He worked hard trying to win approval. When we went to the grocery store, Beckett had a tendency to wander off. I'd find him at the checkout lanes, bagging someone's groceries. Everyone would be smiling at this odd-looking, strange-acting boy.

Beckett looked forward to the trips to the discount stores where he could spend his allowance. He carefully looked over the selections. If he did not have enough money for the things he wanted, he would stick items in his pockets or down his pants. As we got to the car, Beckett was acting suspiciously so I checked him for shoplifted items. When confronted, he stared at me, unblinking, and said, "It belongs to me. I do not steal. I have it so it is mine." In his mind, possession was 100% of the law. I marched him back into the store to talk to the manager. One look at Beckett and they were clueless how to handle it. He'd swear, "It is mine, I have it." Even though I knew it was a waste of time, I continued to turn him in. Eventually he was searched before we left the store. Beckett was, in fact, incapable of understanding any sense of immorality or dishonesty. His brain was just not wired that way. He did have some sense that he would be yelled at if he did something he was told not to do, but he didn't understand the right or wrong of it. He had a totally innocent mind.

In his quest for approval, when making purchases, he would tell the stunned clerks to keep the change. I made sure he got his change. However, on the walk to the car he would ask various strangers if they wanted the money cupped in his hand.

There was another side to Beckett. He would beg for money and he knew how to work it. He confronted complete strangers asking for money to buy soda and candy. He was quite gifted at panhandling, perhaps due to his odd appearance.

Every weekend I took the boys to a matinee movie because afternoon movies were cheaper. The movies were the only good thing about those long, endless weekends. I gladly forked out the admission price for a nap while the boys were being entertained. During one movie, Jacob jabbed my shoulder, attempting to awaken me. He whispered loudly, "Go get Beckett. He's sitting by an old man and woman, asking if he can share their popcorn." I went down the aisle to find Beckett sitting by the elderly couple. I told him he would have to sit by me. He announced loudly in the quiet theatre, "No, they are going to give me popcorn." After a noisy argument, he agreed to sit by me.

The cheerful school counselor called asking what size coat Beckett wore. They were taking up a collection for the poor foster kid that did not own a coat; because, the weather was turning cold. I was not amused. I told the jolly counselor, "He not only has a coat, he has two very nice coats and there will be no need to buy him one. If you won't believe everything he tells you about me, I won't believe what he tells me about you." As Jacob was eating his afternoon snack, he said, "Beckett is at it again. He told Ms. Jones you won't let him eat breakfast. I told Ms. Jones, Beckett had two bowls of cereal and a pop tart for breakfast."

The people of Hoisington were kind to Beckett. He had no boundaries, but had such an innocent quality that no one seemed to mind. I took Beckett various places for testing to get a diagnosis. The school was convinced he had Fragile X Syndrome. He was tested and did not have it. There was never an official diagnosis but something was clearly not right.

Sometimes Beckett was overcome with anger and pummeled his large head with his fists. He also banged his large head into the wall, leaving dents and holes. Once, he sat on the floor trying to choke himself, telling me to, "Call the boys in so they can watch me die."

One day I got a call from the school principal. She was chuckling, "I got a call from the mother of a little girl in Beckett's class. In the girl's homework she found a note from Beckett. It read, Do you want to have sex? There were boxes to check for 'yes' or 'no'. The girl had checked "yes."

Eight months after Beckett moved in he was transferred to a residential facility. Two-and-a-half years later I was asked to take 12-year-old Beckett back as a therapeutic placement. He came back with more baggage than he left with. The residential facilities are also referred to as treatment centers. They have intense therapy, both group and individual, and the children are supervised around the clock. The children in these facilities have severe behavioral problems and they learn new negative behaviors from each other.

Carrie's rights had been terminated so there were no family visits. Beckett had been sexually abused and acted out sexually. I always kept a baby monitor in his bedroom. There were other boys in my home who had been sexually abused so I had to be vigilant, monitoring Beckett 24/7.

Connor was in my home during the same time period as Beckett. They both had a history of severe sexual abuse and exhibited inappropriate behaviors. Connor and Beckett could never be left unsupervised, even in the next room. They never missed a chance to whisper, always watching me, waiting for an opportunity for a sexual encounter. They drew pictures of penises, explicit pictures of naked men and women performing the sexual act. Beckett told me he could not stop thinking about "little boys' butts".

I had to take the stool brush out of the bathroom. Beckett would stick it in his anus. The handle of the brush would have poop on it and on one occasion, there was runny poop all over the brush and floor. When I noticed blood on the stool, I knew Beckett was responsible. I asked him if there was a problem. He said, "I am bleeding out of my butt." This definitely meant a trip to the doctor. I knew and the doctor knew that he had stuck something in his anus and cut himself. The doctor gently questioned Beckett. He stared at him with unblinking eyes and said, "I did not put anything up my butt." Since he would not admit to anything, the doctor ordered a lower GI. After the unpleasant test, Beckett admitted to "putting a toy up his butt."

The boys walked in on Beckett licking the dog's private parts while masturbating. With eyes as big as saucers, Beckett said in his slow way of talking, "I do not know why I like to lick the dog's pussy." Later on while we were watching TV, the dog started barking, wanting to come in the house. Caden got up saying, "Beckett, your girlfriend wants in." Someone else added, "How does Beckett call his girlfriend? Woof! Woof!" Caden came right back with, "How does Beckett get his girlfriend in the mood? With a dog biscuit." I told the boys, "We don't keep secrets; however, this is not something you should go to school or anywhere else and talk about." When I next met with Melanie, I told her the story. She laughed saying, "That's too good for them to keep to themselves."

Beckett had been in the bathroom long enough to cause concern. Bert knocked on the door and said, "Beckett, what are you doing in there?" Beckett replied, "Playing with myself." Bert groaned and said, "Beckett, don't tell me that. Say you're constipated." He said, "OK, I am constipated."

The problem was escalating. Beckett spent most of his day at school in the resource room. The teacher called to inform me Beckett was constantly rubbing his penis while sitting at the table. I didn't even know how to respond, other than to say, "We will discuss this with his counselor." Beckett was told all the reasons he should not masturbate in public. He agreed not to do it again. That would last until the next time the urge hit and he'd be back at pleasuring himself.

I was with the boys in the water park. All of a sudden, a huge bucket of water dumped on the swimmers. Everyone was laughing, enjoying it, and running around. When I got the water out of my eyes, I discovered Beckett was gone. I panicked and alerted the boys to keep an eye out for him. I contacted security and told them, "Beckett is a special-needs child and he is missing." The teenagers in security took the information but never put forth any effort to find him. In fact, they never left the building they were in. An hour later, Jacob told me, "Beckett is back in the pool, rubbing a little black girl's legs." I hurried over and sure enough, there was Beckett rubbing a little girl's legs while she lay on a tube. Her mother was watching, apparently not at all concerned. Beckett had soda and candy. He had told several people he was lost and they had bought him stuff.

Profiles were written for the children who were to be placed for adoption and sent across the country. An example would be, "Waiting Children, Seeking Forever Families."

If I were to decipher some of the profiles, I would translate the phrase, "needs a family that is able to provide a nurturing household with clear expectations, consistency and dependability," as being a special needs child with ADHD; needs lots of structure, be prepared to hang on for the ride." There was no way for anyone to second-guess Beckett's behaviors from his profile. It stated, "Beckett likes animals and small children," which is downright scary.

As I drove up to the respite provider's, my boys were sitting on their bags at the end of the driveway. I immediately thought, "This cannot be good." The respite providers were further up the driveway waiting. As I drove up and got out of the van, they approached me. The first words out of their mouths were, "Don't ever bring these kids back."

They had a toddler, maybe 18 months old, and Beckett was playing with the child. Beckett put the baby above his head, twirled it around, and let go. I said, "Beckett, why would you do something like that?" With unblinking eyes focused on me, he responded, "I wanted to see if the baby could soar." Truthfully, one look at Beckett and you knew all the lights were on but no one was home. The family was licensed by the state which meant they should have had adequate training. Shame on them for leaving their child unsupervised with Beckett.

A deputy, a detective, Melanie, and I were sitting at my kitchen table, discussing a problem concerning Caleb and Connor. The younger boys were questioned as to whether Caleb had ever sexually abused them. Beckett would say anything to get attention and had a knack for zeroing in on hot topics. I thought, "Uh oh. He knows how to play this and he's going to give them a story." I was right. I had a baby monitor in the room where Caleb and Beckett shared bunk beds. I never heard anything. Beckett said, "Caleb wakes me up five or six times every night wanting to have sex." The detective asked, "What type of sex did you have?" Not the least bit embarrassed, Beckett answered, "He put his wiener in my butt." The detective continued, "Would you mind showing me what position you were in when he did this?" Beckett hopped up, assuming a position with his hands on his knees and his knees slightly bent. Beckett was excused. The detective smiled and said, "Unless Caleb is well endowed, this never happened." Melanie chimed in, "He lost me at five or six times a night."

Beckett was now a large, teenage boy. My grandsons, who are considerably younger than Beckett, came to visit. I watched as Beckett sat on the floor with them, pushing little cars around and playing with little action figures. It made my blood run cold. If he felt comfortable playing child-like games with little boys, a natural progression would be masturbation games. In his mind, he was like the little boys, but he knew no boundaries when it came to masturbation. This put my grandchildren in serious jeopardy. Once that cat is out of the bag, there's no going back. Innocence is precious. Loss of innocence is contagious. For the safety of my grandchildren, I asked to have Beckett removed.

My new husband, Vince, did research on the internet and found out that Beckett, now in his thirties, is living in a mental health facility for adults.

19

GIRARD
The Huffer

"Ellen, we need an emergency placement for a 14-year-old boy until a bed is available in a rehab. Girard is addicted to sniffing paint, gasoline, or whatever he can find to get high on." I agreed to take him and five days later, a bed opened up. .

After six weeks he was released, and I got the call. "Ellen, Girard is being released today. Will you take him?" Again, I said yes. The next morning I enrolled him in school. He had no short-term memory. Huffing gas kills brain cells. He could not remember what classes he had previously, and wasn't even sure what grade he was in. It didn't take long to figure out that rehab had been a waste of time. He was huffing everything he could find. He even huffed the freon from the neighbors air conditioner, ruining the unit. She still talks about it to this day. Everything that could be inhaled had to be locked up.

Girard was a budding little voyeur. I'd catch him staring at me through the downstairs windows as I went about my chores. The older boys who shared a bedroom on the main floor frequently caught Girard peering in at them. They screamed, "Get that pervert out of here. He gives me the creeps." Quite frankly, when I would catch Girard sneaking around, spying on me, it made the hair on the back of my neck stand up.

The school counselor from the resource room called saying, "Ellen, Beckett reeks of urine. The students are complaining about the smell. You are going to have to come and get him." I took him home, and said, "Get in the shower." He was a bed-wetter so I assumed he had a wet diaper on under his jeans. I went to his bed to wash the sheets and was amazed to find they were dry. Beckett appeared oblivious to his foul smell. When the boys came home from school, Jacob said, "Girard peed in a jar and threw it on Beckett. It sure was funny." Beckett looked at me with his unblinking eyes with his mouth hanging open then told me in his low drawl of a voice, "That is what happened."

Steaming mad, I turned to Girard pointing my finger, "You just lost every privilege." The remainder of the night I listened as he ranted and raved about what a fucking bitch I was, and how much he hated me. The next morning he stomped into the kitchen saying, "You fucking whore. If you think I'm staying in this hell hole and following your stupid-ass rules, you ain't got a brain in your head. I don't have to take this shit." He grabbed two pop tarts and stomped off, slamming the door behind him. I watched as he headed down the driveway to the highway, then I notified the police and the sheriff's department to keep an eye out for him.

Jim, the police chief, was driving his daughter to school in his squad car. As the call came in over his radio, his daughter pointed to Girard walking through the park and said, "That's him." Jim called for a younger officer saying, "I'm too old to chase a teenager." They picked up Girard with little effort. Maybe he had forgotten where he was going. He was placed in a residential facility.

20

BILLY
Tall Tales

M any of my placements came from a trailer park, where they had been living with an absentee single mother, who was involved in drugs, and had a string of boyfriends. Billy fit this profile. He was 14 and running wild.

Many foster kids have a problem with embellishing the truth; however, Billy took it to a whole new level. Beverly suggested I post the alleged lies and maybe, if he read them, he would realize how ridiculous they were. I tacked the following to the poster board in the kitchen, entitled, Billy's Tales.

1) Me and my friends used to go duck hunting all the time. I would spot the ducks on the pond and ask, 'Hey, Guys, how many ducks do you want?' Then I silently slipped under the water, gliding to where the ducks were, grabbed a bunch by the leg and swam back to shore.

2) I aimed my shotgun to the sky and pulled the trigger. Ten ducks fell from the sky, right by my feet.

3) We cleaned them ducks, cooked and ate everyone of them before we went home.

4) My mom's old boyfriend is storing a vintage 1957 car that he will give to me when I am 16.

5) Mustard makes me high.

6) The Christmas that Tickle Me Elmo® was hard to find, my mom saw it at the store and gave $10,000 for it because I wanted it.

He was proud to have the sign posted so everyone would realize how wonderful he was.

Billy referred to Auggie as the crippled old son-of-a-bitch, behind his back and to his face as, "You crippled old man." To this day, I can't believe Auggie didn't flatten his face.

I took the boys to the mall in the city. I didn't feel like going home and cooking dinner, so I said, "Boys, as a treat we are going to eat at the buffet." Cheers went up. While we were standing in line, Billy looked around and screamed, "I ain't eating in no restaurant with niggers." I reacted before I had a chance to be embarrassed. With my face two inches from his, I said "You are rude and disrespectful and, if you think I am going to put up with it, you are wrong. We are eating here and you will be respectful." We continued on as if nothing had happened.

Billy slept on the top bunk. I noticed cigarette ashes when I changed the sheets. I saw visions of my home in flames so I confronted him saying, "There are ashes in your bed. You do not smoke in here. You will burn the house down." With perfect eye contact he said, "You're crazy. I ain't smoking in here. Where's the butts?" The ashes continued to show up when I pulled the sheets off of his bed. It dawned on me that the butts had to be somewhere, so I investigated. I discovered he was taking the return air vent off of the wall and using the hole for an ashtray. From that point on, no matter what the age, the boys were allowed to smoke outside on the patio and only outside on the patio.

I told Melanie, "I want Billy moved. He's either going to burn the house down or Auggie's going to kill him." No other foster home was willing to take Billy and there were no available beds in the residential facilities. It was obvious Billy could not remain in my home. To my knowledge, this had never happened before, nor has it happened since, but they sent Billy back to his mother until there was an opening in a residential facility.

21

PAXTON
Another Boy Joins the Brotherhood

Something about Paxton was so darn likable. I'm not saying he didn't deserve to be a behavioral placement, but his personality and humor did make him a joy to be around. I knew before the sun set the first day, that this boy was a good fit in our home. As usual, I was provided with background information when I agreed to accept him. He had run from his previous foster home and had been in a bit of trouble involving a yacht in California. When I drove to children's welfare to pick up Paxton, out walked a slender 15-year-old boy, with his head shaved except for a Mohawk strip in the middle that grew into a long ponytail down his back. He carried a small duffle bag that contained all of his earthly belongings. As soon as we were in the car, he felt the need to explain why he ran away from the foster home. He said, "That skinny bitch made me uncomfortable. In the mornings she woke me by running her freaky, long fingernails down my back. That's not all, I couldn't face another night of having polish sausage for dinner."

When we walked into the kitchen, five foster boys and Bert were there to greet him. Their curiosity satisfied, most of the boys wandered off. Auggie, Bert, and I, remained to get acquainted. Auggie asked, "What's your story? Why are you here?" Paxton answered, "I stole a yacht in California." Auggie said, "Bullshit, how did you get it started?" Paxton truthfully answered, "It wasn't easy."

I picked up more information from the files, and Paxton filled in the details. When he was 13 years old, his father had died. The father, Pete, was an alcoholic as far back as Paxton could remember. He sobered up for a few months and decided to take his six children fishing. Paxton was mad at him and refused to go. He said, "I hope you drop dead." Pete had a heart attack and died while fishing with his children that afternoon. Paxton was devastated and regretted his statement. I told him, "You cannot hold onto this guilt. You were a child. If your dad could talk to you he would say, 'I know you didn't mean it, Son'." He discussed it with counselors, but was unable to let go of the guilt.

123

Over the years I had three of Paxton's sibling group in my home as foster care placements. Sometimes their stays overlapped. Paxton came first, a year and a half later, Parker joined us and finally four years later, there was Butch. I became familiar with the family, which also included, Roxanne, Beth, and Will.

His mother, Ruth, as well as some of the children had a range of special needs. Paxton, Butch and Roxanne, were intelligent. Pete had been a frequent guest of the local jail and occasionally the county jail. He had seen to it that his kids were fed, gathering food from the dumpsters behind the restaurants. The kids served as lookouts while he stole money from the donation box of a religious shrine in the area.

If a child got in trouble at the school where they attended, one of the parents had to go for a conference, no exceptions. The exception to the "no exception" rule was Ruth and Pete's clan. Ruth was not capable of comprehending the problem. Pete would show up intoxicated then get off his bicycle and stagger down the halls. On top of that, the conference was pointless because no one could understand Pete due to his slurred speech.

When Pete died, Ruth survived on disability. Only the youngest, Will, who had a low IQ, remained with Ruth. There was speculation that a 40-year-old man who had befriended Will, might be sexually abusing him. Will loved this man and, therefore, did not cooperate in the investigation. So the relationship continued.

Ruth was provided with a brand new subsidized apartment. Paxton told me she sold her trailer home for $300. I said, "She sold an entire home for $300?" He answered, "Yeah, and she was lucky to get it." Of course, with the apartment came rules she was unable to follow. Only she and Will were allowed to live there; however, she was unable to say "no" to down-and-out relatives or to a boyfriend, who wanted to share her good fortune. She was evicted and moved to a trailer similar to the one she had sold for $300.

Ruth was looking forward to a settlement from a car accident she had been involved in. Finally the check arrived. Ruth and her boyfriend walked to a nearby used car lot where they purchased a car, putting both names on the title. He dropped her off at home and she never saw him or the car again.

Roxanne dropped out of school in the seventh grade, married at 15, and was never in the foster care system. Her husband was a violent man, and he shot her in the neck. The scared young girl told authorities it was an accident. Years later, when they separated, she changed her story, but the statute of limitations had expired. Roxanne is currently attending junior college full time and working full time, in addition to being a single mother of three children.

A couple of weeks after the death of his father, Paxton was aimlessly walking around the small town, when two of his 13-year-old buddies drove up beside him and said, "Get in." Someone left the keys in their car so the kids took it, viewing it as an opportunity too good to pass up. Paxton hopped in, asking, "Where're you goin'?" They responded, "California."

The three 13-year-olds were on their way to a destination halfway across the country. It did not matter that not one of them had any money or even a clue how to get to California. There is an old saying "Ignorance is bliss." They stole gas and food the entire way. They broke into a house where they found a pan of lasagna ready for someone's dinner. It turned out to be their dinner. They enjoyed the warm meal that was not pre-wrapped food from a gas station. Since that was the only thing they took, I have often pictured the mother explaining she really did make lasagna for dinner and she doesn't know what happened to it.

They made it to California without a bit of trouble. Their next goal was to steal a yacht and go to Mexico. They nonchalantly checked out the yachts, trying to decide which one they wanted. When they agreed on the perfect vessel, they boarded and managed to get it started. They were giddy with excitement, off on their adventure to Mexico, but headed in the wrong direction. Suddenly there were helicopters hovering over them and a SWAT team talking over loud speakers, informing the boys that they had guns pointed at them. Imagine the SWAT team's surprise when they discovered three 13-year-old boys, missing from the central United States, had stolen the yacht and were heading to Mexico, going the wrong direction. Turns out, the yacht belonged to an illegal arms dealer and had an arsenal of guns on board.

The boys were placed in a detention center for several months. California was anxious to get the youngsters out of their jurisdiction, so they put them on a plane to be met by children's welfare. Paxton was placed in a foster home.

Paxton was not in my home long when I decided to take a respite weekend. I dropped the boys off for respite care, including Paxton. Mike, Todd, and my son stayed with me. When I picked them up, Paxton said, "All I did was watch the clock and keep figuring out how much longer I had to be there." I thought, "He gets along well with the older crew and I don't mind him being here. He doesn't need to go to respite." I didn't send him to respite again.

One respite weekend I took Paxton and Bert to an upscale movie theatre in the city. Paxton patiently stood in line to get his popcorn and soda. The young lady in front of him could not decide what she wanted. Her friend suggested the chocolate-covered caramels. She gasped, "I cannot eat candy out of a box." Paxton was infuriated. This was a boy who had eaten meals from a dumpster. He said, "Who does that uppity rich bitch think she is— can't eat candy out of a box?"

I was watching the movie, when I noticed chocolate caramels flying through the air aimed at the young lady, some hitting her in the back of the head and she never had a clue that it was all because she wouldn't eat candy out of a box.

Auggie had his favorites and Paxton was one of them. He frequently took him along on his runs to the city to take care of business. On this particular day, Auggie was investigating a claim that freight had not been delivered.

The first person Auggie talked to remembered the driver who had delivered the freight and the day it came in. All was going well until the supervisor butted in. He grabbed the signed bill of lading out of his minion's hand and looked at it. The supervisor barked at Auggie, saying, "We never received this freight. The signature is scribbled and the owner didn't sign it so this paper don't mean shit." Bert knew all hell was about to break loose.

Auggie, staying relatively calm, explained to him, "Your employees remember my driver and getting the freight. My driver will be here in about 20 minutes to straighten this mess out." The supervisor had a really bad attitude and the argument continued to escalate. Auggie told him, "You're nothing but a goddamn paper jockey so get the fuck back in your office and do your fuckin' job." After that comment Auggie and the boys were instructed to wait outside for the driver.

They were outside maybe three minutes when Auggie announced, "I'm thirsty, how 'bout you guys? Let's go in and get a soda." With the boys trailing behind Auggie, they marched back into the building searching for the vending machines. A secretary gave directions to go through the office and outside onto the dock. Auggie couldn't have been happier than when the crew had to traipse in front of the supervisor's office where he would see them.

With sodas in hand, they went outside and stood at the bottom of the metal stairs leading up to the little porch where the door was. Before the sodas were even opened, Auggie's wish was granted. The supervisor stormed out of the door screaming, "I told you to wait outside and get the fuck out of this building. Now, leave!"

Auggie calmly responded without raising his voice, "Jesus, all we did was buy a soda." The supervisor screamed, "You got 10 minutes to get off of this property before I call the cops." Auggie's response was quick and to the point, "You have five minutes to shut your fucking mouth before I turn your facial hair inside out."

The manager flew down the stairs, maybe touching two out of the 10 steps on his way down, where he exploded in front of Auggie, "Motherfuck-er, what did you say? I'll kick your ass." Bert handed Paxton his soda preparing to help his dad. Paxton stood there with a bewildered look on his face. Auggie leaned against the wall for balance and looked like he was ready to strike. Every time the manager would yell, Auggie would interrupt by telling him, "Kiss my dick." This verbal confrontation went back and forth with Auggie and the manager nose to nose. Bert stood three inches away from his dad's side. Paxton stood 10 feet away, looking dumbfounded, holding a bottle of soda in each hand.

The confrontation ended when the man started to yell something and Auggie quickly interrupted, "Hey! Maybe you didn't hear me the first 10 times, but I said kiss my dick." The supervisor stopped dead in his tracks, so mad he couldn't form a word. He backed away, walked up the steps and said, "Fuck this. I'm calling the police. You're trespassing." Auggie calmly told him, "Go ahead. By the time the police arrive, I'll be sitting in my car on the other side of the fence." The supervisor went inside slamming the door. The boys climbed in the car with Auggie and he drove until they were two feet past the fence where they waited for the driver. Paxton was silent for a bit and then said, "Wow, Auggie, when you asked me to come along and help, this was not what I expected." When I heard the story from the boys, I thought, "That child has only been in our home a few months and is already banned from a major truck line."

Paxton applied for a job at the local pharmacy. I was surprised when he got it. Everyone in Hoisington knew of the foster home right outside town, and the reputation of the boys. No one gave them a break. The pharmacist trusted Paxton with his vehicle to deliver the prescriptions to the local nursing home. I will forever be grateful to that pharmacist.

The partially-shaved head with the long ponytail was long gone. Paxton bought a car. Hoisington High School was small so students were allowed to drive to school with few restrictions. It was my opinion that the school targeted my foster boys. I guess the small town was typical of many small towns. Everybody knows everybody and most have been there for generations. The principal, who was notorious for ogling the well-developed girls, approached Paxton, "You're going to have to move your car. You are not allowed to park there." Paxton felt this was unfair since other students parked in that same spot. Glaring at the principal, he said, "I guess if I had tits I could park there." He walked out of school and refused to go back. He aged out of the system without a high school diploma.

Paxton heard me playing Für Elise by Beethoven, on the piano. He listened and said, "Blondie (a term of endearment used by many of the boys), that is a beautiful song, teach me how to play it." I looked at this boy who had never touched a piano but was confident he could play Beethoven. I said, "I'm not a piano teacher, and it's been years since I had lessons. The best I can do is write the notes on the music and show you where the keys are on the piano." He agreed like it was no big deal. What was a big deal is the fact he learned to play the piece flawlessly. The next surprise came when he asked if he could take piano lessons. Stunned, I said, "I'll pay as long as you practice." After a few months of lessons it was time for a recital. We proudly found a seat toward the front of the church basement and waited for Paxton's turn. The teacher announced him and went on to say, "Paxton has only had a few lessons." She stopped until she gained control of her emotions, "Every once in a while I get a student who is truly gifted, and that is Paxton." He sat down and with his fingers going up and down the keyboard, made beautiful music. He made me proud. To this day when he visits, he gives us a private recital.

Paxton aged out of the foster care system but continued to live with us. He found employment with a construction company, making decent money. Eager to be independent, he and Todd joined forces and rented an apartment. He packed all of his possessions into his car and the back of Auggie's pickup. Ready to roll, he looked at me and said, "You know, Blondie, when I came here I carried everything I owned in a duffle bag, now, I am leaving with the back of a pick-up and my own car packed full." Occasionally Paxton ran into financial problems and came knocking on my door. I always told him, "Get your stuff and come on back."

Paxton was a handsome guy but he only had eyes for Kylie. I'm not sure if it was love, lust, or obsession. When things were good between the two of them, he was happy. If they were fighting, he was inconsolable. All I heard was "Kylie-Kylie-Kylie" as he followed me around.

Living in the country, we were under the jurisdiction of the sheriff's department, however, our well-known foster home was only one mile from Hoisington. The police were acutely aware of my boys. On occasion I would get phone calls inquiring if I had knowledge of local crimes.

It was 4:00 AM when the phone rang, pulling me out of a deep sleep. I answered to hear Tony, the assistant chief of police say, "Sorry to bother you, but we have Paxton in a cell. He's drunk and belligerent. He and Kylie were fighting. Can you come get him?" Well, that certainly woke me up. I got dressed and drove to the police station. Tony met me at the door saying, "We decided to transport Paxton to the county jail. He's out of control and won't calm down." I asked Tony if I could talk to him. He said, "Sure," and led me back to his cell. Paxton's rage intensified when he saw me come through the door of the lock-down area. He yelled, "Why did you call her?" I yelled right back, "Knock it off right now. I'm here to take you home with me." They unlocked the cell and he meekly followed me. As we approached the last door, he turned around shouting at Tony, "Fuck you." As he plopped down in the car, he said, "Thanks, Blondie, for picking me up." He continued on, explaining the events that led up to the present. When I pulled in the driveway he said, "Fuck her! She can't even give a good blow job." I gave him a blanket, pointed to the couch, and said, "Sleep it off." The next morning I told a sober Paxton he owed Tony an apology. He said, "I'm not apologizing. I'm not sorry. Tony was being a prick." I pointed out that Tony went way beyond the call of duty with him and he damn sure did owe him an apology. It took a year, but Tony did get a sincere apology.

Apparently the lovers made up because Kylie was pregnant. No surprise there. Her mother and sisters gave her a baby shower. It was the typical shower with the borrowed folding chairs circling the room, everyone holding their cup of punch, chatting to the person next to them. Caroline and I went together and we were a little early so the chairs next to us were empty. Ruth and her two daughters, Beth and Roxanne, arrived. She didn't know anyone so she sat by me. She talked about her health while the room was filling up. She announced in a loud voice, "Beth is pregnant." I said, "Beth, I didn't even know you had a boyfriend." Ruth responded, "Oh, she doesn't. Someone she went to school with just stopped by." Beth chimed in saying, "He told me he was fixed." Ruth said, "I told Beth—fixed, he's 19! What could be broken?" You could see the jaws drop all around the room.

Kylie and Paxton had a love-hate relationship. They couldn't get along with each other and couldn't get along without each other. While Kylie was not with Paxton, she dated other guys. Kylie told Paxton there was a possibility he was not the baby's father. An expensive DNA test proved he was the daddy. Six months after the birth of their son, Austin, Kylie left, leaving the infant with Paxton. They were no longer together but engaged in frequent sex which led to yet another pregnancy. She moved back in and gave birth to another son, Trenton. It was a rocky relationship at best. They didn't speak to one another. They texted back and forth, but there was always sex.

Paxton was family, and I was grandma to the sweet little boys. I had a barbeque and Paxton, who never missed one, was to come. It was getting late and everyone was saying, "Where's Paxton? He said he'd be here, and he always shows up." He finally called Mike, and the mystery was solved. He was in jail. He told Mike, "I'm in so much trouble, I can't even be bailed out. Kylie and I were fighting. Her sister called 911. The police took Auggie's pistol. They locked me up." The gun was mine. After Auggie died, Melanie told me to get rid of his pistol. It was just a matter of time before it would come up missing, just like Auggie's pain pills. Paxton had a locked gun cabinet, so I asked him to keep it for me. Paxton was jailed for a month.

Coincidentally, Kyle was also in jail at the same time as Paxton and was happy to see a familiar face. When Paxton was released, he showed up at my door again, asking if he could move back in. I love that boy unconditionally and I felt bad for him, but I had to tell him, "This is a state-run foster home and since you recently had a visit at the Cross Bar Hotel, I can't take you back in."

Kylie moved on with a new boyfriend and they had a daughter. One day Paxton called me because something was weighing heavily on his mind. He said, "Kylie told me the baby was conceived December 27 with her boyfriend. I had unprotected sex with her on December 25, you know, a Christmas present. I'm thinking I might be the father." Oh my goodness! There was never a dull moment dealing with Paxton. Time went on, Kylie's boyfriend moved out. After seeing the new baby girl, Paxton became convinced he wasn't the daddy this time. Kylie and Paxton lead separate lives, but still have sex.

Vince hires him to help out occasionally. He likes the young man and claims he is an excellent worker. Paxton gave me an update on Will. "He's in prison." I said, "Oh that's terrible. He's mentally challenged. He doesn't belong in prison." Paxton looked at me amazed and said, "No, he's happy. He has a bed to sleep in, three meals a day, and all the sex he wants." Paxton is currently living with Roxanne and has enrolled in community college.

22

MAX AND DAX
The Twins from Hell

Under the oak tree in the front yard, I made a sickening discovery. Baby birds lay scattered from a nest knocked from a tree. With thin sticks, the dead babies had all been skewered through from mouth to back end. The twins had struck again!

The next day while I was hanging clothes on the line, the twins were playing in the nearby fort. My mind was racing, thinking children's welfare had dumped the "twins from hell" at my doorstep.

The silence of the morning was broken by a thump and a screeching howl. I ran to the fort, with Kyle one step in front of me. The thump I heard was a cat landing on top of the small metal shed that was next to the fort. Kyle positioned himself to catch the next cat launched from the top of the 15-foot tall fort. The cat flew down into Kyle's waiting arms. You can't catch a flying cat without some major scratches. Exasperated, I marched the twins off to spend time in their room, noticing a cat on the porch roof softly meowing looking for a way down.

The disturbed boys, Max and Dax, were fraternal twins. Dax was about six inches taller than Max, with darker hair, and clearly not as intelligent as his brother. The 9-year-old twins were left unsupervised every day while Mom worked. They lived in a trailer court, not to be confused with a mobile home park. Mom instructed the boys, "Don't go out of the trailer while I'm at work." Max said Dax had gone out the front door to pee off of the steps when some nosy neighbor hotlined them. Peeing off of the steps was only the tip of the iceberg. Hotline calls had been placed by the school they attended. When the social worker brought the boys, she said their lunch bags often contained bizarre things, like just one big onion. Max was in my home about five minutes when he told me, "I heard you're a good cook." When we sat down to dinner, the hungry boys devoured the food. Apparently, it had been a long time since they had enjoyed a full sit-down meal.

Living in the country, we always kept barn cats for rodent control. In the spring the boys spent hours playing with their beloved kitties. As soon as a new litter was born the boys would fight over which kitten would be theirs.

All the kitties had names such as, Figaro, Hot Lava, John Robert, Juvenile, Sweetie, Felix and so on. I immediately noticed the twins were rough with the kittens. They would toss the kittens up in the air and swing them around which struck me as being cruel. As the days went by, the cruelty escalated. I walked behind the house to find Max and Dax swinging the kittens in front of the dog. They were tormenting the dog, trying to make the dog attack the kitten. Luckily the dog was disinterested. I expressed my concern to Beverly, the psychiatric consultant. "I won't be surprised if they kill a kitten," she said. Before long, Max did kill a kitten. I'm not sure how, but that poor kitten was all twisted with stuff coming out of every orifice. It was Kyle's kitten and he was steaming mad. The other boys told him, "Wait 'til Mom goes in the house, then kick his fuckin' ass." Kyle did just that. I heard the screaming and ran outside to break it up. The boys were all cheering for Kyle, and blood was gushing out of Max's nose.

 The boys were eagerly marking off the days on the calendar as they looked forward to a trip to the amusement park. I took off with a bunch of happy, excited boys. After a couple of hours of fun, it started to cloud up and looked like rain. The sky burst open and there was a downpour. We messed around, hoping it would pass over, but it wasn't letting up. Trying to keep six boys entertained in the rain for two hours at an amusement park is a true test of endurance and I had reached my limit. I told the boys, "If it doesn't stop raining in 30 minutes, we're leaving." For 30 minutes we watched the lightning show, listened to the rumbling thunder, and witnessed the torrential downpour. The lightning let up, but the rain did not. We made our way through the deluge to the van.

 Max and Dax started whining. It changed to crying, then bellowing. They were not to be calmed down. I told them, "We'll stop for burgers and fries on the way home but there's no sense standing here in the rain." The wailing continued on the drive to the restaurant. Their burgers and fries sat untouched in front of them as they bellowed. I thought, "Why me, God?" The other boys responded to the bellowing by telling Max and Dax to "Shut up!" It was the day from hell.

 Caroline had a barbeque and included the foster kids. I supervised the twins, aware that disaster could strike at any moment. Unfortunately, I did not follow them from room to room. Max went into the kitchen to get a drink. The family dog, Mitzi, had the misfortune of taking a nap in the entrance hall between the kitchen and the living room. Caroline was in the bathroom off of that hall when she heard Mitzi yelping. She came running out, buttoning her pants on the way. She found Max with the dog cowering and whining, so scared she peed on the floor. Max denied doing anything, and we never figured out what happened. Afterward, every time Max went near that dog, she peed on the floor. Max was not allowed back in Caroline's house.

Kurt, who was the boyfriend of Max's mother, was a suspected pedophile, not convicted, but a lot of red flags had been raised. When she called the boys, I was required to monitor the conversations. Mom was aware I was on the other line, but I did not intrude on the conversation. I overheard Mom tell the boys, "Kurt loves you boys so much."

At supervised visits in the park, Mom always wanted to sit on the bench with me and chat. "You need to spend this time with your boys," I would remind her. She responded, "Oh, I'll just sit here with you and watch them." Each week I was more emphatic, "This is your time to be with your boys." She appeared to have no maternal instincts and the boys were unable to bond with her. With a complete lack of emotion, she often shared horror stories with me such as the boys cramming their kittens into the heating vents. She once found an adult cat cut wide open under the kitchen table with the bloody scissors left on the cabinet. Mom had a psychiatric evaluation. I wasn't privy to the confidential information; however, I was told her story was so horrible it would make you want to cry.

Dax was a picker. He picked his nose. He picked his scabs and chewed holes in his shirts. At my wit's end, I sprayed his shirt with repellent used to keep a dog from chewing on things. Big mistake! His face broke out. His hands were often down his pants playing with himself. He was in his own little world, not caring. Everyone was disgusted by his public masturbation. He sat by me at the movie theatre and quickly consumed his snack. He asked if he could share my popcorn. I gave him the entire box. No way would I eat another bite knowing where his hands had been.

The boys rarely saw their father and did not like their stepmother. "She's so fat she can't get out of the car without help, and our dad's mean to us." They did not go into detail.

Several boys had their trading cards spread out on the front porch where I could keep an eye on them while I worked in the kitchen. Beckett accused Max of cheating and within 30 seconds fists were flying. Max's anger escalated into the most severe temper tantrum I have ever seen. He was totally out of control. Like a rabid dog, he was foaming at the mouth and developed a nosebleed from his soaring blood pressure. I managed to get him into the house and down on the floor in the hall. I was holding him, talking calmly, thinking, "Oh God, I'm going to have to call 911! He's so mad he could literally explode and die." I did everything I was trained to do and nothing worked. After what seemed like an eternity, he calmed down. I got myself together and waited for the next crisis.

My wait was short. I discovered, to my absolute horror, another nest of little kitties were all dead. All four kittens had been squeezed so hard their insides came out of their mouths and flies were buzzing over them. When I got through gagging, I called children's welfare.

Beverly was in the process of giving a behavioral training session. She told me later, she had immediately changed from the intended session content and went with, "Children who kill."

Max was the kitten killer in this incident. I requested that Max be taken out of my home, thinking Dax was not quite as disturbed. I could not have been more mistaken. One morning shortly after the boys got on the school bus, I took the trash to the garage. I like kittens too. So I decided to check on the remaining litter. All of the kittens were dead, just like the previous batch. The mama cat lay dead a few feet away. Each school day the boys walked to the end of the driveway to catch the bus. Dax had stopped off at the garage on the way. In the blink of an eye he had managed to kill the mama cat and all the kittens. I called Melanie begging, "Move him before the sun sets." I called the school and alerted the counselor. She informed me that they had not been able to wake Dax up since he arrived at school. Dax had most of his classes in the resource room. Later, while discussing this situation with his counselor, I was told that Dax had an emotional release after he killed the kittens. He relaxed and fell asleep. He was picked up and placed in a psychiatric hospital.

There was a psychic bond between the twins. They never argued or fought with each other. They always seemed to be on the same wavelength so to speak. Time spent with other children ended in conflict, usually with the pair ganging up on another lone child. Fortunately, I had enough children around to keep the odds equal and I was also fortunate that the twins never injured any other child in my care. When they were outside playing basketball or skateboarding on the basketball court or playing with trading cards or riding bicycles, one would never suspect that these two cute little boys were capable of the horrific deeds they could perpetrate. They were capable of acting either in unison or separately when torturing or killing animals.

Max spent about a year in a residential treatment facility and, in their infinite wisdom, they decided he should be released. In my infinite wisdom, I agreed to take him back.

It was apparent that Max was still a disturbed boy. I was taking Max to the counselor on a regular basis, documenting all his behaviors for children's welfare. Things were going along as near normal as was typical in my house. Max was not bothering the cats, which was a huge improvement. I was stunned and horrified as I entered an old shed on my property. Nailed to a board, I found snakes, lizards, and frogs. My blood ran cold as I stared in disbelief. Immediately I called Max's counselor who, in turn, called children's welfare. "Get that kid out of her house. He's dangerous. Nailing his trophies to a board is an indication of Jeffrey Dahmer Syndrome. Past history proves this kid should never be placed in a foster home." The next day Melanie called. "Pack his bags. A transporter is on the way to pick him up." Max was taken to a psychiatric hospital. Once again both boys were in a residential facility.

The twins were held until age 18, at which time they were released into their mother's custody. The pedophile boyfriend, Kurt, had been replaced by a new boyfriend, whose worst offense was never having a sober moment. The family was monitored until the boys turned 21. At the last court hearing, Melanie told the judge the situation was not good but it was as good as it could get. Case closed!

It wasn't long and there were problems with Mom and Dax. Dax had grown into an obese boy with a nasty temper. In a fit of rage, he broke Mom's arm. He's currently residing in an adult facility.

My home phone number was a simple number. A lot of kids never forgot it, especially those doing a stint in the county jail. Eight years passed and Max started calling me. Sometimes he called twice a week, sometimes going six months between calls. The last time he called, I told him I was getting married, giving up fostering and moving to the city. He asked, "Where in the city?" "Not too far from the south side mall," I replied. He was ecstatic and exclaimed, "That's where I live!" I immediately had my home phone turned off and have never heard from him again.

23

PARKER

Hopping Off to Jail
Used Prosthetic Leg for Weapon!

E arly one Sunday morning a man was jogging along the railroad tracks when he came to a scene that stopped him cold. Lying next to the tracks was a young man who appeared to be dead. His severed leg lay in the middle of the tracks. The young man, Parker, had been a foster child in my home. Saturday night found him walking home, high on drugs. He made it as far as the railroad tracks and passed out. Parker lay there several hours with his leg separated from his body before the jogger found him.

Parker's mother, Ruth, called asking to speak to Paxton. I said, "Paxton's at a summer camp. He won't be home for several days. Is there a problem?" She answered, "Yeah, Parker got hit by a train." Stunned I said, "Oh my God. Is he all right?" She answered, "Yeah, but he broke his leg." I said, "He's real lucky if he got hit by a train and only has a broken leg." She said, "Yeah, he broke it clean off."

Parker had been placed in my home at the age of 16, after being released from a residential treatment center. He joined his brother Paxton in our home. I found him easy to get along with and a likable kid.

He found employment at a fast food restaurant. The standard initiation prank that was pulled on all the newly-hired kids was to tell them to take something to the basement. Parker fell for it hook, line and sinker. He searched inside and out, looking for the door to the non-existent basement.

He had pictures of Jennifer Love Hewitt all over his room. He would say, "You just watch, one of these days I'm gonna to marry her." Like so many boys who passed through my home, hygiene was a problem for Parker. The boys decided to take matters into their own hands. They found a large piece of plywood in the garage, stuck it at the end of the driveway with the words, "Parker doesn't change his underwear," painted in big bold letters. When he got off the bus that afternoon, he came walking up the driveway carrying the sign and calling the guilty parties, "You stupid bastards."

Paxton was not the only one in that family with musical talent. Parker could play the spoons. It was amazing the way he could take two spoons and make a snappy tune.

Parker had been in my home almost two years and was fast approaching his eighteenth birthday. He got along with his foster brothers, didn't cause problems, and was basically easy-going and likable. It was clear he would not graduate from high school, even with an IEP (Individual Education Plan) and resource room assistance. For him to attain any type of independence, he needed job skills. He was placed 200 miles away in a vocational facility to be trained for employment. After several months of schooling, arrangements were made for Parker to have an off-campus visit. He went home to his mother's and didn't return to the school. Ruth called occasionally, talking about how her life was going. She complained about the heat in her trailer. I felt sorry for her knowing her life sucked and that trailer had to be hotter than hell. She said, "Parker got drunk and busted the windows out. I have blankets hanging over them."

After the accident, Parker got a prosthetic leg and learned to walk with it. He got a job selling magazines and ended up in Texas. He called me and said, "Hey, Blondie, I'm in Texas. I got fired and they're giving me a bus ticket home. Can you pick me up at the city bus stop? I'll be there about 3:00 AM." The bus station was 80 miles away. By this time I was a widow with a houseful of troubled teenage boys. There was no way I could leave them unsupervised, or get them out of bed to drive 80 miles in the middle of the night. I explained, "Parker, I'd like to help you, but I can't get the boys out of bed, and return home in time for them to go to school. I'm sorry." He called from every bus stop and finally the bus station. I continued to tell him, "I'm sorry but I can't do it. Call someone else." The next afternoon, Parker called, "Hey, Blondie, just wanted you to know I made it home all right. I hitched rides and walked." The next day there was another call, "Hey, Blondie. They had a warrant out for me. I'm locked up. Will you bail me out?" Maybe I should have, but I didn't.

As the years passed, we ran into each other occasionally, and he was always happy to see me. He said he had a son but didn't get along with the baby-mama. He was a little misguided but had a good heart. I took my boys to a pool party sponsored by the foster parents' group. I watched the kids jump into the water as I unloaded my potato salad and brownies beside the mountain of food on the picnic table. I wandered over to a shady spot to sit by Melanie. I glanced at the baby she was holding and said, "Oh my God, that's Parker's baby." I had never seen the baby but there was no denying it looked like Parker. The baby had developmental delays.

I heard Parker was in jail. He got in a fight and took his leg off to hit a cop. The leg was considered a weapon and was confiscated. While in jail, he hopped around on one leg. The county built a new justice center with a video system that allowed prisoners to be arraigned from the jail without having to go to the courtroom. There was an article in the local paper describing what an advantage that would be. Right there on the front page was a picture of the first inmate to use it; it was Parker.

It is easier to build strong children than to repair broken men.
—Abolitionist Frederick Douglass

Ellen on Dozer

I wish I was half the man that ol' dog thought I was!

— My Dad

24

TYLER
The Boy Who Cried

Through the years many children came and went through my foster home. They were delivered to my doorstep and informed, "This is your new home." They had no choice but to adjust. I was a stranger to them. It always amazed me that they seldom showed any emotion. The question was never, "How long do I have to stay?" but usually, "What are we going to have for dinner?"

Fourteen-year-old Tyler was the exception. He had the deer-in-the-headlights look, when the social worker brought him as a behavioral placement. He hated the thought that he was now a foster kid. He asked if he could use the phone to call his mother. The windows were open so I listened as I fixed dinner. He sat on the front porch, crying, begging his mother to get her life together so he could live with her. From Tyler's end of the conversation, I could tell Mom wanted no part of the responsibility for her son. She was crashing with some friends and there was no room for him. After 30 minutes of begging, the conversation ended. He continued to sit on the step, petting the dog, and crying.

Tyler's parents, Doug and Bailey, had been separated for years. Both were homeless, with their most permanent address being the local jail. Both were skinny drug addicts. Between the two of them, they had five teeth.

Tyler had two older sisters, Morgan, and Samantha. The Caucasian girls dated only African-American men. Morgan, age 18, had spent the year in a relationship with a 55-year-old drug dealer. When he was not in jail, he was selling drugs and making babies. His children of all ages had been through the foster care system. I declined when asked if I would take one of his sons, a 12-year-old who pooped his pants.

Tyler was roaming the streets with his homeless father, not attending school. They were stealing food and whatever money they could. Children's welfare was alerted, tracked Tyler down and started the search for a foster home. Tyler had fallen through the cracks and this was his first time in foster care.

The first night as all the boys gathered around the table for dinner, I noticed Bert and Ryder were up to their usual practical jokes. They walked in holding hands, dressed in pink and chartreuse pants they had bought at a thrift store for a Halloween party. They sat down blowing kisses at each other, openly flirting with Tyler. I managed to get the two off to the side and said, "Don't do this. This boy is very upset." They quit immediately. I introduced Tyler. Someone said, "So he's the new kid." From that time forward he was called "New Kid".

Tyler was a tall, handsome boy with a diagnosis of bipolar. Even with medications, his moods were all over the place. Tyler had a hard time accepting the fact that he lived in a foster home; however, he seemed to adjust fairly well to the rules and structure. He did not get into any serious trouble at school or at home. I was informed he would be downgraded to a traditional placement.

Children's welfare knew I would be seeking another higher-paying placement and they would have to find a new place for Tyler. But Tyler intervened. One afternoon I received a call from Brooke, supervisor at children's welfare. She told me the school principal had contacted her. Tyler told the principal, "I want you to know I'll be getting in trouble because I don't want to be moved. If I keep my behavioral status I can stay." Brooke informed me an exception would be made for Tyler. He would be down-graded but stay in my home. They would also give me another behavioral placement so my income would not be jeopardized. Actually, I got a raise! Woo! Hoo!

I sent Ryder, Bert, Paxton and Tyler to get a truckload of rocks. A friend wanted them removed from his yard. After they surveyed the job, Paxton and Tyler suggested Bert and Ryder could unload the rock from the wheelbarrow into the truck and they would bring the rock to the truck in the wheelbarrow. Bert and Ryder agreed. Paxton and Tyler got busy shoveling rock into the wheelbarrow and pushed it uphill to the pickup. Meanwhile, Bert and Ryder found a plank and made a ramp up into the bed of the truck. Paxton and Tyler hadn't figured on the ramp. Using the ramp to run the wheelbarrow up into the truck, Bert and Ryder had it unloaded in two minutes. Paxton and Tyler realized they had made a mistake. The longer they worked, the madder they got. Bert and Ryder egged them on saying, "Could you hurry up? We're bored waiting for the rocks." Tyler and Paxton cussed and complained but they did not quit.

Tyler was a good fit in our home. I enjoyed time spent with him. Auggie filled up his tank with gas, while Tyler ran into the station to get a soda. He came out with one for Auggie. That was the only time a foster child ever bought him anything and Auggie was moved by the kind gesture.

As the months slipped by, he became defiant and refused to follow the rules. His young life had been spent watching his parents in a drug-induced haze and he followed suit, self-medicating with marijuana. One evening I told him it was time to do his chore. He told me to fuck off, and walked out the door. He was street smart and disappeared from the radar for several weeks. When he was located, his spot in my home had been filled. My friend, Alexandra, had an opening and Tyler moved into their home. He stayed a year and ran again. No one bothered to look for him this time. Eventually the court emancipated him.

A couple of years went by and I heard from him. Obviously high, he called, inviting us to a barbeque. Alexandra and family would also be invited. Money was no object. He would pay for everything. It was his way of saying thank you for being kind to him. The barbeque never took place.

Tyler called occasionally, giving me updates about his life. My traditional placement was now in his twenties and on disability due to mental illness. He thought getting those checks was like winning the lottery. He told me he was living with his dad, who was also on disability. The years of drug abuse had taken a toll on Doug. He was spending his days in a wheelchair, suffering with diabetes, and still abusing drugs.

I accepted the collect call from the county jail. It was Tyler, with drug-related charges. I felt sorry for this young man who was born into a family that made him destined for failure. I was happy to talk to him. I did tell Tyler I could not afford the collect calls; however, we could keep in touch by writing. I never received a letter.

Years went by with no contact, then one day he walked into my kitchen. He proudly showed me a picture of his daughter and said his life was great. He went outside and shot a few hoops with the boys before he left. Kyle innocently told me, "Tyler had drugs he was trying to sell to us. We told him we didn't have enough money. Tyler said he would be back in two weeks and that we should save our allowance." Two weeks later, right on schedule, I saw Tyler's car rolling up the driveway. I walked to his car and said, "Get the hell off my property and don't ever come back." I never heard from him again.

25

TREVOR

Loved Buckwheat Pancakes

A few of the boys who came through my home liked the structure and impersonal lifestyle of the residential treatment centers. Trevor was one of those boys. He had been in a residential facility for two years and the state office said, "It's time to move him to a less-structured environment. We'll find a therapeutic home." That meant me.

At the time Trevor was placed in my home, I had the six-foster-child limit, plus, four emancipated boys, Bert, and a nephew, Richard, in residence - twelve boys in all. Trevor arrived in the afternoon, unpacked, and joined us at the dinner table. A typical meal was total chaos, usually a happy time, with the boys laughing, joking and being silly. The huge table was loaded with a mountain of food to feed the hungry boys. Trevor showed little emotion as he pulled up a chair to join the gang. I had buckwheat pancakes for dinner and he must have liked them. Richard said, "Hey slow up on them pancakes boy, you've already had five. We want some too!" From that day on the boys referred to him as "Buckwheat".

Trevor did not recall ever meeting his father. His mother didn't want to be responsible for her two children and dumped them at her sister's house. Trevor was angry at the world, which resulted in rude and defiant behaviors. His uncle resented their intrusion into his peaceful world, especially Trevor's presence with his bad attitude. His uncle resorted to physical punishments and was hotlined. The children were placed in foster care. Trevor's behaviors went from bad to worse, and thus, he ended up in a residential treatment center.

Trevor was an obese 15-year-old boy. He was intelligent and loved to read. It was difficult to get him out of his room. When I walked by his room and saw his large body lying on the bed with his face stuck in a book, I would say, "Trevor, why don't you go outside for awhile and get some exercise?" He was never interested. It would take a bomb to get him moving.

After a brief honeymoon period, Trevor emerged as the defiant, obnoxious child, his previous caregivers had witnessed. Two, of many things responsible for irreparable damage in children are total lack of structure and traumatic abuse. After suffering these and many other problems, hours of counseling doesn't seem to help them move on. From the very depths of their being, they hurt emotionally and spiritually. Children need a safe and stable environment where they can count on consistency. Neither Trevor, nor any of the other parties involved, ever revealed the extent of the abuse within his family. The consultant told me she would like to say, "I'm putting my pencil down. Just tell me what's going on."

I suspect Trevor was denied food as punishment or the availability of food was limited. He ate huge quantities of food but was never satisfied. I limited him to two helpings at meals. Sitting at a picnic table, unaware he was being watched, I witnessed him put the plate up to his mouth and push the food in with his fingers. He had stashes of food hidden in his room and in the garage. Food was his source of comfort.

The charts did not work for Trevor. The only motivator for him was food, and since he was easily 100 pounds overweight, that was not an option. Grounding him didn't work. He grounded himself, being completely content to stay isolated in his room with a book, shut off from the rest of the world. His feeble attempts at chores were aggravating. His view of my home was a bed to sleep in and the knowledge that there would always be enough food at the next meal. Trevor was more intelligent than most of the foster boys who came through my home. His grades were good. If his life had been in order, he could have soaked up knowledge like a sponge.

Occasionally Auggie had a project where he expected help from the boys. He had a load of dirt in the back of his pickup and wanted the boys to shovel it out and spread it. When the boys worked as a group, pity the poor kid who didn't do his share. The other boys shouted out, "If Buckwheat ain't gonna work, I ain't either." Auggie told Trevor to pick up the pace. He threw his shovel across the yard, defiantly glaring at Auggie with his dark eyes, and said, "Fuck you. You're dumber than a garden salad." He stormed away with his middle finger held up in defiance. Auggie was so mad he was sputtering. The boys were delighted, finding it hilarious which only added to Auggie's state of mind. Shoveling dirt was over for the day.

Shopping for groceries was an ordeal. It was a job shopping for the huge amount of food required to feed the boys. When they were out of school, they had to accompany me, because I could not leave them at home unsupervised. After one shopping trip, Trevor jumped out of the car and headed to the house. I yelled, "Hey there, not so fast. You have to help carry in groceries." He walked back to the van, picked up a gallon of milk

146

and threw it across the yard. I watched the jug crack, milk seeping out with happy cats lapping it up. He stood there with his huge body perfectly still, staring at me dead center, defying me to say something. I stared right back at him and said, "That wasn't very smart."

Trevor's aunt showed up at the support meetings, and appeared to be taking an interest in him. His sister, Autumn, was in foster care for a brief time, and then had returned to live with her aunt and uncle. Occasionally, Trevor was allowed an overnight visit. Paxton had lived in the same foster home as Autumn. He claimed, "I talked her into having sex with me. She was a virgin. I popped her cherry for her."

Trevor was a loner. He had no friends at school, and did not interact favorably with his foster brothers. One evening while we were eating dinner, Trevor was in a surly mood and he was baiting Tyler. Tyler, not being one to turn the other cheek, jumped up, his chair crashing behind him. He started swinging at Trevor. The fight was on, with me screaming for them to stop. Trevor's huge body went through the wall between two studs, leaving a gigantic hole. Over the years, my walls sustained many holes, but Trevor holds the record for the largest.

All the boys just stood there with their mouths hanging open. Bert yelled, "I had nothing to do with it." The rule was, you break something, you fix it or pay to have it fixed. Trevor earned very little allowance due to his unfavorable charts. At the rate he was going, it would take five years to repair the wall. To my amazement, he gave me $50 toward the repair. He had written a paper for school that had been entered in a state competition and he was awarded a $50 prize.

Completing chores was a trigger for Trevor. I maintained consistency by requiring each boy to complete a daily chore. Few of them did their chore willingly. It was a hassle for me to have to supervise them and it drained my energy. One evening, it was Trevor's chore to clean the bathroom. I walked by the bathroom several times. Trevor was sitting on the stool with his elbows on his knees propping his head up. After observing his inactivity for 30 minutes, I said, "Trevor, you'd best be getting started. Dinner'll be ready soon." He glanced at me as he stood up and said, "Fuck you and fuck your stupid chores. I'm outta here." I heard the front door slam shut. I did not miss a beat. I called the sheriff's department, reported a runaway, and went on fixing dinner.

A few hours later, the sheriff called from a small neighboring town. He said, "We have Trevor in custody. You need to come and pick him up." The authorities are always anxious to get the juveniles picked up as soon as possible. Auggie left immediately. When he arrived, Trevor said, "I'm not going home with that old son-of-a-bitch." The sheriff stated, "Son, you need an attitude adjustment. I'll be happy to keep you in my jail. You'll do chores here and you'll learn to like it. Even a pillow's an earned privilege." Trevor begrudgingly left with Auggie.

As soon as they returned, Trevor said, "I'm hungry, I missed dinner." I said, "Dinner was served at the usual time. You made a choice not be here. You're welcome to a piece of fruit." He was furious. He called the hotline stating his case. He was told dinner was served. It was his choice not to be there to eat it. He sat at the table silently eating his apple and probably thinking of ways to get even.

Trevor's attitude and defiant behaviors were not improving. No one could get along with him. Children's welfare decided he needed to go back to a residential facility, but not a kiddy camp such as the one he had been in before. He was sent to the strictest facility in the state, Genesis a New Beginning Detention Center. Just the name, Genesis, strikes fear into the toughest kids. I never heard from him again. Hopefully, they were able to turn him around. It would be a shame to waste his intelligence.

26

GABE
An Ongoing Saga

The mountain man had a special treat for his 14-year-old bride, Lynette. On her wedding night, Lynette had to watch while her new husband had sex with his 13-year-old girlfriend. The mountain man figured this act of foreplay would get Lynette in the mood. Until the wedding, she had lived with her father in the Appalachian Mountains. He traded her to her new husband for two hawgs and a mule. A few years later, the child bride, along with her three children, left the mountains and went to the west coast. The mountain man disappeared from her life but a steady stream of lovers replaced him.

She gave birth to nine more children, seven of whom survived. Lynette took her two-year-old comatose toddler to the emergency room. It was obvious he had suffered a blow to his head. Lynette claimed he had fallen off a cabinet. The child died after being in a coma for two years.

There were too many children to fit in the car with Lynette and her most recent baby-daddy. Their solution was to strap the baby into the car seat and stick him in the trunk. When they opened the trunk, the baby was dead. Lynette said the father was responsible. The father said it was Lynette's idea. The police believed Lynette and the father went to jail and was forever out of Lynette's life. Children's welfare monitored Lynette's every move and eventually all of the children were removed from her home.

With all of her children gone and the baby daddy in jail, she decided to leave the watchful eyes of children's welfare and headed to another state. There she met her soul mate, Jeff. Lynette was intelligent. She boasted, "My dad's a member of MENSA." Jeff's IQ was in the low normal range. He reminded me of a bull, thick, with a mean face. I could visualize Jeff snorting, pawing at the ground, and charging. As a child, Jeff lived in a series of foster homes. He fathered numerous children before he and Lynette crossed paths. Jeff had Lynette pregnant immediately. She gave birth to a girl, then had three more children between his stays in jail.

Lynette stayed under the radar until Chase, baby number 16, was born. The social worker from children's welfare arrived to find the family was living in a slide-in camper on the back of a pickup. The living conditions were deplorable. In the yard were several dogs and three filthy, unsupervised children playing around a pile of smoldering leaves. She knocked on the door and Lynette invited her into the smelly camper. Lynette had obviously not bathed for a long time. Her long, stringy hair was unwashed and she wore a stained tee shirt that said, "Tell it to somebody who gives a shit." While they were talking, Chase vomited. Lynette grabbed a baby blanket and used it to clean up the gooey mess. She threw the blanket out the door to one of the dogs, that promptly began licking off the vomit.

The family moved from the pickup camper into a mobile home without running water. It was an improvement. They had a bucket set up in the living room for a bathroom. A bucket of water in the kitchen served for cooking, drinking, and washing.

Hotline calls came in at an alarming rate. There were several reports of four small children at the crossroads of two major highways, picking up aluminum cans. The police questioned the parents who were waiting patiently in the car. Lynette told them, "The kids broke a window. They have to pay for it by picking up soda cans." Services were stepped up.

To punish the children, Lynette would get down on her hands and knees, naked, and the naughty child would have to sniff her butt until Jeff decided they had learned a lesson. The family was monitored with regular visits. On one visit an enraged Jeff pushed the terrified social worker into a bedroom and did not let her out for several hours. Children's welfare decided the living conditions were unsafe and placed the children with foster parents. The children were in and out of foster care with children's welfare working diligently to keep the family intact by providing numerous services. Lynette and Jeff cost the taxpayers a fortune.

Jeff told the family counselor, "I know where you live. I sit in my car and watch you. Don't be messin' with my kids, puttin' crap in their heads. I'll make you wish you'd never been born."

The entire family was infested with head lice. This is a foster parent's nightmare. We struggled to get rid of the lice, only to have the children become re-infested at family visits. Eventually Jeff and Lynette were checked for lice before visits. Often visits were cancelled as a result.

In spite of the best efforts of children's welfare, no progress was being made. All the powers that be said, "It is time to start proceedings to terminate parental rights." A guardian ad litem (GAL) was appointed for the children.

With Thanksgiving approaching, the GAL decided to give the family a chance to spend the holiday together in his home. He traveled many miles, picking up the children from various homes for the special day. They had the traditional dinner and to the attorney's horror, he discovered Lynette and Jeff didn't care. They told the children to go to the basement so the adults wouldn't have to listen to a bunch of screaming kids.

The children had behavioral issues. Ava, age nine, was placed with Alexandria. Brittney, age eight, and Bryce, age seven, were placed with Vivian. Chase had turned five just two weeks before he came to our home as a therapeutic placement. Initially Chase had been placed at Vivian's; however, Bryce was aggressive and Chase was his target. The brothers had to be separated. I thought, "A five-year-old therapeutic placement—how hard can it be?" I would soon find out.

Chase arrived in time for dinner. Everyone was gathered around the large table listening to Chase talk about feeding and taking care of his pet dinosaur. Bert asked, "Where is your dinosaur?" Chase answered, "I walked outside one morning and he just lay there dead."

Chase was a cute little boy with personality and a lot of spunk. The first morning at 5:00 AM, I was awakened by noise in the kitchen. I jumped out of bed thinking, "OMG, that child can't possibly be up." Chase smiled brightly when I walked into the kitchen. He had my big pepper shaker and had peppered every nook and cranny. I sat him down with a bowl of cereal and started cleaning up the mess. I was hoping he would quietly watch cartoons, so we headed to the living room. Stunned, I surveyed the damage. I glanced at Chase, still smiling brightly. He had unrolled some of my player piano rolls and there was paper everywhere. I sank into a chair, contemplating the mess and the ruined piano rolls. That was the last time he ever got up before I did. The first day ended with one more catastrophe to add to the list. He destroyed my irises that were in full bloom.

That long summer finally ended and I enrolled Chase in kindergarten. He entered school the same way he entered my home, creating havoc. Within the first few weeks of school, a personal aide was hired to be with him the entire day. He was disruptive in the classroom even with an aide, so part of his day was spent in the resource room. His behavior did not improve; every day was a struggle. My phone was constantly ringing with reports of Chase assaulting the staff, bullying the children, running away, and the inevitable, "Come get him." It seemed he was suspended more than he attended school. By the age of seven, the school was calling the police and filing assault charges. Parents were warning their children to stay away from Chase.

There were problems at home also. Chase caught little frogs from the creek and squeezed the life out of them. With no remorse, he put a cat in the swimming pool and watched it struggle until it died.

By the end of each day, I was exhausted. I slumped down in a chair and stared at the TV. One evening Chase dashed into the room, pulling me out of my zombie-like trance. Clearly upset he said, "Come quick, there's maggots all over my bed." That got my attention, and we trotted down the hall to his bedroom. I assured him there were no maggots. His little body rammed into me. He pummeled me with his fists, screaming, "You're lying, get rid of them." I carried him to the living room and held him until the maggots were forgotten.

Same scenario, different night; agitated, Chase said, "Bryce and I were playing. Now he's hiding and I can't find him anywhere. I call his name and he won't answer." I patiently explained, "Bryce isn't here. Maybe your imagination is playing tricks on you." Starting to cry, Chase said, "You're hiding him. Tell me where he is? You're mean." I knew the more I tried to convince him Bryce was not there, the more agitated he would become. I suggested, "Chase, how about some hot cocoa? When you're finished, you can continue to search." He agreed, drank the hot cocoa, crawled in bed and fell fast asleep.

Parental rights were finally terminated. Vivian decided to adopt Bryce and Britney. Ava was adopted by a couple 400 miles away. Auggie and I adopted Chase, a vulnerable little boy, who needed a family. He was seven at the time.

I told Chase being adopted meant he could change his name. I had a book of baby names. I started reading, telling him to stop me if he heard something he liked. He did not say a word until I said "Gabriel". He said he wanted a different middle name also, so I kept reading. He stopped me when I got to "Royce". Melanie said, "I didn't think he could sit still long enough to get to the G's, much less the R's."

Sometimes I would pray, "Lord send me some angels to help me out." I was thinking an angel would make a good babysitter. On the day the angel made its presence known, I had a house full of kids.

Apparently the angel was on baby-sitting duty, watching the boys riding their bikes up and down the long gravel driveway. Sixteen-year-old Paxton hopped in his car, honking the horn, hollering "Get out of my way." Max turned around to see where Paxton was, and ran into the back of seven-year-old Gabriel, who was approaching the bridge. The horrified boys watched Gabriel go off the side of the bridge, head first, with the bike following. It was an eight-foot drop to the rocky bottom. Paxton was carrying Gabriel, running, screaming hysterically, "Call 911. He's hurt bad." I didn't stop to ask why. I just dialed. The operator overheard a terrified Paxton yelling, "Gabriel fell off the bridge on his head." Minutes later an ambulance arrived, followed by the good old boys that volunteered. Their pickups were adorned with flashing lights and blaring sirens. They all came to help the little boy who had fallen off the bridge.

While the paramedics were strapping Gabriel to a board, he insisted, "I'm not hurt, an angel caught me." There was blood on his head. I followed the ambulance with its screaming siren.

While the doctor was cleaning the small cut on top of his head, Gabriel was explaining, "An angel caught me, I'm all right. I gotta pee." The doctor said, "The bathroom is down the hall. Go ahead." Gabriel jumped off the examining table and ran down the hall. The doctor looked at me and said, "I believe an angel did catch him. Everyone witnessed his fall. There's no way he could've fallen eight feet and landed on his head without getting hurt."

Gabriel returned. I asked, "What did the angel look like?" Without hesitation he said, "It was a little boy like me. He caught me, then floated up to the overhead wires, and just sat there and watched everyone." The amazed doctor said, "He's fine. Take him home." When I returned home, I found the mangled bicycle at the bottom of the creek.

Through the years, I found that my foster boys were rarely sick. Their rough early life seemed to build in them very strong immune systems. Most of them were from drafty, dirty homes where hygiene was not encouraged. A special meal was macaroni and cheese out of a box or a frozen pizza. When you are mentally ill or high on drugs, nutrition and hygiene are not important. The boys all had Medicaid and I took them to the clinic for various reasons: wellness check-ups, flu shots, a lot of drug testing and so on. I was a familiar face. I gave the doctor a copy of Gabriel's psychological evaluation. He sadly shook his head and said, "Wow." From that point on, we were jumped ahead of everyone else at every appointment, so they could get us out of their office as quickly as possible.

Gabriel participated in equestrian therapy. He had weekly appointments with his counselor, Darrena. And twice a month, he met with Marcie from the mental health program. Marcie decided to go beyond the call of duty and take Gabriel fishing for a couple of hours. It was a disaster. He just couldn't sit still long enough to fish. He ran around, threw things at her, and hid. She tried to get him into the car; however, she couldn't catch him. She approached a couple of good old boys who were fishing and asked for help. It took all three of them to catch Gabriel and get him into the car. That was the last time she ever took him anyplace by herself.

Gabriel was a whiny little kid. I constantly had to monitor his moods. If he was whiny or agitated, I had to nip it in the bud before he slipped past the point of no return. The tantrums involved screaming, jumping up and down, throwing things, name-calling, aggression with intent to hurt, running away, deliberately breaking things and wetting himself. There were disagreements with the other boys that led to tantrums. That made sense. The senseless part was when there were no discernable triggers to initiate his anger. There was one telltale sign that Gabe was agitated. He would begin circling the dining room table and I would think, "Brace yourself, he's going to explode." It was noted in his psychological evaluation that his anger levels reached a peak where he became suicidal.

One afternoon Gabriel came into the house whining. Within minutes he was throwing things, upsetting chairs, and jumping up and down. I didn't think much about it because that was common behavior for him. The phone rang and an upset neighbor, Amelia, was on the line. It was difficult dealing with the aftermath of his path of destruction. Gabriel was nine and had been at the neighbors playing with their five-year-old son, Oliver. Noah, Oliver's father, was outside working on his car, not paying a lot of attention to the boys. When he heard the raised voices, the work was forgotten and he slipped into the protective father mode. Gabriel was taunting Oliver. They were dancing around with Gabriel trying to hit Oliver with a stick. Gabriel threatened, "I'm gonna kill you. If I can't kill you with this stick, I'll make a weapon to kill you. I won't stop until your blood and guts are all over the yard." Amelia said, "Gabriel will never be allowed on this property again. Keep him at home."

Each child was required to do a daily chore. It would have been easier to do the chore myself. The simple chore of sweeping the floor could mean a total meltdown. Jack was with me in the kitchen when we heard the banging noise in the living room. Running in there, we found Gabriel banging on the hardwood floor with the broom. Jack grabbed the broom. Gabriel doubled up his fists and began pounding away on Jack, screaming, "I'm not sweepin' this fuckin' floor."

I was consistent. Gabriel would not be allowed to do anything until his chore was completed. A 15-minute chore often lasted several hours. If I ever gave in, Gabriel would know he could outlast me.

As time went by, Gabriel became harder for me to manage. I kept a chart with rewards and consequences to encourage better behaviors. Gabriel earned a star if he was dressed and ready to go in 30 minutes every morning. I walked into the kitchen to find Gabriel changing the timer. I told him he had lost his star. I noticed his wet adult diaper on the table. I said, "Gabe, that's disgusting. Go put it in the garbage can." He picked it up and put it on the cabinet. I said, "No," and pointed outside. He grabbed it and I started spraying disinfectant on the table and cabinets. Suddenly I was hit from the back with a heavy, sopping wet, diaper. Before I could react, he grabbed the disinfectant spray and sprayed me. He was swinging the wet diaper, trying to hit me again. Frantic, I managed to corner him and get the diaper and disinfectant away. He picked up a chair, slamming it against the floor, breaking it. I was grateful that he did not slam the chair into me. Everything on the cabinets went crashing down as I tried to grab him. Gabriel was almost as tall as me and was becoming very difficult to restrain. I managed to get him to the floor in a restraining hold. All he could do was spew out a list of vile names at me. I knew I could not show any signs of being upset. I repeated over and over, "Gabe, I'll let you go when you calm down." I could feel the fight leave him and I knew the struggle was over. The boys were yelling they were going to be in trouble for being late to school. Smelling like piss and disinfectant, I took the boys to school because they missed the bus. I called the psychiatric hospital and a transport was sent for Gabriel. Within two hours of being admitted, he had an anger attack and pushed the nurses station computer to the floor then ran through the halls, dodging the staff.

A few days after Gabriel completed his three-week-stay in the hospital, he was back in the kitchen swinging a wet diaper. I thought, "Here we go again." I asked Gabriel to put the diaper in the trash. Glaring at me, he threw the drippy diaper toward me. He took off out the door, ran down the driveway and onto the highway. The boys made their way to the end of the driveway to wait for the bus. Jacob charged back into the house, panting. He told me, "We saw Gabriel. He's hiding in the culvert, under the highway." I walked out to the highway, going over in my mind how to handle this newest crisis. I sweetly said, "Gabriel, are you having fun in there?" No answer. "Gabriel, there are snakes and wild animals in there with you." No answer. "Gabriel, damn it, get out of there right now! At the count of three, I'm calling the sheriff. If he shows up, you'll end up going back to the psychiatric hospital." He crawled out, grinning and filthy dirty. He took a shower and I drove him to school.

My father was in the hospital for by-pass surgery. I wanted to be with him but knew pulling the boys out of school was not an option, even if I could have found respite. I needed to be there to support my mother and to be there physically for my father, but caring for the boys consumed my life.

My former daughter-in-law, Kathleen, came to the rescue like a knight in shining armor. Her husband was in the Navy and she had often stayed with us while he was deployed. The boys liked her. She made home-made chicken and dumplings as well as chocolate chip cookies, and took them to fun activities. She was familiar with their behaviors and up to the challenge. Bert was there overnight while she worked the night shift. She planned to sleep while they were in school. The first day, she was awakened by pounding on the door and someone yelling, "Open up, this is the Sheriff's Department." The school principal had called the sheriff's department to report that I was not answering the phone (before cell phones) and could they see if I was home. Gabriel was suspended and the principal wanted me to pick him up. Kathleen told the deputy that I was out of state and unreachable. The principal did not have authorization to allow Kathleen to pick up Gabriel, but she was so thankful that someone showed up to get him that she wasn't about to question who it was.

Sleep deprived, Kathleen picked up Gabriel. On the way home, she pulled to the side of the road and said, "Gabriel, there are no witnesses. I'm warning you. Don't give me any shit or you'll live to regret it." Dealing with their behavior was a way of life for me. Having six boys with behavioral problems dumped on her at one time was overwhelming, but she did an amazing job.

There was never any reasoning with Gabriel, even when the obvious was in his face. One cool morning on the way to church, Gabriel said, "Turn off the air conditioner." I told him it wasn't on. He insisted it was. I turned it on and showed him which button was lit up when it was running. The five irritated boys chimed in, "Are you stupid? Just look and you can see it's off." No one likes to be called stupid and no one likes to be proven wrong. Gabriel took it to a new level. As soon as the word "stupid" was out of their mouths, I thought, "Brace yourself, it's going to get bad." When we got home, he jumped out of the car and ran into the kitchen where all hell broke loose. He kicked and shoved the free-standing island. While kicking the door, he was screaming, "You're a fucking bitch. I'm going to break everything you own and butcher you with the broken glass." He charged toward the island, knocking it over and breaking nearly everything in it. He ran out the door, down the driveway and was gone. I had to call the sheriff's department. Eleven-year-old Gabriel was a danger to himself and anyone he encountered. Several hours later, a patrol car pulled up with Gabriel in it. They had found him about four miles from home, stuck in sticker bushes. They yelled, "We see you. Get up here right now." He responded, "I can't, I'm stuck in the sticker bushes." They had to cut him out. The deputies found this amusing and Gabriel thought it was hilarious.

One evening I invited friends and family for a barbeque. Keeping an ever-vigilant eye on Gabriel, I noticed he was tormenting the kids. He was chasing them, trying to hit them with a bungee cord. Telling him to stop was like spitting into the wind. I had to physically walk him over to sit with me. I was sitting on a bench, subduing him with a semi-restraining hold. I was embarrassed as 10 people watched me being hit, kicked, bit and scratched. Finally one gentleman said to Gabriel, "If you hit that lady one more time, I'm gonna get involved." Gabriel did stop hitting; however, he sat there grunting and growling like a wild animal for another 30 minutes.

Gabriel was disruptive in church so I had taken him outside. There were three cement steps down to the parking lot. We were sitting on the top step and I was trying to hold him to prevent him from attacking me. Unbeknownst to either of us, there was a man sitting in his car and apparently he could see us even though we didn't see him. We heard this deep voice saying, "Boy, don't touch that woman again." Gabriel thought it was the voice of God, and sat quietly until the service was over. I had enrolled the boys in PSR religion classes; however, the priest requested that I not bring them back. He politely said, "We feel you should instruct the boys at home."

After an entire afternoon spent with Gabriel exploding into one tantrum after another, Bert and Richard decided Gabriel needed an exorcism and they were the ones to do it. They were shouting, "Demons, depart from this boy." Gabriel thought it was great fun. Either there were no demons or well water doesn't make a good substitute for holy water.

The boys were playing outside with their toy cars, building roads and content until Gabriel decided he wanted all the cars. Not getting his way, he kicked Beckett and took off running down the highway. We watched him dart off the highway into a wooded area. My boys thought tracking Gabriel was an adventure. The boys knocked on the doors of the few rural neighbors, inquiring if they had seen him. We eventually spotted him and convinced him to return. I found out later a phone chain had been organized with the message conveyed, "One of Ellen's foster boys ran away—get in your house and lock the doors."

One of Gabriel's running away escapades was preplanned. He filled his backpack with a can of frosting, a box of sweetened cereal, a shirt, three diapers and a screwdriver. It was a couple of hours before dark when he left. I watched as he headed through the pasture, past the pond, and into the woods. There were coyotes in the fields and woods surrounding our house and he was afraid of them. Just as it was getting dark, he came flying through the back door, yelling, "Mom, I've been attacked." I looked in horror as blood was dripping off Gabriel. He said, "I was attacked by 'possums." I grabbed towels to soak up the blood and we headed to the ER. The staff was stunned and repeatedly asked, "What happened?"

His face was covered with the frosting. His clothes were shredded. His arms, chest, and legs were covered with scratches, some of which were quite deep. After Gabriel was examined, we waited for hours while the search was on for enough rabies vaccine. During the wait he explained what had happened. While he was traipsing through the woods, he stopped to examine what the rustling sound in the leaves was. As he was bent over, two opposums sprang up, one latching onto his leg and the other onto his chest.

He managed to grab the one on his chest by the neck and flung it off. He took off running and the second oppossum let go. He endured the painful rabies shots and his scratches eventually healed.

Every summer I enrolled Gabriel in day camps, crossing my fingers he would last a few weeks. Two weeks into the camp, I answered the phone; it was an upset camp supervisor. He said, "Come 'n' get him and don't bring him back. Our staff can't handle him. This morning, the children were transported by bus to the park. Another camper asked Gabriel to move, and he said, 'Fuck off'. I told him to sit in time-out for five minutes. He was rude, telling me what he did was none of my business. He ran away and stood in the middle of the creek. We called the police to help catch him. The officer agreed to ride on the bus to escort Gabriel back to the camp. Gabriel found a safety pin and jammed it into the unsuspecting officer. When we got back to camp, he took off running to a port-a-potty, kicking and punching it, and swinging the doors. Before we could catch him, he ran into the street. We finally got him in the building then he took off his shoe and hurled it across the room, hitting a camper's mother in the head. The officer and four staff members are watching him. He needs to be picked up immediately." The psych hospital agreed to admit him, and sent a transport.

While in the psychiatric hospital, Gabriel confided to the psychiatrist that he had made up the story of the opossum attack and had actually cut the scratches on his body with a piece of razor blade. The psychiatrist was impressed that Gabriel had such resolve to maintain the integrity of his opossum story that he had submitted to the series of very painful rabies shots.

Gabriel accepted no responsibility for any of his actions and blamed the boys for things they didn't do. I watched Gabriel walk past Kyle, who was sitting at the kitchen table with his foot stuck out. He started screaming, "Kyle kicked me in the balls for no reason." Kyle was not one to let a false accusation go by. He jumped up, ready to fight. I managed to get between them, yelling, "Gabriel, I saw what happened. He didn't touch you." He said, "Yes he did. You always stick up for him." Kyle walked away—Gabriel knocked over chairs.

Taking Gabriel shopping was an ordeal that I dreaded and hated. On every trip I told him, "Do not shoplift. There will be consequences." He'd slip away from me and I'd wander around searching for him until my feet hurt. When he was younger, sometimes I'd find him hiding under clothing display racks with his contraband. When he got older, the men's room was his hideaway of choice. I'd get one of my boys to check it for me. Often they'd find Gabriel in there wolfing down candy, chips and soda. I'd find the manager and report that Gabriel was shoplifting. Not once did Gabriel hear more than, "Don't do it again" or "It's not nice to steal." To Gabriel, this meant nothing will happen when you steal.

I paid for my items at the discount store and went out the door to the van with six boys following me, when I decided to check pockets. Looking guilty, Jacob said, "I'll be right back" as he dashed into the store. I discovered that Gabriel had a candy bar and a flashlight in his pocket. We marched back in and I asked the clerk to get the manager. We waited and waited. Gabriel was noticeably agitated and defiant. Finally, I told the clerk, "I'm done waiting. I'll call the police myself." Gabriel made a wild dash out of the store. The police showed up and I had to explain that Gabriel was shoplifting and he ran away. The officer called for help and, after searching for over an hour, they found him. The officer scolded him then asked me if he could talk to Gabriel alone. I readily agreed. The officer grabbed Gabriel's collar and marched him off. He brought him back and told me, "I tried to put the fear of God in that boy, but it did absolutely no good."

As if I didn't have enough problems, a new one popped up. Gabriel was seeing strange little beings, some black, some white, about three-feet tall, with red eyes. He was older now, but he found them as disturbing as the imaginary maggots from an earlier time. He saw them circling the kitchen table, hiding in his closet and walking around in the garage. He'd tell me, "I know they're not real, but I see them. Sometimes they follow me around. The black ones are evil. The white ones are good." He'd also hear voices, sometimes in his left ear and other times in his right ear. When he told me, "The devil whispers in my left ear," my blood ran cold.

Our dog, Bosco, was a mid-sized Aussie mix shelter/rescue dog. She slept by Gabriel's bed every night and trotted behind him wherever he went. Bosco could sense when Gabriel started to escalate and stayed faithfully by his side. She'd look up at him with sad puppy eyes as if to say, "It's not your fault. I'll protect you." Poor Bosco would occasionally be struck or kicked by Gabriel. Yet she remained his loyal companion.

One of my enjoyments in life was looking out the kitchen window at my flower garden. I was attacking the weeds in my flower garden, yanking them out with a vengeance. Bosco, is a world class "moler." Her frantic barking got the attention of several of the boys, who came to check on the cause for all the commotion. Bosco had a mole cornered and was frantically digging, trying to catch the elusive critter. It wasn't long and the mole was in Bosco's mouth. As was her custom upon catching her prize, Bosco paraded around triumphantly showing off her catch. Gabriel felt sorry for the critter. (I didn't. It was destroying my flower garden.) He was determined to rescue it. He managed to get it out of Bosco's mouth and into his hands. After successfully extricating the critter from Bosco's mouth, within seconds, the mole clamped down on Gabriel's thumb, leaving a nasty bite mark. Gabriel screamed as he threw the mole back to Bosco, "You son-of-a-bitch, you deserve to be eaten."

Bosco's other favorite pastime was to chase the cattle in the pasture behind our house. One day I noticed Bosco lying in the corner of the pantry. The pantry was her preferred refuge. She would not come out so I crawled into the pantry to check on her. She was clearly in pain. She was lopsided with her back end noticeably off center from her head. I suspected she had been kicked by a cow. I took her to the vet who said, "Her injuries are consistent with having been kicked. If she can empty her bladder, she'll be all right." I took her home and gently laid her on a blanket in the pantry. Gabriel was very nurturing. He sat in the pantry with her, talking gently and petting her. After a while, he lay down with his head on her belly and fell asleep. Bosco recovered. She never chased the cows again.

Lynette had two more children. Children's welfare was at the hospital each time to take custody. The last baby was born a few days before a court hearing. The judge mentioned that the child was number 18 for Lynette. I doubt if that woman ever had a period.

The kitchen window was open to let the warm spring breeze drift through. As I peeled a mountain of potatoes, I could hear the boys playing on the front porch. Gabriel's blood-curdling scream brought an abrupt end to the peaceful afternoon. I glanced out of the window on my way to the front door to see Gabriel running and screaming across the yard. Now I could hear the boys on the front porch laughing hysterically. I went out to investigate. By then I was sure they were up to no good and Gabriel was their victim in some sort of prank. The boys said Gabriel was stung by wasps. I managed to get him into the house and eventually he quit screaming. The boys gathered around to watch me pluck out the stingers and put baking soda paste on the quickly-rising welts, as they related to me Gabriel's theory on wasps.

There was a wasp nest in the birdhouse off of the front porch. The birdhouse was built for me by my dad and was placed so that I could enjoy watching the little sparrows as they were busy about the birdhouse. Gabriel told the other boys, "Wasps won't sting you if you stand perfectly still." They told him, "You're crazy. I wouldn't try it. If you do, you're gonna be sorry." Gabriel was determined to prove his theory to the other skeptical boys and he hit the birdhouse with a stick. Sure enough, the swarm of angry wasps came racing out of the birdhouse. Gabriel stood perfectly still for about 30 seconds then came to the conclusion his theory was not working.

The boys in our home tolerated Gabriel but had little to do with him. The blond hair and blue-eyed boy told me, "I figured out why no one likes me. It's because my mother is black."

Every day as I watched Gabriel get on the school bus, I'd cross my fingers, hoping he wouldn't get kicked out. The small country school clearly could not handle him. They often called for me to pick him up. Auggie was being prepared for surgery when the irate principal called, insisting I pick Gabriel up immediately. I explained, "I'm at the hospital and my husband's about to go into surgery. I can't pick him up today." The snippy principal informed me, "He's your responsibility and if you don't pick him up, I'll hotline you." I refused, saying, "Go ahead. He's kicked out more than he attends. I won't be there today." She called children's welfare and was told to handle it until I was available.

During recess, Gabriel stood on a pile of dirt armed with rocks and threw them at the other students. One of the rocks hit a little girl in the head and she was taken to the emergency room. Gabriel was expelled and I was told that the state required home-bound students to receive two hours teaching each day, either in the home or at the school after the other students have left. My previous experience with home-bound students was that no one wanted the job and there was seldom anyone available.

Gabriel's previous suspensions had been for short periods. This expulsion was for good. I knew my limitations. I could not handle his severe behavior all day, every day, without a break. My only free time had been the brief hours he was in school and often I had to cancel plans because he was suspended.

I contacted everyone I could think of to try to get Gabriel into an alternative school. The local school district from which he was expelled was responsible for the cost, but flat-out refused to even consider it. We lived more than 60 miles from any alternative school. There would be transportation and tuition cost. Children's welfare, Gabriel's counselors, and the mental health facility were all helpful and sympathetic; however, no one could get past the pious principal. Hoping it was true that every child deserves an education, even special-needs children, I contacted state officials. A meeting was set up in my home and we discussed every option. The representative from the state requested a meeting with the school team. I was optimistic. However, she threw me under the bus, agreeing that the expulsion set in place by the school district would stand. She stated, "Gabriel is a threat to the safety of the students, but an alternative school is not an option." I was livid. Waves of hopelessness washed over me.

Justin, a case manager with the mental health facility, found a parents' advocacy center in Ellsworth. They were expensive, but maybe they could help me. The fee was $500. The mental health facility agreed to pay half. I set up an appointment at which I explained the circumstances. They were like a bat-out-of-hell tackling the problem. I had kept every notice of suspension and scrap of paper sent home with Gabriel. They found that he had been suspended for more days than was legally allowed. The school would have to take him back, but that was not what I wanted and it sure wasn't what the school district wanted. I worked with a wonderful lady, Audrey, who was both knowledgeable and efficient. We had several meetings outlining a plan. She set up an Individual Education Plan (IEP) meeting with the school district.

The IEP meeting started in the morning with everyone seated around a table. Audrey had the entire thing choreographed like a fine dance. It went on and on with no break for lunch. When Audrey laid her pencil down, that was my cue to say, "Gabriel has a history of running away. If he is hurt in any way, I will sue you for not supervising him." There were angry glares and dead silence for a couple of minutes. Audrey and I glared back, refusing to break the silence. Finally, I heard what I was waiting to hear, "What do you want us to do?" Audrey forged ahead with her plan. I had to leave when school was dismissed to be home when the boys started to arrive. Audrey stayed to iron out the details. She told me she finished up around 7:00 PM.

I chose an alternative school 65 miles away. Auggie, being disabled and retired, was offered the job of transporting Gabriel. The alternative school was more tolerant of Gabriel's bizarre behaviors, but there was no improvement. I received the following letter:

Gabriel's current negative behaviors are increasingly becoming more severe. The number of outbursts is becoming more frequent during the course of the school day. He has difficulty following school and classroom rules and staff directions. His behaviors frequently escalate into explosive outbursts of verbal and physical threats, singing, making noises with his voice and/ or other body parts, sprawling out on the floor, inappropriate sexual behaviors and comments, taking off his socks and picking his feet, shoving staff, overturning/throwing furniture and other objects, and running out of the classroom. He has difficulty with personal boundaries evidenced by roaming the classroom, instigating peers, placing hands, bare feet and objects into the personal space of both peers and staff. Gabriel divulges inappropriate personal information and asks inappropriate questions with the intent of drawing attention to himself in order to shock and surprise. When redirected, he takes little to no responsibility, frequently stating, "It's not my fault", "I was just playing", or "I didn't do anything wrong". "I didn't do anything," is a daily response when redirected and/or when given consequences. He belabors his innocence; screaming and crying as if he has been severely wronged. His reactions are hugely out of proportion to situations/incidents. He is able to maintain uncontrollable and inconsolable overreacting/tantrum behaviors for long periods of time. Gabriel is manipulative. He creates power struggles with authority figures, justifying or minimizing his behavior.

The letter accurately described every aspect of Gabriel's life. Though he was a handful, the staff did an excellent job of working with Gabriel. He had only been suspended on two occasions—once when he stabbed another student with a pencil and a second time when he pushed a student over a desk.

Gabriel was frequently hospitalized. He was released with significant amounts of psychotropic medications. The same medication, given by injection, that had briefly helped Kyle, had no effect on Gabriel. He was diagnosed with attention deficit hyperactive disorder, impulse control disorder-explosive type, reactive attachment disorder and conduct disorder.

During one of many psychiatric evaluations, Gabriel was shown a flash card representing a male authority figure. He yelled, "That's the devil and he is pooping." The psychiatrist had to pay him to continue the test. Through the years, he has had several IQ tests. Each time the numbers varied from retardation to low middle range.

After spending an endless day dealing with Gabriel's aggression and tantrums, I knew it was time for another hospitalization. None of the hospitals that provided transportation had an available bed. I called the state hospital children's section and was told, "We only accept patients from nine until five, Monday through Friday. So, you'll have to get him admitted at the adult psychiatric hospital, then they'll transport him here by ambulance." That sounded like a hassle but the thought of facing another day like this one didn't sound too good either. I put Gabriel in the car with snacks and a hand-held video game and we took off for the city. When we arrived, I was told to go through the double doors to admitting. I glanced at the waiting room. Every chair was filled and the overflow was sitting on the floor. I asked, "How long is the wait?" The answer was, "Five hours." I looked at Gabriel, who was bouncing off the walls and said, "I don't think we'll wait." Then the bomb dropped. I was sweetly told, "Once you come through those doors, you can't leave. You'll have to leave your purse, cell phone, book and the game with us." Another person magically appeared and said, "Follow me." She led us to a small room with an examining table, a chair, and a picture on the wall. I was told, "You'll wait in here. Some of those people in the waiting room are coming down off drugs or have serious mental problems. Your child isn't safe out there." She walked away and was replaced by an armed guard who never left the door. I'm claustrophobic and now I was locked in a small room with a distrubed child for what would probably be hours and no means to give him any medication. About this time I was thinking I could use some medication. I came up with an I Spy game of what was in the lone picture and all sorts of other guessing games. A couple hours into the ordeal, they brought Gabriel a ham sandwich and a glass of milk.

Right on schedule, five hours later, we were escorted to another tiny room to speak with the doctor. He agreed to hospitalize Gabriel. I was thrilled, thinking the wait was over until the doctor said, "You'll have to wait until an ambulance is available and follow them to complete the paperwork for admitting." We were escorted back to the first room, where we waited another hour. By now it was 2:00 AM and Gabriel showed no signs of being sleepy. At long last the paramedics arrived. They strapped down Gabriel's hands and legs to the gurney. He was laughing, having a great time. Finally, they wheeled him into the ambulance. I was so happy, I wanted to kiss the ground. At last I was out in the fresh air. I followed the ambulance in my car, finished the paperwork, and finally arrived home at 4:30 AM. I got an hour of sleep before I had to get up and get kids going, fed, and off to school. It was a brutal day.

Auggie had a massive heart attack. Mike came over to stay with the boys while I went to the hospital. When Mike heard the news that Auggie had died, he approached Gabriel, who was eating cereal and watching cartoons, and gently told him his father was dead. Gabriel made no comment. He just continued eating his cereal and watching cartoons. Vivian graciously agreed to keep Gabriel during this difficult time. She accompanied him to the visitation and funeral. While I stood by the casket with him, he said his good-bye, showing little emotion. He slipped his hand into his pocket, pulled out a dollar, and stuck it in Auggie's suit pocket. In the days that followed, he helped Kyle spread the word that I had poisoned the chicken soup and killed Auggie.

After Auggie died, Jack took over transporting Gabriel. Jack was kind to him, offering rewards for good behavior for the daily 130-mile round trip. He transported Gabriel for two years with no problems. Jack was the only person Gabriel responded to and was more help to me than the professionals who worked with Gabriel. Jack spent a lot of time at my house, frequently sitting on the patio, grilling our dinner. His steady, quiet demeanor had a calming effect on the boys.

A couple of months after Auggie died, I reached my breaking point. Gabriel was smacking the boys with a sword-shaped balloon. Jacob lunged at him to get the balloon. Gabriel, in full combat mode, picked up a chair and threw it toward him. It missed Jacob, but crashed through the wall.

I tried to restrain him so he wouldn't hurt anyone. Before I could get the proper hold on him, he grabbed my hair and literally pulled out a handful. Bert was getting ready to leave for work, but hesitated, concerned about everyone's safety. I assured him I could handle it. He left, but a nagging little fear prompted him to call Caroline and Mike to come over and check on me.

Gabriel was like a wild animal stalking his prey. As soon as Bert was out the door, he resumed his path of destruction. Repeatedly I restrained him. He kicked me in the face, breaking the frame of my glasses. While I was trying to salvage what was left of my glasses, he continued to kick me with his bare feet. He accidentally kicked a cabinet and howled in pain. I took the opportunity to crawl away. I was battered, bruised, and exhausted. Gabriel glared at me deadly calm and said, "Too bad your husband is dead. Makes you wanna cry, doesn't it?" He came charging at me one more time, then ran out of the house. I didn't have the strength to see if he was on the run again. I sat down at the kitchen table and cried uncontrollably. I cried for the hopelessness of the situation. I cried, exhausted from being on guard day and night. And I cried for the beating I had endured. Mike and Caroline arrived to find me totally defeated. They were awestruck as they surveyed the path of destruction. They calmly talked to me until I was in control of my emotions. Mike headed outside to deal with Gabriel. I called a psychiatric hospital. A transport was sent and he was admitted. He averaged two or three hospitalizations a year. During his absences, I healed and built up my strength to keep going.

The hospital report from this visit stated that throughout his stay, Gabriel was out of control. He was continually verbally aggressive, argumentative and extremely defiant. He had frequently attacked or attempted to attack peers. He had attacked staff members on numerous occasions, punching or kicking them. He was placed in seclusion and required physical restraint, mechanical restraint and chemical restraint.

Bryce, Gabriel's older brother, was a patient in the same hospital a few weeks later and broke a nurse's arm. The doctor on staff called me and said, "An entire staff cannot handle Gabriel. How do you do it?" He recommended Gabriel be moved to a residential facility. Gabriel had numerous hospitalizations and they clearly were not working. Every type of medication had been tried on him but nothing worked. I explained to the doctor, "I know Gabriel needs residential placement; however, I know the system. After he has been there six months, the state will start pushing for his release because of the cost involved. I went through this with another adopted child. They will send Gabriel home and the situation will be even worse. If I have a six-month break, I won't be able to start over." Gabriel was released into my custody with everyone aware it was a dangerous situation.

I made fun activities available for the boys. Gabriel's unending behavioral problems often turned these into misery. Each summer we had season tickets to the amusement park. Gabriel liked to play rummy and was good at it, and was good at a domino game called chicken foot. Every weekend we went to the movies. For me, movies meant nap time. It was worth every penny of the admission price. I made the sixty mile drive to the big mall so the boys could play the arcade video games. On the way home from one of the arcade visits, it was obvious that Gabriel was agitated. He began kicking the back of my seat, and moved on to beating on the windows with his fists. He attempted to open the door to jump out but I had the safety locks set. I pulled into a weigh station on the interstate. I knew that no one in the car was safe, nor was it safe to keep driving. Gabriel said, "I'm so mad and I don't even know why." He calmed down enough for me to take him to the nearest psychiatric hospital. He was admitted. The bright flashing lights in the arcade had triggered the psychotic episode. I never took him to an arcade again.

I always watched for discount coupons for fast food restaurants and buffets. We ate at fast food restaurants between the endless appointments. We visited the buffet weekly. While we were at a buffet, Gabriel burped as he passed a table. The guy sitting at the table, grabbed Gabriel and threatened to hurt him. Bert saw this and calmly intervened until the rude man said, "Sorry your kid's not right but I don't have to put up with that shit." This really set Bert off. He screamed, "Come on, let's take this outside." Bert and the guy were nose-to-nose, ready to throw punches. I yelled for them to stop and tried to get between them. The guy backed down and told his family to get in the car and they left. We finished our meal.

Gabriel grew to be a large boy who towers over me. He was always instigating fights with the other boys. I was responsible for their safety. Restraining him was difficult. I had bite marks, pinch marks, kick marks, and hit marks. Of course, spitting and name calling do not leave marks. Many times I called the sheriff's department, begging them to send a deputy before Gabriel hurt someone or himself. The deputy would arrive, threatening Gabriel with. "We'll put you in a place you don't want to be." He didn't believe them because he knew nothing would happen. They may as well have a revolving door on the psychiatric hospital. He'd be admitted and then sent home to start the cycle over again.

About this time Vince entered my life. He is an amazing man who was willing to become involved in my life, even with the boys. He asked me to marry him and I happily accepted. To have time for courting, I needed respite providers. There were none in a 200-mile radius willing to keep Gabriel. I pleaded to get residential respite. I provided letters from psychiatrists and counselors who insisted that I needed help. The respite was approved for every other weekend with two places available. I cheerfully drove him to the city, eager for a break. (Vince lived in the city.) When I picked him up after the third visit, I was informed, "We're truly sorry. We understand your predicament but his behaviors are more than we're prepared to handle. We can't keep him anymore." With fingers crossed, I took him to the last chance.

One pleasant Sunday afternoon while Gabriel was at respite, Vince's daughter drove to the country to meet me for the first time. Reluctantly I had to leave for the 140-mile round trip to pick up Gabriel. She said she would still be there when I returned. On the return trip home, I heard a disturbing noise in the back seat. I turned around and Gabriel was masturbating. I didn't handle it well. I screamed at him to stop. He refused, saying, "There's nothing wrong with satisfying my urge. It's a normal thing. If you don't like it, don't look." I screamed, "You're not satisfying that urge in front of me." A full-blown tantrum followed but at least he quit whacking off. When we got home, Gabriel jumped out of the car, yelling, "It's normal to jack off! Mom's a bitch! I'm outta here!" He ran down the driveway with Bert following him. Bert explained, "Masturbating is normal; however, it's always done in private. If you run, you know you'll go back to the psych hospital." Gabriel returned. I was so embarrassed. Bert, like Jack, was my rock.

Gabriel entered the ninth grade and was transported by the special school district in one of their short busses. I sent him with handheld video games and snacks for the hour-plus ride. He loved video games so I was surprised when he appeared to have lost interest in them.

The school counselor called, "There's a problem on the bus. Gabriel masturbates daily. You'll have to provide transportation if this isn't stopped." I told her, "That explains why he's no longer interested in the video games. He found something else to play with." Two counselors and the mental health facility stepped up counseling.

I answered the phone to hear, "Hello, this is Officer Elkhart from the police station. We have your son, Gabriel, in a cell. You need to pick him up immediately." This was not my first call of this nature, so I calmly said, "I live 70 miles away. I'll get there as soon as I can." The short school bus had picked Gabriel up and stopped for a 10-minute wait at a different alternative school. During the wait, Gabriel decided to masturbate. The bus driver said, "Keep your plaything inside your pants." Gabriel was tired of the bus driver depriving him of his fun. He attempted to kick out the back door and break the windows on the bus. He screamed, "I'm going to fucking kill you, you lousy piece of shit," as he lunged at the driver, attempting to stab him with his ballpoint pen. The driver called the police. Gabriel yelled, "After I kill you, I'm killing myself." He attempted to drink the contents of the cold pack I had sent in his snack bag. The police arrived and he threatened to kill them. They cuffed him and transported him to an adult cell. The police were not sure what to do with a 14-year-old disturbed boy in their adult jail. The aggression disappeared, replaced by a manic state. They brought in a value meal and he calmed down long enough to eat it.

Every few minutes the police called, inquiring as to my exact location, tracking my progress. They didn't seem to care that I was driving while talking on the cell phone. I arrived, smiling, and said, "Bet you're glad to see me." Before they brought Gabriel out, I asked if I could stay long enough to find a psychiatric hospital for him. They said, "No." Gabriel came bouncing out, then ran to the parking lot where he tried to get into the police cars and peered into the windows. A couple of officers were watching but did nothing. The last thing they wanted was another meltdown. I ignored Gabriel and blatantly defied the police by standing there going through my speed dial for psychiatric hospitals. The police informed me again that I could not stay. After being put on hold and transferred several times, I found a bed for Gabriel.

I couldn't drive safely with Gabriel in that condition; however, they didn't care. I was terrified! This could be a life-or-death situation. My mind was racing, trying to figure out how to safely transport him to the hospital. I calmly said, "Gabriel, it's time to go. Do you want something to eat?" I knew he had just finished eating, but he responded, "I'm hungry, let's go." I told him, "Keep your eyes open for a hamburger place with a drive-through window." He was satisfied with this and I took off in the direction of the hospital. He shouted, "Stop right over there. I want a milkshake, hamburger and fries." He was happily munching on his meal, oblivious to his surroundings. When he finished, he noticed where we were and said, "We're going to the hospital, aren't we?" Scared to death of his reaction, I responded, "Yes." He said "Oh, I really screwed up this time." We arrived and he calmly walked into the hospital.

I knew this time I would not be bringing him home. I had been encouraged the past two years to place him in a residential facility and knew he was a threat to everyone's safety. He was admitted to a treatment center, also referred to as residential. It worked on a level system. They start on beginning level, and with good behavior they can work up to level four. The incentive is more privileges and rewards as the child goes up in levels. He was there ten months when Clarissa from the state office said, "Send him home." I attended staff meetings every month where Gabriel's goals were discussed. I read the documentation describing his behaviors:

Gabriel exhibits poor impulse control. He is struggling to control his anger. He is restless and fidgety. He attacks peers and staff. There have been episodes that required his being placed in restraints due to being a danger to himself and others. On three occasions the bus driver who transports Gabriel to his new school from the residential facility had to call the police because of aggression on the bus. If Gabriel is hungry between designated meal and snack times and is denied food, a full-scale temper tantrum emerges. The day before Christmas, he destroyed the tree and broke the ornaments. He picks at his body, creating sores. He refuses to bathe or brush his teeth. His new alternative school has a resolution room with padded walls for out-of-control students. Gabriel is often placed in that room.

The phone calls to me consisted of, "Ellen, Gabriel spiraled out of control, kicking the staff, attempting to run, and had to be placed in the resolution room where he tore the padding off the walls."

He never advanced past the first level to earn privileges. I no longer had the strength to take him back home again. After ten months in a treatment center, he showed no improvement. If an entire staff could not keep Gabriel's behaviors under control, what did they expect me to do? I told children's welfare, "I can't do it." They were kind and helpful. After many meetings, there was a court hearing and Gabriel was placed in state custody. My adopted child was now a foster child and I paid child support. I continued with regular visits but refused to bring him home, even for an overnight stay.

On a cold Sunday afternoon in January, I answered the phone to hear Gabriel's supervisor say, "Ellen, I have to inform you that Gabriel has run away. He went to church this morning and left with four girls." I couldn't believe what I was hearing. Girls ignored Gabriel or made fun of him. I was thinking, "Wow, Gabe, four girls! This has to be the highlight of your entire life." At 11 P.M. the supervisor called back. "Gabriel has been located. Three of the girls are still missing but Gabriel and the fourth girl called her aunt. The aunt called us, saying she would keep her niece overnight; however, she would not keep Gabriel. We arranged for the county to hold him in juvenile detention until tomorrow.

The next day she called, "Gabriel is safe. He didn't have any meds for over 24 hours so he returned angry and aggressive. He'll be grounded for a few days." On my next visit I said, "Well, Gabe, I hear you had a run for freedom." He hung his head, and said, "I don't want to talk about it." I asked, "Are you still going to go to church?" He answered, "They said they forgave me but I'm not allowed to come back."

That summer I married Vince in a small country church. Staff from the residential facility brought Gabriel. Alexandria told me before the ceremony that Vivian would not be attending. Brittney, now 18, was living in an adult facility where they were teaching her independent skills. The day before the wedding, while she was learning to use city transportation, she jumped off the bus at a bus stop, without looking right or left. She ran into the front of a car as was witnessed by two police officers, who were across the street on another call. The forceful impact threw her into the next lane, where an approaching car ran over her, unable to stop. She was stuck under the car as it skidded to a stop. She was severely burned by either the muffler or catalytic converter or both. Her body had actually burst open. She had bruises and broken bones, but survived.

The special boy rescued by an angel, lived in a residential home 70 miles away for two-and-a-half years. Gabriel made it to level two briefly, but could not maintain, mostly alternating between beginning and level one. I called and visited on a regular basis. Gabriel looked forward to my visits. He was child-like in his enthusiasm when he saw me. The frequent phone calls were a link that kept him grounded to me. On every visit I bought him something: clothes, candy, CD's, movies, anything, to let him know he was a special person. I only had a problem with him once. He wanted trading cards and I had already bought his special treat. We were in the discount store and he started to escalate. People were passing by, staring at us. Gabriel, who towers over me, was in his screaming mode by now. I knew if I gave in to him, we would go through this every time. I told him, "Gabriel, if you can't calm down, I won't take you out anymore. All the visits will be on campus and we'll play cards." I watched him struggle to gain control, knowing it wasn't easy for him. He did it, and I never had another problem.

The staff at the facility kept me posted regarding his day-to-day behaviors, both in his cottage and in school. I'd ask, "Gabriel, what happened?" Full of remorse, he'd hang his head and say, "I messed up again." He'd already served his consequence, so I never scolded him for the negative behaviors. I'd listen and comment, "I'm sure you can do better next time." Then he'd go into detail about each incident. I praised and rewarded him for positive behaviors. I was there to give this child unconditional love and acceptance. He needed it and responded to it. He has a good heart, but incurable mental illness has its grip on him.

After Gabriel's seventeenth birthday, the process began to place him in a transitional home. Such a home was located 160 miles away. He was excited about leaving the treatment center. I repeatedly told Gabriel, "Your future is in your hands. If you blow this new living arrangement, you may find yourself back in another residential facility for years." I drove him to the prospective home for an interview. I picked up a proud and happy Gabriel, dressed nice with a borrowed tie. He said, "I'm going to make a good impression. I'm dressed nice and I'll look them in the eye when I talk." He did. I told him I was proud of him and he lapped it up like a puppy.

Gabriel was accepted and the funding was approved. There was one boy a little older in the home, with a housemother. Gabriel is putting forth every effort to control his negative behaviors so he can remain in the place-ment. He has started his senior year of high school in yet another alternative school. His school day runs from 10 AM until 2 PM. He explained, "I get to play blackjack with my teacher every day." Well, at least he's learning some-thing.

The social life and activities in his new placement all revolve around church. This seems to suit him. He said, "I wanted to go to college to be a youth minister but my counselor says my education isn't sufficient to go to college. I've decided I want to be a bus boy when I get out of school." In grade school his goal had been to become either an archaeologist or a fry cook.

I drive the 320-mile round trip once a month, and call several times a week. He still enjoys the visits and frequently says, "I love you, Mom." Now approaching age 70 and retired, I am paying child support for Gabriel out of my Social Security check.

27

CONNOR

Sleep with your door locked

W hen children's welfare arrived at the small dingy yellow house, they were unprepared for the sight of the five-year-old child covered with bruises and blood. His name was Connor. He had been beaten and raped by a group of teenage boys.

In the home, in addition to Connor, were his mother, Becky, who was strung out on drugs, two teenage sisters, Dawn and Tracy, six-year-old Trista, and two-year-old Candice. Becky's boyfriend, George, and his teenage son, Bradley, also lived in the tiny house.

Their investigation revealed the extent of the abuse that had taken place in the little yellow house. Becky and George were usually high. They often gave marijuana to Connor and Trista, then told them to, "Get naked and fuck," laughing at their attempt. It was common practice for the teenage girls to bring home guys and have a very attentive audience as they had sex. Connor had been giving Bradley oral sex with the parent's knowledge.

The neighbors reported seeing the dirty, unkempt younger children wandering around the area unsupervised. They weren't sure if Connor was a boy or a girl.

Bradley bragged to his friends about his good fortune to have such an accommodating little step-brother, one that could give one hell of a good blow job, and they wanted to get in on the action. Arrangements were made to meet in a cave. Bradley told Connor, "We're going on a bike ride to meet my friends. You'll really have a good time. They can't wait to meet you." Connor thought, "Wow, I get to hang out with the big guys."

Bradley's friends had come prepared in case Connor was not as accommodating as Bradley had told them he would be. They had a rope. It started with everyone getting naked. This was not a scary situation for Connor. It was a daily thing for the abused child. But then things got rough. Connor was pushed to the ground. He tried to get up, but again and again, they pushed him down, kicking him when he fell. Connor was terrified and tried to fight back, but he was no match for the four teenagers. The more Connor struggled, the more they beat him. They were in a frenzy, each one inflicting more pain on the helpless little boy.

After taunting him, beating him, and torturing him, he was hog-tied. The boys took turns raping him. When it was over, they untied him and just walked away, leaving him bruised and bleeding. Connor eventually managed to make his way home. Becky refused to call the police. Dawn dialed 911.

The three younger children were placed in protective custody. Connor was transported to the hospital where photographs were taken for documentation. Several hours had passed and his face was swollen to the point of looking non-human.

After his release, he was placed with an elderly widow. She had no clue what to do with the disturbed five-year-old, so she basically did nothing. She complained that Connor stole cigarettes and money from her purse. When she became more vigilant, he visited the neighbors and stole from them. He never passed up a cigarette butt that had a few more drags left in it.

It wasn't long until the neighbors banned Connor from their homes and prohibited him from playing with their children. He was sharing stories no child should hear. His language was inappropriate and he had been observed sitting on the curb masturbating. Much to the relief of the neighbors, the fed-up foster parent asked to have Connor moved.

His next placement was with a preacher and his family several counties away. Preacher Joe and his wife, Darlene, were trained to deal with children with behavioral problems. They were determined that he would learn to sit in timeout even if they had to hold him down. He was just as determined he would not. He struggled so violently, his arm broke. They were committed to help this child, but unfortunately, their marriage ended and Connor needed a new placement.

The court was in the process of terminating parental rights so the search was on for a pre-adoptive home. Children's welfare called on me to take Connor as an emergency placement until such a home was found. Connor required constant supervision, but I had other children who also required close supervision and we had set up secure bedrooms with alarms and monitors to keep everyone safe. Connor stayed with us for four months until his pre-adoptive home was found and he was moved.

Trista and Candice were also placed in pre-adoptive homes. Trista was placed in the home of her counselor, Mickey. Mickey and his wife had no children and were eager to start their family with pretty little Trista. Even though he was a counselor and had full knowledge of Trista's background, he and his wife were not prepared to handle this disturbed child. Her behaviors were sexual and she refused to follow their rules. Fed up, they requested

Trista be moved and she was. A few months passed and they changed their minds and wanted her back. The social worker referred to him as Mick the Prick. After a few weekend visits, Trista did move back. The adoption was finalized. She changed her name from Trista to Felicia. Mickey kept in touch with me for several years, always at a loss as to how to handle her.

A few years passed. Felicia made friends with a girl, Eva, at her school. She was invited to spend time with Eva's family, the Pratts. She decided she preferred the Pratt's home. She knew what it would take to get out of Mickey's home so she told Mrs. Pratt, she was being sexually abused. Mrs. Pratt contacted authorities. Mickey called me, "Everyone knows she makes up stories and has a history of horrific sexual abuse. I don't think I have too much to worry about." He should have been concerned because he was charged with sexual abuse. I don't believe he molested that child. She knew the system and how to work it. Mickey's life was ruined. Felicia moved in with the Pratts and they adopted her when she was 14. She changed her name from Felicia to Victoria.

Candice was placed in a pre-adoptive home with a family that had three young children. They also had three adopted children. The house was miles out in the country and the children were homeschooled. The family was strict. A hotline investigation discovered the children were deprived of food to gain control. Candice was a beautiful red-headed six-year-old child when she was removed from the home, diagnosed with autism, and placed in a residential facility.

Connor was placed with a family that had two children. They were excited to adopt Connor and envisioned their perfect little family. The mother started a journal the day he entered their home. By day two, she was aggravated that Connor had little interest in putting his things away or interacting with the family. As I read the journal, it was plain to see, day by day, that the situation was getting worse. There were few positive remarks. The journal was filled with page after page of instances of problems in school, inappropriate sexual activity, intimidating and bullying her children, and disgruntled relatives. The final entry said, "I'm done. Connor threatened to kill my son while he slept. I'm convinced he's capable of doing it. I never want to hear his name again." He was admitted to a psychiatric hospital then transferred to a residential facility for six months.

He was released to my home. It was clear Connor was a disturbed boy and it was my mission to closely watch the boys in my charge. He was nine years old and parental rights were terminated. We had adopted Kyle when he was seven and were in the process of adopting seven-year-old Gabriel. We thought we could help Connor, and wondered how hard can it be to add one more child with severe behavior problems. I was already committed to around-the-clock supervision. I was soon to find out it was not only hard. It was impossible.

Keeping an eye on Connor was overwhelming. Despite my best efforts, he managed to find matches or lighters. If he was out of my sight for two minutes, he was either starting a fire or lighting a cigarette. Connor picked up discarded cigarette butts wherever he could find them, out of ashtrays and off the street. Occasionally he'd steal a pack of cigarettes. If I noticed Connor missing, it meant danger and I'd better move fast. He'd either be attempting a sexual encounter or I'd find him in the garage huffing gasoline. The closer I watched him, the more he rebelled.

Connor glared at me and calmly walked over and pushed the dishes off of the cabinet, watching them break as they crashed to the floor. When I ran to stop him, he darted under the kitchen table between the chairs, knocking over everything in his path. He threatened me with a kitchen knife saying, "It's gonna hurt when I stab you." He didn't stop until I physically restrained him.

The counselor at school called, "Ellen, you'll have to pick Connor up. He's suspended for two weeks. Several boys reported he was lying on the bathroom floor masturbating. From now on he'll be required to use the bathroom in the nurse's office." Connor was suspended frequently.

Several times throughout the day he'd go into the small hall bathroom. It was close enough to the kitchen for me to hear. I'm sure that was his intention. I'd hear panting and groaning and, when he came out, his face was bright red. I always checked his homework before he turned it in because he often drew pictures of penises on the pages. When I put away his laundry, I'd find more of the same kind of drawings in his drawer.

Beckett was in our home at the same time. Every time I turned around, Beckett and Connor were whispering. It was a full time job keeping those two separated.

I did my homework to find the counselor most suited for Connor's needs. She asked him, "Who's your best friend?" He replied, "My step-brother, Bradley." Connor was diagnosed with reactive attachment disorder, ADHD, bipolar disorder, conduct disorder, and post-traumatic stress disorder.

When Connor was 11, Caroline invited everyone to her home. She lived on a farm with a large house, a barn, chicken house, garage and washhouse. The washhouse was a nice building, which Jack made into his man house. They had a table set up for playing poker. The guys did not bother to throw away the partially-empty beer bottles that had been used as ashtrays and to spit in. Paint, gasoline, and that sort of thing were stored in the washhouse.

Jack came into the kitchen where we were washing the dishes and said, "You'd better come with me. There's a problem." The guys were outside playing catch, keeping an eye on the boys, when Connor had slipped away. He drank all the beer left in the beer-bottle ashtrays, then huffed the paint and gasoline fumes. He was high.

I took him into the house and told him to sit on the steps so I could keep an eye on him. He violently banged his head on the wall and hit the steps. I had to restrain him which was like holding on to a raging bull. The next day his hand was swollen, so I took him to the ER, where I learned it was not broken.

I enrolled the boys in summer day camps, praying they would not be kicked out. Connor only made it a few weeks. After one field trip, an 11-year-old girl, reported, "Connor touched my privates. We were crawling through a tunnel and he wouldn't leave me alone." The next day, I was summoned to attend a meeting with the director of the camp, the girl's mother, and an officer from the sex unit division.

The officer looked at the innocent faces of the two 11-year-old children. She immediately came to the conclusion it never happened. She very gently questioned the girl, leading her exactly where she wanted to go, saying, "Are you and Connor friends--maybe a little more than friends? You kind of like Connor, don't you? Is it possible you really wanted him to touch you?" After 30 minutes of the leading questions, the child said maybe she imagined it. Everyone but me left smiling. When I shared this story with Connor's counselor, she was appalled, saying, "He definitely did it."

I enrolled him in a two-week overnight camp, with all sorts of exciting activities. When I walked into my house after dropping him off, my phone was ringing. "Ellen, you have to come and get Connor. He won't be allowed to stay. He's bullying the other children, refusing to take direction, and ran away. We brought him back. Right now he's in the office on his hands and knees, growling at us." Damn, I didn't even get one night of relief.

Hoarding food was quite common in my home. If Connor was not obsessing about sex, it was food. He opened can after can of food, taking a few bites and then hiding the can with the spoon still in it. I started keeping the can opener locked up with the medications. He was creative in finding hiding spots. It was not unusual to find partial glasses of curdled milk, rock-hard bread, and so on, hidden in drawers, air vents, under the bed, and behind stuff in the closet. In the bathroom there was a short drawer with the water pipes behind it. I pulled the drawer out and discovered a plastic container of ice cream with about four inches of mold growing on top. Every day I fixed breakfast, lunch, and dinner, plus an afternoon and bedtime snack. Many of the boys came from homes where they could not depend on a meal every day, so they were compelled to hoard food—just in case.

Connor had the bedroom off of the kitchen with alarms on the door and window for the safety of the other children. His window was by the back door. More than once, the boys reported, "Connor's standing in front of the window jacking off." If they didn't notice him, he would tap on the window.

I arranged for respite, which was no easy task, so I could go to a resort for a three-day training session. It is a requirement to have training hours to keep the license for therapeutic foster care. I was looking forward to getting all those training hours in a resort area and having fun with my foster parent friends. I was happily attending to all the last minute details. The boys were in an upstairs bedroom listening to music and playing video games. Safety in numbers is a myth. Gabriel told me, "Connor gave Marco a blow job." I bolted up the stairs where five pairs of eyes stared at me as I asked, "What the hell's goin' on in here?" No response. I continued with the information from Gabriel. Eleven-year-old Connor admitted to the sexual encounter with 16-year-old Marco. Marco had paid him $5.00. I was struck dumb for a few minutes. I told Marco and Connor to go to their rooms and under no circumstances were they to leave.

Good-bye weekend vacation, hello weekend from hell. I called Brooke to explain the situation and was instructed to stay home and keep Marco isolated in his room until there was an opening in a sex offender facility. That wouldn't happen until Monday morning. For the safety of the other boys, they all had to sleep on the floor in our bedroom.

On a visit to the amusement park, Connor said, "I gotta go to the bathroom." I answered, "We'll wait right outside the door." There were five hyper boys waiting with me, wanting to go on rides, not wait outside of a bathroom. It seemed to me that he was in there a little too long, so I sent the oldest boy in to check on him. He found him lying on the floor masturbating. Now I had five unhappy hyper boys because we were going home. I called the admissions office for the psychiatric hospital, which was on my speed-dial. They agreed he should be admitted and they sent a transport. He averaged three or four hospitalizations a year.

Trips to the discount store were a challenge. Shoplifting was a huge problem. It was difficult to keep track of the boys, and they were always begging me to buy them stuff. By the time I was loading the van with my bags, I was exhausted. One day, as I was taking the items out of the cart to put into the back of the van, Connor slammed the hatchback door on my head. I saw stars. I said, "God dammit, Connor!" Feeling dizzy and nauseated, I sat down for a few minutes.

I went home with a huge knot on my head and explained to Auggie what had happened. Auggie was furious and told Connor to go to his room.

Connor started beating on the door with his shoe. Auggie asked him to stop. He would not. Auggie opened the door to take the shoe away and Connor hit him with the shoe. Auggie grabbed the shoe, put Connor on the bed and told him to stay there. He did not. The banging continued.

Auggie called the hotline to report Connor was out of control. He was put on hold. While he was on hold, he told me, "We've gotta get that little shit outta here." That statement was recorded and we were hotlined.

The investigator came to our home to evaluate the situation. She asked Connor what I did when he slammed the door on my head. He responded, "She said, 'God dammit, Connor'." The investigator gasped and said, "You know better than to talk to a child like that! What were you thinking?" Then she lit into Auggie for his statement. Fortunately the hotline call was unsubstantiated.

Many times when a child was out of control, I was told to take him to the ER where they would evaluate and admit him. The ER was not a good experience. Often I had many children with me and would wait endless hours in one of those tiny rooms. One of the psychiatrists told me that when a child was out of control, I should give them an antihistamine pill. When I gave the child the antihistamine, he calmed down before the doctor evaluated him and, 100 percent of the time, he was not admitted.

On one visit, I sat in the ER for four hours, and they determined Connor should be admitted. He was sent by ambulance, with me following, to a hospital 70 miles away. By the time we got there, it was about 10:30 PM. and Connor was getting sleepy. We were escorted to another examining room and waited three hours. When the doctor finally came in, Connor was sound asleep. The doctor woke him up, and said, "Are you all right?" He sleepily said, "Yeah." The doctor said, "Take him home." At 3.00 AM, I walked into the house looking at the holes he had put in the wall earlier in the afternoon.

It seemed like we were always running out of shampoo. Occasionally I would check how much shampoo was in the bottle before the showers started. I noticed when Connor showered, the bottle appeared to be fuller, and watered down. I was cleaning the bathroom and, on a hunch, I smelled the shampoo. Oh my God, Connor had been peeing in the shampoo, knowing everyone was washing their hair in his piss.

I called Brooke, the supervisor at children's welfare, and said, "I have pages of documentation of Connor's behaviors. I feel he's a danger to the boys in my home. Nothing I try seems to work. What do I have to do to have him placed in a residential facility?" Brooke said, "He doesn't need to go to a facility. I'll call the mental health program and arrange to have a counselor in your home 20 hours a week." Yikes, I'd rather eat worms than have a counselor in my home 20 hours a week. I was upset.

Linda, the supervisor of the mental health program, read the stacks of documentation. She made an appointment with me to discuss Connor. I braced myself. She looked at me and said, "I told Brooke this wouldn't work. That boy's dangerous. He's going to hurt someone. He needs to be out of your home today." Oh my God! What did she just say? I loved Linda. She sat at my kitchen table and made arrangements to have Connor transported to a psych hospital to be evaluated for residential.

Twelve-year-old Connor was sent to Genesis, a New Beginning detention center, which was 400 miles away. It was the strictest facility in the state, with a unit for teenage sex offenders. He might benefit from the counselors or he might pick up new techniques from a dormitory full of young sex offenders. The children were monitored at all times. When they went from one building to another, they walked in formation, arms by their side, eyes straight ahead and no talking allowed. The boys were allowed few personal possessions. The rules were strict and the consequences for not following them were extreme. This was the end of the line for boys who refused to conform to rules. I received updates from the concerned counselor saying, "Connor is proud of his sexual issues. He bragged to the group that he had been paid $50 for giving Marco a blow job, which he would have done for free." I told the counselor he stretched the truth by $45.

The calls continued to come. Either Connor was involved in a fight or inappropriate sexual conduct. One call was to inform me that "Connor and another child wanted to study together. Each boy has his own room and they are never allowed to enter another room. Connor sat on a chair in the hall while his study mate was in the doorway. The phone rang, I turned my back for two minutes and when I turned around, Connor was giving the boy oral sex." I was relieved that this did not happen in my home.

Two years went by and I was informed that Genesis was closing down. Shortly before the facility was to close, I received a written report stating that Connor and another boy were sitting in lawn chairs watching other boys play basketball. It was a cool day and both boys had sweatshirts over their laps. The boys were giving each other reciprocal masturbation.

I was informed that I would be responsible for finding Connor a new placement. Many facilities will not accept a placement with Connor's issues. I frantically made phone calls and to my dismay, I could only find level four placement facilities. The cost of placing a child in level four is at least double, if not more. The state refused to pay and I could not afford it. Finally I found a facility willing to take him that could accommodate his sexual issues.

This facility insisted on family counseling. I was terrified that he would be sent back home. During a counseling session the clueless counselor asked Connor," When was the last time you sexually acted out?" He said, "It's been so long, I can't even remember." I chimed in, "Connor it was a few weeks ago. You and your friend were pleasuring each other under your sweat shirts." He looked at me innocently and said, "I have no idea what you're talking about." He was asked to sit in the waiting room while the counselor talked to me. She said, "I know when a child is telling the truth. Connor is telling me the truth." I sat there astonished thinking, "I can't believe what I'm hearing. This woman's a clueless idiot." I told her, "He's lying." She rebutted, "No, he's not." I was livid. I went home and found the letter that detailed the sexual encounter. I left a message for the incompetent counselor, explaining that I had found the dated documentation I was referring to. She did not return my call and there was a new counselor at the next session.

While Connor was at this facility, Auggie died. I called to tell Connor, but the sympathetic house attendant said he could tell that I was too upset, and he would let Connor know. He also brought Connor to the funeral.

The new placement was not as strict and Connor was constantly in some kind of trouble. He was aggressive, which generally ended in a physical altercation. He ran away several times. On one occasion, after several days, he flagged down a policeman because he was cold and hungry.

Due to his behaviors, he was permanently housed in the lock-down portion of the facility. Clarissa, who was from the state office, decided the state had spent enough money on 16-year-old Connor and that he should be released into my custody. I was in shock. He was being released from lock-down to a widow with a house full of boys. Beverly agreed to talk to Connor. He told her, "I'm looking forward to getting out of here. Now there won't be so many eyes watching me." My blood ran cold, and I was powerless to do anything to stop the drama that was about to unfold.

I moved him back home and braced myself. The first night I dreamed someone was walking around upstairs. The second night, not quite awake, I heard someone walking above me. Instantly awake, I thought, "Oh shit, there's no upstairs above my room." I ran outside in time to catch Connor crawling back through the upstairs bathroom window. I ran up the steps and asked, "Just what the hell do you think you're doing?" He calmly answered, "I thought that would be a good place to smoke."

The principal must have had my number on speed dial, or used it enough to have it memorized. The calls started coming in at an alarming rate. "Connor's a bully, Connor starts fights, Connor's cutting classes. The students are afraid of him. Come get him—he is suspended." The police were called to pick up Connor numerous times. I arrived at the police station to find him handcuffed to a bench, waiting for me. I was informed there

s a special meeting called to discuss Connor. He was expelled. If he was
ght on the school campus he would be arrested. They would be willing to
a teacher work with him two hours a day, five days a week, at the public
ry. I would be required to be present.

Connor had weekly appointments with a counselor and the mental
facility, in addition to his equestrian therapy. I was told to sleep with
my door locked.

I was reading the local paper when I came across an article stating there had been a recent rash of car burglaries during the night. I laid the
paper down and went to Connor's room. I knew I would find evidence that
he had done it. I was right. I called the sheriff's department. They showed up
with plastic gloves and put the stolen items in an evidence box, but I never
heard from them again.

While I was sorting the laundry and chatting on the phone with
Linda, I emptied Connor's pocket, telling Linda, "This is strange. There's
an empty prescription bottle that he obviously pulled out of the trash. What
is that yucky stuff in there?" Linda hollered, "Don't touch it!" as I stuck my
finger in it. Horrified at my stupidity and ready to puke, I ran to the bathroom to wash my hands over and over in the hottest water I could stand.
Spending two years in a sex offenders unit apparently did some good. He
wasn't masturbating in public anymore.

It was the Fourth of July and the boys always looked forward to fireworks. Connor did not bother to take his outside. He shot off bottle rockets in
his room, leaving black marks on the walls and burn holes in the carpet.

With my stacks of documentation, I sat down at Brooke's desk and
started begging, "I can't do this." The state agreed to cover the cost of a
residential facility up to level four. He was accepted in a different facility
and the behavioral pattern continued, along with the informative phone calls.
A few months later I was told he could no longer stay there. The grand finale
came when Connor, unprovoked, attacked a boy who had only been a resi-
dent for 30 minutes. An ambulance was called and the child was transported
to the ER to evaluate his wounds and stitch him up. Once again it was time
to look for another facility.

I dreaded the process of relocating Connor. It was like going through
a maze with dead ends everywhere. Every time he was settled into a new
facility, I braced myself for the inevitable call that started out, "Hello, this
is Mrs. Smith from the treatment center. Connor has informed us that he was
raped and molested repeatedly while living in your home." The allegation
nearly caused panic attacks. I would explain, I'm Connor's adoptive mother.
This occurred while living with his biological mother and her parental rights
were terminated. This did not happen in my home. They would call two or

three more times before the timelines were established. I called Melanie, in a panic, "Ms. Smith can't get it through her thick skull that Connor was not abused in my home. Do something." Unconcerned, Melanie answered, "Relax, we have all the documentation."

I called every facility in the state, and was told repeatedly, "His behaviors warrant a level four placement, we can't accept him." I had saved $18,000 from Auggie's death benefit. I placed Connor in a level four, with the state covering the cost up to level three and I paid the difference. In less than six months the $18,000 was gone. Clarissa said six months was long enough and the funding was totally cut off. I paid out of pocket thousands of dollars for a few weeks. There was no way I could keep that up and I could not bring him home.

One time, his sister, Victoria, along with the Pratt family, drove several hundred miles to visit Connor. On a whim, I called Mrs. Pratt and said, "Connor enjoyed your family visit, and was delighted to see Victoria after so many years of no contact. He's being released. Would you be interested in keeping him? There's a healthy death benefit plus an adoption subsidy." She immediately said, "Yes."

I met them at the level four lock-down facility to sign papers for Connor to be released into their custody. Thank you Jesus! I drove the 200 miles to his new home for visits and brought him home for weekends. I refused the weekend visits after he stayed out all night and came home high on drugs.

After keeping him for four months, the Pratts kicked him out on his eighteenth birthday when the money dried up. They did keep him long enough to refurnish their house with all new good quality furniture. He drifted away and the years slipped by. I follow his life of crime on the court docket via the internet. At the present time, he's in prison.

28

CADEN
Wore a Red Velvet Suit to a Funeral

The first time Caden was in my home, I was relieved when he left. The second time Caden was in my home, I was saying, "Thank you, Jesus," when he left. Yes, I took him back a third time. The final time he left, I was so grateful, I wanted to do cartwheels up and down the driveway.

He arrived at my doorstep as an angry-at-the-world, 14-year-old boy. He and his 15-year-old sister, Christine, had been living with their great-grandmother in a run-down trailer court. The kids did not know their sperm-donor father, who had never been part of their lives, or their mother, whose only service to her children was that of serving as an incubator for nine months. Great-Grandma called children's welfare, requesting to have them placed in a foster home. She was old and didn't feel good. The kids did not respect her, wouldn't obey and were physically abusive.

Caden was initially an emergency placement with Vivian. An uncle expressed an interest in family visits with the kids. After one such visit, Vivian was listening to her voice mail. It was clear Caden had stolen his uncle's drugs, as she heard, "You thievin' little bastard, give me back my mother-fuckin' drugs, or I'm coming over with my gun and blow your fuckin' head off." Vivian called the police.

Caden had experienced many losses in his life. He didn't know his mother or father. His great-grandmother washed her hands of the siblings. And, now his uncle was mad at him. Christine had been placed in a foster home not far from our home and she was his only link to family. He called repeatedly to talk to her but the foster kids in that home would say, "Christine doesn't live here anymore. She left a message for you to go fuck yourself." I called the foster mother pleading Caden's case, and was told, "Christine has no interest in talking with her brother." A few months later, the paternal grandmother, Margie, surfaced and offered Christine a home with her. Caden was in my home as an emergency placement until he was moved to a neighboring county.

He had been gone about six months, when he returned as a therapeutic placement. The previous home made no attempt to keep a reign on Caden. He rarely attended school, stayed out all night, tested positive for drugs, had nine new piercings on his face and lots of homemade tattoos. His dyed-black hair and clothes, covered with chains, made everyone turn around for a second look.

On his earlier brief stay, I found him to be angry, whiny, and full of self-pity. The second time around, his attitude took a turn for the worse. Every conversation involved complaints about somebody that had done him wrong. Caden was hurt. Margie had taken Christine into her home, but said there was no room for him. She wasn't interested in setting up family visits and Christine didn't care. I understood Caden's anger. He had been rejected by his entire family. I drove Caden to her home, hoping to rekindle some sort of bond.

Margie worked part-time for a veterinarian and could be classified as an animal hoarder. Driving into her yard, the first thing I noticed was the clutter. There was a corral with too many horses in it. On my way to the front door, skinny dogs, with flies buzzing around them, approached me. Before I walked into the house, the smell hit me. There were dogs stretched out on the filthy floor and occupied dog crates that needed to be cleaned in every available spot.

It was hard to pretend I didn't notice Margie's black eye or the bruises on her arm. She shrugged her shoulders and said, "It's his house. I can't leave my animals and I got nowhere else to go." I was thinking, "Caden's the lucky one. There's no room in her life for grandkids. This place is a shit hole." She agreed to visits but rarely followed through. Sometimes we waited in a parking lot for an hour before Caden, totally dejected, said, "I don't think she's gonna show." When we'd arrive home, I'd call her and she'd invariably say, "I was there, looking all over for you. We must have just missed each other." Margie and Caden had one thing in common—if their lips were movin', they were lying.

Caden would steal anything that was not nailed down. I knew he stole, so I frequently searched his room, finding movies, CD's, tee shirts and whatever else interested him. When confronted, the lies slipped effortlessly from his lips, claiming someone gave it to him or that he'd found it. I called the clueless people to confirm they "gave him" the stuff. Upon hearing their negative responses, he would be grounded. Returning from the park one afternoon, he told me he found $30 lying on a park bench. I said, "Caden, I don't know where you got the $30, but I do know you didn't find it on a park bench." He stormed to his room screaming, "You don't believe anything I tell you." The next day Todd said, "I had $30 hidden in my sock and it's gone. I've been looking everywhere." I didn't bother to respond to Todd, but started screaming, "Caden, get your butt in this kitchen right now." He walked in defiantly and I said, "Until you return Todd's $30, you're grounded. Either you pay him or I'll pay him out of your allowance." Caden swore he didn't take it and stomped away. A few hours later he laid $30 on Todd's dresser.

Caden detested Paxton, claiming he used to beat him up at the trailer court. Paxton's response was, "You're a fuckin' liar. I don't even remember you. Why would I beat you up?" Caden never let it go.

I took Caden to the clinic to get a physical. He peed in a cup and the nurse returned, saying, "The urine is fine." Caden lit up like a Christmas tree as he said, "I passed the urine test!" The nurse gave me the look and I told her to retest the urine for drugs—he failed.

Girard moved to our home, and became Caden's new roommate. Caden was giving him the rundown of what it was like to live in our foster home. He said, "The boys who live here will steal all your stuff. You can't trust any of them. If you have any money, I'll show you where to hide it." Grateful for the heads up, Girard stuck his money in the secure hiding spot. That evening Girard told me, "Caden showed me a safe place to hide my money, but it's all missing." I listened to him and started screaming, "Caden, give Girard back his money!" Caden denied taking it. I said, "I'm not even asking you if you took it. I'm telling you, give his money back. No privileges until you do." He admitted taking it but added, "I walked to the store and already spent it." I said, "Fine, you're grounded until your allowance covers the theft."

Caden was never caught shoplifting from a store. I would call the discount store and describe the stolen items. The answer was always, "We can't prove he took it." With a sullen Caden in tow, I returned the items, stating he was shoplifting. His loot probably went in the trash or home with some of their employees, but I didn't care. It was not going to be in my house.

Caden failed every drug test. He was self-medicating, using marijuana to mask his unhappiness. The drug gave him a sense of euphoria. The consequences and rewards system was not working and his attitude sucked. I called Melanie and said, "I'm giving my two-week notice to have Caden moved." Arrangements were made to pick him up at school. They stopped by the house to pick up his belongings, which I already had all packed up. Melanie, anticipating trouble, brought John with her. He was a newly-hired gung-ho young man, who turned out to be my favorite person to work with. John told Caden, "Piercings aren't allowed at your new facility. Take them all out before we leave." He mumbled something to the effect, "Fuck all of you."

He was transported to the same strict detention facility, Genesis, New Beginnings, where Connor and Trevor had spent time.

Caden was aggressive and an instigator. His fellow inmates didn't 'take no shit off nobody' and knew how to keep Caden in his place. During the night, four boys quietly crept into Caden's room, stuck a sock in his mouth and blindfolded him. They beat him severely. The facility was plagued by fights, allegations of abuse from staff, and poor-quality food. Caden's beating, plus an accumulation of reports caused the facility to be closed. Over 100 boys needed to be placed in a new lock-down facility. The availability of beds was limited, so many were placed in less restrictive environments. Caden was moved to a less strict facility.

Only God knows why they called me when Caden was soon to be released because he was almost 18. Only God knows why I said, "Yes." Now I was the contact person, kept up to date on his progress, or lack thereof. The staff ignored trouble, knowing release was imminent and charged ahead with the transitional program. He began to earn more privileges and was finally allowed unsupervised off-campus visits. With this privilege came required random drug tests. He failed.

I sat in on a phone conference with Caden present to discuss the situation. A failed drug test meant being confined to the dormitory. Trying to convince us of his innocence, he was half crying, "The only reason I failed the drug test is because I had a fever. That's why I tested positive. I didn't take no fuckin' drugs." Everyone was kind, but firm, pointing out that he had failed the drug test because he took drugs. I could feel his anger through the phone. He said, "I'm not staying in this hell-hole one more minute. If you don't let me go, I'll kill myself." He was escorted to his room and put on suicide watch.

Caden was given every opportunity to get out of the facility, but he never progressed enough to earn release. He was finally released because he turned 18, had a foster home to go to, and the people who controlled the purse strings in the state office, namely Clarissa, realized how much money they could save. Margie agreed to meet us to give Caden the things she had been storing for him for two years. The cardboard boxes she handed us were falling apart. She had stored the flimsy boxes on the dirt floor in her garage. They had not only been wet, but were covered with mouse turds.

Caden settled in with the same sullen attitude he'd left with. He did not have a high school diploma so I signed him up for GED classes. I drove him countless miles so he could fill out job applications. Finally, he was hired at the same discount store he had earlier stolen from. The GED classes were three blocks from the discount store, so he could walk to work. It was a brutal experience, driving him back and forth. I was held captive in that car while he complained from the second he got in the car, barely coming up for a breath, mile after mile, for 15 long, endless, agonizing miles. According to him everyone employed there was an asshole and he was the only one that did any work.

It wasn't long before he stopped attending the GED classes saying, "There ain't no one big enough to make me go." I thought, "Oh joy, I get to spend more quality time with him." I picked him up one afternoon and received some fantastic news. He had a girlfriend and wanted to hang out at her apartment after work. The only thing going through my mind was, "Hallelujah, I'll have a few extra hours that I won't have to listen to Mr. Complainer."

They both worked at the same discount store. He was a cart pusher and she was a cashier. I am not sure if she wanted a boyfriend or a threesome for herself and her lesbian girlfriend. After a few visits with the girls, he felt the need to share details of their little love nest. I said, "Caden, you are 18 and legally old enough to make decisions about your sex life. I am 62, old enough to choose not to listen to your ménage a trois escapades." Knowing I didn't want to listen was like throwing fuel on a fire. He wouldn't shut up, saying, "You're too uptight to try anything like that. There were fingers and tongues all over my body. Those girls love sex and nothin's off limits." Every night when I picked him up, I would say, "Don't start, I don't want to hear it," and I would turn the radio up in an effort to drown him out.

One Saturday morning, I was getting ready to drive Caden to work, but was a little apprehensive about leaving Auggie. He had had a rough night and I was trying to convince him to let me take him to the emergency room. He refused. I decided to call 911. I told Caden, "Call work and tell them you'll be late." The paramedics put Auggie in the ambulance and took off with the siren screaming. His heart stopped beating before they arrived at the hospital. I had no idea what happened to Caden the remainder of the day nor did I care.

On Sunday, Caden said, "I went to the discount store and told them they needed to set up a memorial for Auggie. He's the one-legged man who comes in every day and rides around in the cart, talking to everybody." The memorial never came about, but the gesture was Caden's finest moment. The store did send a flower arrangement.

The visitation was Monday evening. A large crowd gathered to say good-bye and there was Caden in a red velveteen suit. It was June and it was hot. The suit sort of looked like something Santa Claus would wear, minus the white trim. Friends, relatives, and acquaintances hugged me, offering their condolences, and whispered, "Who's the young man in the red suit?" Auggie's gone. Memories fade. But the red suit'll never be forgotten.

Christine was harassing Caden by sending him obscene text messages and leaving disturbing voice mails on his phone. I told him to report it but he refused. I suspected he felt that any communication from his sister was better than none. I'm sure he was sending her similar messages.

Caden was fired from the discount store. I never knew whether it was his negative attitude or if it was because he had taken off frequently to indulge in the ménage a trois. The end of the job meant the end of his sex life. He didn't go to school nor did he go to work. His new pastime was to follow me with his constant complaining. About the time I decided I couldn't take it another day, he started hanging around with two African-American brothers who lived with their parents in Hoisington. The kids referred to Caden as a "Wigger"—a white who wants to be black. His new friends went to school and were star football players. I approved of their friendship.

It was a chore trying to get Caden to lift a finger to do anything. One afternoon I asked him to paint a bench. He looked at me and said, "You're fuckin' with me, right? I ain't paintin' no goddamn bench." I responded, "Well you aren't doing anything else and I'm not driving you anywhere." It wasn't long until a car came up the driveway. Caden was waiting with all of his worldly possessions in two black plastic bags. He got in the car and it disappeared down the driveway. I thought, "Good riddance." Children's welfare emancipated him so he was on his own. He moved in with his new friends. Their mother worked at the local gas station. A week after Caden had joined their family, the mother told me he was lazy and hard to get along with. The next time I needed gas, he had already left their home.

A year passed with no word about Caden. One day I was sitting in the park with several foster parents waiting for the family visits to end. One visit was with a pregnant mother in her mid-thirties with two young children. Parental rights had been terminated on three of her older children. It was mentioned that the father of her baby had recently been a foster child. I said, "Oh my God! That's Caden's baby she's carrying.

29

RESPITE

Not Always There When You Need It

Respite is the most treasured part of the foster care system. It is close to impossible to find someone to keep the troubled children in placement. When I attended the beginning training courses, it was mandatory to use respite. Now it is a privilege. We were given a list of licensed respite providers several pages long; however, I was lucky to find anyone actually willing or able to do it. Many on the list had already quit. Many specified that they wanted babies or children of certain ages. Some took only girls, some only boys. Many had a list of unacceptable behaviors. I always had six or seven boys, mostly teenagers. Most respite providers will only take one or two children at a time. Therapeutic placements paid $40 per day. Traditional and behavioral placements paid $20 per day. Who wants to give up their weekends for that kind of money? There were times when a respite provider figured out that keeping all of the boys paid well. I would be ecstatically happy, dancing around thinking, "Oh boy! Oh boy! I get a break. Thank you Jesus!" Invariably after two or three visits, I was either told politely, I'm so sorry, this is not going to work out for us." Or, "You've gotta be out of your mind to keep those boys. Don't ever bring them back here."

Day and night, seven days a week, there was no break from the responsibility. To keep everyone safe, I had baby monitors in their bedrooms and alarms were placed on the windows and doors. I suffered from lack of sleep the entire time I was a foster parent. Watching them get on the school bus was a tremendous relief, but it was short lived. I was lucky if I could go more than two weeks straight without someone being suspended. I sent snacks and drinks, and paid out-of-pocket to the respite providers at the same rate as the state paid so they actually got double pay. Even that didn't keep the providers. I would drive more than 100 miles for respite from Friday evening to Sunday afternoon. It was not uncommon for the providers to bail on me at the last minute with flimsy excuses such as, "I've got a headache (or a hangnail) or I don't feel I can handle the boys this weekend." With one such call, I simply said, "Would you feel better if I gave you an extra $100 on top of the double pay?" They accepted but were never willing to do it again.

One of the first respite homes I dealt with after moving to Parish County was that of Lorena and Alan. They were the go-to people if you needed respite, rarely turning anyone down. It was not a long drive for me to their isolated country home. They lived in an old schoolhouse that had been converted into a home. Pulling into their driveway, I was greeted by five licking, sniffing dogs of various unknown breeds, and a couple dozen little goats that roamed free. At first glance, Lorena appeared to be a foster child. She was in her early twenties, very petite, maybe 5'2" and 100 pounds. Alan appeared to be 10 or 15 years older than Lorena.

They had no children of their own but kept as many foster children as the state was willing to give them, plus the respite kids. Often Lorena's niece, a toddler, was in her care. Lorena planned to adopt the child, who was the daughter of her drug-addicted sister. Alan and Lorena were also in the process of adopting a teenage girl.

They preferred to keep teenagers, male and female. Alan and Lorena slept downstairs and the boys and girls slept upstairs in the old school. The stories drifted around that the second floor was a free-for-all sex orgy. Jacob came home, complaining that his top bunk had been bouncing from the sexual activity below him. He said, "I yelled at them to knock it off so I could sleep, but they yelled back telling me to shut up." Alan and Lorena did have a rule that there was to be no sex inside the house. I guess the rule was not enforced. I knew I could not use that respite house again.

The boys thought Lorena was sizzling hot. She got buddy-buddy with them and confided personal information to them which they then passed on to me. Such as, "Lorena's thinking about leaving Alan because he loves her more than he loves Jesus," and "Alan loves Lorena so much, he allows her to date." Also, "Alan and Lorena never have sex because of her bad back." And finally, "Lorena is taking guitar lessons. The teacher comes to her house several times a week." That guitar teacher cured Lorena's bad back because the next thing I heard was, "Lorena's pregnant with the guitar teach-er's baby." Alan moved out and the guitar teacher moved in. Even though he moved out, he continued to come over to chop wood for the wood-burning stove. Lorena did not adopt the teenage girl or her niece. The mentally-chal-lenged niece was adopted by a Parish County foster family and the story had a happy ending. Lorena could have visited the child but never did. She had another child with the guitar teacher and faded off into the sunset without the teacher.

Cecelia operated a daycare in her home and she was licensed for ev-ery level of respite. She agreed to take my boys. They enjoyed being there, so the second time I sent extra money, snacks, and an abundance of vegetables out of my garden. When my beloved respite was over, I was greeted with, "Can I go back? I love that place. We had so much fun." I happily answered, "You bet you can."

Eighteen-year-old Butch no longer went to respite. He approached me with, "Blondie, I need to talk to you in the bedroom." As he followed me to the bedroom, I thought, "This is not going to be good." He started out, "I don't want to be a snitch but you need to know what happened at respite. That man there let the kids look at pornography. He gave them beer and weed, even to six-year-old Gabriel." I was stunned. I called Brooke, and was told to hotline the respite provider and to have the boys drug tested. I marched them to the doctor's office and they admitted using marijuana. I was amazed how many people were sitting around my kitchen table the next day. Children's welfare was represented by the supervisor, case manager, hotline investigator, and a behavioral specialist. Cecelia lived in the city, so two supervisors were representing the city children's welfare office. Two city detectives were also seated at my table. Fortunately my table was 10 feet long, since I had so many kids.

Individually they interviewed each child at the kitchen table with me present. The boys 'spilled their guts,' loving the attention, talking to detectives, just like on television. As I listened, I knew they were telling the truth. Each boy told the same story, providing details down to the size of the large can of beer. Cecelia's brother, DeAndre, lived in her basement. He had provided their ill-gotten gain with her knowledge. They gathered the information, thanked us and left to question DeAndre and Cecelia.

The detectives called a few days later, claiming they could not find any information on this character, DeAndre. Caleb calmly told them, "His full name is Lexington DeAndre Howard. He won some kind of award and there was a plaque on his bedroom wall with his name on it." They quickly found that Howard had a record. The house was searched, the weed was found, but no pornography. Again the kids told them, "It's in a box behind the furnace. DeAndre told us to enjoy the pictures." There was another visit to our home and the questioning continued. The boys stated, "We hung out in DeAndre's room. He smoked weed all the time, and let us have hits. He encouraged Gabriel to smoke cigarettes and drink beer and thought it was hilarious." It was also revealed that Cecelia had a barbecue in the park for the families of the children in her daycare. DeAndre did the grilling and was generous with his beer supply. The only stipulation was that the boys had to drink in the bushes. After the festivities in the park, DeAndre made a stop by a crack house to pick up drugs. The boys loved to be the center of attention, and continued, "Cecelia is mean to the little kids in the daycare. She yanks them around by their arms and spanks them."

Obviously Cecelia was upset that everything was coming down on her and DeAndre. She called me, saying, "What are you trying to do to me? Everything I worked for will be gone. You have ruined my life. Your boys brought the marijuana to my home. They said Butch grew it." I responded, "I'm not going to discuss this with you. Anything you have to say can be said to the detectives." They searched my property for a marijuana patch, but found nothing. In the back of my mind, I expected them to find marijuana. After all, it was Butch.

After the investigation was over, we received a letter from the prosecuting attorney advising that the defendant had pled guilty to five counts of 1st Degree Felony - Endangering Welfare of a Child and three counts of 2nd Degree Felony - Endangering Welfare of a Child.

"DeAndre" was sentenced to four years in prison, but Judge Deighton suspended his sentence and granted him probation, which was to last five years. As special conditions of the defendant's probation, he was to serve 60 days shock time in the county jail with credit for time served. He was also to receive drug-alcohol evaluation, follow recommended treatment, and to have no contact with the victims. Cecelia lost her license for fostering, but not for daycare.

A few years later, I heard on the news and read in the paper that Cecelia had lost her daycare license. In the report it was referenced that she had been in trouble before with foster children.

Richard and Gloria agreed to do respite. They were fostering two boys. Their huge farmhouse off of a gravel road was isolated, miles from the nearest town. I followed their directions and finally pulled up at the back of the house where four dogs slowly walked over to sniff me. The boys tumbled out of the car and I went in to get acquainted. I opened the old screen door and was met by a cloud of smoke. Gloria yelled in her deep, raspy, smoker's voice, "Come on in." The kitchen wasn't particularly clean but they held a state license, so I thought, "It can't be too bad." I smelled something cooking through the haze of smoke and asked, "What are you cooking? Smells good." She said, "Richard trapped a rabbit, so I'ma makin' a potta stew." The boys didn't mind Richard's house, except for Trey, and they stayed there twice. I was feeling pretty confident. I had finally found a respite provider. So I called Richard to set up the third respite. Richard said, "Guess I can't do it for a while. Gloria's in the hospital and she's pretty dad-gum sick." A month passed and Richard called, "Gloria's dead, but I reckon I kin still do respite. My step-granddaughter's a-movin' in with her guy. She's gettin' ready to drop a young'un afore long." Amazingly, Richard was back in the respite business.

I took the boys back to Richard's home, and the same cloud of smoke met me as I came through the screen door. The granddaughter, Hannah, and her boyfriend were sitting at the table puffing away. I used this home a few more times in the next eight months even though the conditions were far from favorable. Hannah had the baby and was pregnant again. The boyfriend left, taking the baby, claiming she was an unfit mother. Along with Hannah and the two foster boys, Richard's daughter, son-in-law, and their three kids moved into this large farmhouse that was getting rather crowded. One weekend I dropped five boys off for respite.

The son-in-law's three children from a previous relationship were visiting. I did the math. That house was full. Trey told Melanie, "I'll never go back to that pig-sty, with wall-to-wall people." The other boys enjoyed the crowded house. The next time I called Richard to arrange respite, he said, "Fuck it, I quit."

Few of the respite homes fed the kids more than peanut butter and jelly, frozen pizza and bologna. No matter what time I picked them up on the last respite day, you can bet they had not been fed. Usually I would pack a lunch to tide them over until I could get home and fix a meal. The boys complained bitterly about the food and the lack of it.

I drove 90 miles to the respite home of Frank and Rachelle. Frank was employed at a lock-down facility for youth offenders. Rachelle taught school. Their children were adults and lived a distance away. It appeared they did respite for all the right reasons. When I dropped the boys off, she had activities planned. After church on Sundays, they were treated to a meal in a restaurant.

Many of the foster/respite homes weren't so nice, but Frank and Rachelle's home was beautiful. Their basement was fixed up with teenagers in mind. The boys slept in the downstairs bedrooms, which was not a good idea. When it was discovered that Caleb and Connor were engaging in sexual behaviors while everyone slept, Frank and Rachelle discontinued doing respite.

A new name popped up on the respite provider list. It was 90 miles away but I would have driven further to have free time. I gave the lady some background information and she agreed to do respite. She had recently begun a relationship with a man who had custody of his two young sons. She was full of the spirit of the Lord and praised His holy name for the opportunity to reach out and love the boys I was dropping off. Frankly I was praising the Lord for a chance to have respite. In the tiny little apartment, her deadbeat boyfriend was lying on the bed until I was ready to leave. He followed me to the car asking, "Hey, how about giving me some extra money? I want to give them youngun's a little extra treat just from me. You know it costs a lot to take care of them kids." He was well aware that I had left extra money with his woman, and I knew the kids would never see a dime of anything I gave him. I gave it to him anyway. They lived within walking distance of a mall. The boys told me they wandered around the mall and didn't stay home much. I guess the spirit of the Lord and the love wasn't enough to keep her there. In no time she was long gone!

On my quest to find another respite home, I found one, miles away on a desolate farm with the usual pack of dogs making me apprehensive about getting out of the car. The first visit did not go well. Connor scratched the side of their pickup with a rock. She was not happy but agreed to keep the boys again.

On the second visit, she ended up in the emergency room with Connor. He slept on the top single bunk without a safety bar, with a double bed below. During the night Connor rolled out of bed and fell to the bottom bunk, breaking his collarbone.

To my surprise, she agreed to do respite for the third time, which was the final time. Kyle found nicotine gum on her dresser. Even though he was only 10, he never missed an opportunity to steal a cigarette left lying in an ashtray. Feeling generous, he shared the gum with six-year-old Gabriel. The two boys were chomping on their gum until time for dinner. Gabriel announced, "I don't feel so good," followed by projectile vomiting, covering the food on the table. With a little detective work it was determined that the nicotine gum was the problem.

They contacted poison control and were told to monitor him and, if he didn't feel better soon, to take him to the emergency room. He recovered quickly. When I arrived to pick up the boys, I was met with, "Don't bring those boys back here." On the ride home the boys were jabbering away, claiming that Gabriel was the first green human being they had ever seen.

30

EPILOGUE

"You should write a book."

During my years as a therapeutic foster parent, as I related the stories of troubled placements to psychiatrists, psychologists, counselors, children's welfare agents, children's welfare managers, police officers, other persons within the system, school counselors, teachers and principals, at one time or another they all inevitably made the comment, "You should write a book." Several years have now passed since the end of my career. I was inspired by my husband, who helped me learn to use a computer, encouraged me every time I doubted myself, and helped with editing. My son, who lived it, helped jog my memory and even filled in some of the secret stories years later that I wasn't privy to back at the time they happened.

I've told my story honestly, as I related the effects that taking in troubled foster children and adopting troubled young children had on me, my family, my acquaintances and even my community. I explained my views on a system working with a strained budget that is not perfect. I was fortunate to have been trained and supported by some incredible, sincere, caring people that always went the extra mile for me. I am grateful for having been given an opportunity that enriched my life and provided unique experiences on a daily basis—there was never a dull moment. My only regrets are the pain it occasionally cost my family.

Many of the behavioral problems are kept in check by medications supplied through Medicaid. As the children age out of the system, they are no longer eligible for Medicaid and can't afford the expensive medication, so their mental health problems return at a time when they are being freed from direct supervision. They are sometimes released as homeless, walking the streets, susceptible to the temptation to self-medicate with illegal drugs. To support their habit, they turn to crime and end up in rehabilitation centers and in the justice system at a much higher cost to society than if the foster care system could have been more successful in their preparation for emancipation. Incarceration costs taxpayers from $20 thousand to $100 thousand per year per inmate.

The foster system of charts for rewards and consequences, the hours and hours of counseling, the monthly visits to the psychiatrists for medication management, the hours of training I underwent to help set the boys on the right path, hopefully will trickle in through their entire lives. I will probably never know the impact their stay in my home has made on their lives. Many of those children were damaged, having lived through abuse most of us can't even begin to imagine. They didn't care whether they earned the big reward at the end of the week or whether they had a consequence. It didn't matter to them if they lost their TV or video game privileges or missed a dessert. How effective could any consequence I imposed be if they were used to being locked in a dark, air-less closet after a beating? My lesser consequences were meaningless.

The reward system was equally a challenge to administer. If the reward was a movie and there were six boys and one didn't make it, was it fair to keep five boys home because the sixth one had a consequence? Should I have allowed the boy who did not succeed to attend the movie when the other five had succeeded? I had to be very creative. All six boys went when I went or stayed home when I stayed home. They couldn't be left unsupervised. My husband was not always able to help because of his job and, later, due to health problems. After his death, my son-in-law was a godsend.

Residential care facilities can desensitize kids from the ability to live in a family setting. They condition themselves to accept living their lives in an institution and learn no family skills. Children who move through a good foster home have a better chance of becoming productive, tax-paying citizens. After some of the boys were emancipated from the system because they had aged out, we allowed them to continue to stay in our home. They continued to live in our home until they were able to comfortably transition to independent living. They are productive citizens with families and they are still part of my family.

Life will be what you make of it.

If you decide your life is miserable, it will be.
If you decide you will be happy, you will be.

Don't ever lose hope.
No matter how bleak things appear, it will pass.

There are many blessings in our lives every day.
Take time to find them.
Be aware of them and appreciate them.

—Ellen Harlie (Written pre-fostering period)

Order Form

Mail to: **Bobby Mac Press**
P. O. Box 270544
Sunset Hills, MO 63127

Orders can also be placed at bobbymacpress.com

Price per copy soft cover: **$16.99***

Price per copy hard cover: **$31.99***
(Note: Hard cover is in limited supply.)

*Price Subject to Change.

Select from shipping choices at our website.

Name _____

Street _____

City/State/Zip _____

Telephone / Email Address _____

Note: Special pricing and shipping discounting is available for orders of 10 or more copies to the same address if prior arrangements are made. Contact rob@bobbymacpress.com.

Contact Ellen Harlie at: ellen@ellenharlie.com

Follow Ellen Harlie at: ellenharlie.com

and on social media sites Facebook & Twitter

Summer of 2015:

Ellen Harlie Blog Site at: ellenharlie.com

Fall of 2015:

Release of Ellen Harlie's Second Book

ISBN 978-0-9889601-0-7

9 780988 960107 >

Printed in the State of Missouri, USA